Ex Libris

J.E. JeNNiNGS
2011

OVER FIELDS OF FIRE
Flying the *Sturmovik* in action on the Eastern Front 1942–45

Anna Timofeeva-Egorova

Edited by Sergey Anisimov
Translated by Vladimir Kroupnik

Soviet Memories of War Volume 3
Series editor: Artem Drabkin

Helion & Company Ltd

Soviet Memories of War series, edited by Artem Drabkin. Previous volumes in this series:

Volume 1: *Penalty Strike. The Memoirs of a Red Army Penal Company Commander 1943–45* by Alexander V. Pyl'cyn

Volume 2: *Red Star Airacobra: Memoirs of a Soviet Fighter Ace 1941-45* by Evgeniy Mariinskiy

Helion & Company Limited
26 Willow Road
Solihull
West Midlands
B91 1UE
England
Tel. 0121 705 3393
Fax 0121 711 4075
Email: info@helion.co.uk
Website: www.helion.co.uk

Published by Helion & Company 2010

Designed and typeset by Farr out Publications, Wokingham, Berkshire
Cover designed by Farr out Publications, Wokingham, Berkshire
Printed by Gutenberg Press Limited, Tarxien, Malta

Text and photographs © Anna Timofeeva-Egorova 2008

Text edited by Sergey Anisimov, translated by Vladimir Kroupnik

Publication made possible by the I Remember website (http://www.iremember.ru/index_e.htm) and its director, Artem Drabkin.

ISBN 978 1 906033 27 9

British Library Cataloguing-in-Publication Data.
A catalogue record for this book is available from the British Library.

For details of other military history titles published by Helion & Company Limited contact the above address, or visit our website: http://www.helion.co.uk.

We always welcome receiving book proposals from prospective authors.

Contents

1

Led astray by a rainbow

I'd made my choice – I was going to be a professional pilot! Nothing else would do! One cannot split oneself into two halves, one can't give one's heart to two passions at once. And the sky has a special claim on one, completely engaging all one's emotions …

I remember the send-off as a bright sunny festival, although the day was quite likely to have even been overcast. But … my friends' smiles, laughter and jokes – all this so dazzled me and so turned my head, and my joy, overfilling me, so fogged my vision … When the train had taken off I, by now on the carriage platform, stared ahead for a long time, blinking with half-shut eyes, failing to make anything out …

In Ulyanovsk, I rushed straight from the train station to the *Venets*[1]– the highest spot above the Volga. And such an inconceivable space opened up before me from up there, such an expanse that it took my breath away! Here it was before me – the mighty Russian river that had given Russia the *bogatyrs*[2] … And what a wonder, above the Volga covered by young December ice, a rainbow began to shine. It threw its multicoloured yoke from one bank to the other across the whole blue sky – and this in the wintertime? Yet maybe I had just imagined it? But I was already laughing loudly, sure that it was a rainbow, and that it was a sign of luck. Again just like back at the Kazan train station in Moscow, waves of joy were coming from my chest and their splashes were curtaining the horizon with a rainbow mist. It had been no easy ride – exams passed brilliantly, approval given by a nitpicking medical board – and I had been enrolled as a flying school cadet!

… We had already been issued with uniforms: trousers, blouses with blue collar patches, boots with leggings. It seemed I had never worn a better outfit in my life although it was obviously a bit big for me. In a word I liked everything in the school from reveille and the physical exercises up to marching with a song before bedtime. We studied a lot. I did well in the classes. But once … I still see that day as a terrible dream.

"Cadet Egorova! The school commander's calling you."

When I entered the office and reported as one should, everyone sitting at the table met me with silence and just stared at me gloomily. I remember standing at attention and waiting.

"Do you have a brother?" I heard someone's voice, and answered:

"I have five brothers."

"And Egorov Vasiliy Alexandrovich?"

"Yes, he's my elder brother."

"So why have you concealed the fact that your brother is an enemy of the people[3]?"

For a moment I was taken aback.

"He's not an enemy of the people, he's a Communist!" I shouted in anger, wanted to say something else, but my throat dried up straightaway and only a whisper came out. I

---

1 Translator's note – lit. 'crown'.
2 Translator's note – Mediaeval warrior heroes comparable with West European knights-errant.
3 Translator's note – a common designation for people subjected to repression during Stalin's purges.

could no longer see the faces of those sitting in the office and heard little – only my heart throbbing stronger and stronger inside my chest. It seemed that my brother was in trouble and I knew nothing about it … From somewhere I heard, like a sentence:

"We are expelling you from the school!"

I don't remember leaving the office, changing into my civilian clothes in the cloakroom, the gates of the flying school shutting behind me. They had taken the sky away from me … That rainbow had led me astray … I hadn't found happiness… And again I found myself on a steep river bank, but this time not up on the *Venets* but far out of town. I searched through my pockets, found my passport, *Comsomol*[4] membership card, a small red certificate with the Metro emblem on the front – the Government's token of appreciation for my participation in the first stage of the Moscow Metro construction. That was all I had.

In agonising torment and anxiety I decided to go to see my mother in the village. There, in my native land of Tver I would be always understood and supported. But I suddenly thought: I haven't even got a kopeck – not even enough for a passage ticket. And then I headed for the City *Comsomol* Committee …

4   Translator's note – Young Communist League.

2

My native land

Basically our village of Volodovo, lost in woodland between Ostashkovo and ancient Torzhok, had only one street. By 1930 it had only 45 houses. In summer everyone went to pick mushrooms and berries in the forests and coppices of Glanikha and Mikinikha, in Zakaznik and up on Sidorova Hill. But the main occupation of many generations in our land was flax. When it was in blossom it was impossible to tear your eyes away from the blue sea, and when it ripened it would become a sea of gold! And what great air there was in the many-grassed fields and meadows! And how crystal clear the springs were in Veshnya and Pestchanka, Lotky and Yasenitsa!

After I finished year four of the Sidorovskaya village school my mother decided to send me away to Torzhok and enroll me in a gold-embroidery school. But in a week I began to ask to go home for I understood that I would be unable to sit all day long over embroidery. I had understood even with my child's mind that one has to have to have a vocation for such a craft. They didn't make a gold embroiderer of me. But there was no place to continue my education, for there was no secondary school in our area and my elder brother decided to take me to Moscow.

I liked it at my brother's, especially the warm arms of one-year old Yurka. He wouldn't let me away from him day or night, and if I chanced not to be next to him he would begin crying so, that he awoke everyone in the apartment. I didn't go to school for I had a headstart on studies by two months. I went for walks with Yurka, with children from our courtyard in Kourbatovskiy Lane, helped at home, and ran to the bakery to buy bread.

In the winter they set up a skating rink in our courtyard. With home-made wooden skates tied with strings to our *valenki*[1] we managed to trace out some kind of figures on the ice. I happened to be at the circus when Grandfather Dourov[2] performed in person. My brother took me once to the Bolshoi Theatre. I remember that the opera *Prince Igor* was on and I remembered Prince Igor's aria for the rest of my life.

Looking ahead somewhat I recall that once I would have to listen to this aria as a POW of the Germans. An Italian POW named Antonio would sing it until he was shot dead by the Hitlerites … Years later when my second son was born I would call him Igor …

Thus, with all the variety, discoveries and delights of early teenage life my first Moscow winter went by. The next summer Yurka and I were sent to the village. It turned out that at long last they had opened a seven-year school in Novo village and it was decided that I would go there to study. The new school was a seven-year CYS[3] and I entered Year 5 there. Seven kids from our village went there. Every day we had to cover five kilometres there and five kilometres back – in frost, under rain, on roads covered by snow and through impassable mud. Only two of us stayed on till year 6: Nastya Rasskazova and I.

---

1   Translator's note – felt boots.
2   Translator's note – a famous animal trainer.
3   Country Youth School.

Nastya and I went to the graduation ball dressed "to kill" as they said in our village. We wore black skirts made of 'devil's skin'[4], white calico blouses with sailor collars and white socks and rubber-soled shoes on our feet. We sang, recited poetry and danced at the ball. They entreated me and Nastya – would-be sailors – to dance to *Yablochko*[5] and we joyfully kicked up our heels with all our might.

Along with our graduation certificates we all received recommendations for further studies. Guryanov and I were recommended for teachers' college, Nastya Rasskazova for agricultural school. Nikitina, Mila, Lida Rakova were recommended for 9-year school and to continue studying at university.

4   Translator's note – leatherette.
5   Translator's note – literally 'little apple' – a popular song in the Red Navy.

3

The underground

The papers were calling us to the 5-year-plan construction sites and almost all of our graduating class left for different places. Everyone wanted, as it was said back then, to take part in the 'industrialisation of the country'. We were eager to work and to study.

That summer my brother Vasiliy spent his vacation in our village. He helped mother mow hay for the cow and stocked firewood for the winter. He told us a lot about Moscow, construction sites, and about the underground railroad – the Metro – which was to be built in Moscow.

"What for?", mother asked.

"To get to work faster", Vasya[1] answered. "In many developed countries Metros were built even in the middle of last century, in London, New York, Paris …"

We were all were surprised by my brother's knowledge and most of all by the fact that a Metro would be built in Moscow. This word had not been heard before! I had already decided for myself that I would go with my brother and try to find a job on this mysterious construction. But when I advised mother of this she began to object, and lamented "I've brought my kids up and now they all are going to fly away from their native nest and I'll be left alone". Vasya convinced mother I would definitely keep studying in Moscow and on that we left.

Upon arrival in the capital the first thing I did was to go and look for a district *Comsomol* committee. I gingerly entered the building and began to guess which door I should knock on.

"What are you looking for, young lady?" a man dressed in overalls asked me.

"I want to work for *Metrostroy*[2]!"

"Are you a *Comsomol* member?"

"Yes!"

"Write your application", the chap suggested, and asked a passing girl: "Where shall we send her?"

"And what can she do?"

"Nothing yet" he answered for me.

"Then send her to the *Metrostroy* Construction School FZU"[3]

"Alright!"

And right there in the corridor, on the window sill, the man immediately wrote me the school's address on a piece of paper: 2, Staropetrovskj-Razumovskiy Passage.

---

1   Translator's note – diminutive from 'Vasiliy'.
2   Translator's note – abbreviation for Metro Construction.
3   Translator's note – FZU – Factory-Plant School – a common educational establishment for young industrial workers in the USSR in 1930s.

And off I went. In the FZU during the entrance examination I was told that the *Metrostroy* badly needed fitters. I didn't know what fitting was or what it was for but answered firmly, "Alright, I'll be a fitter!"

The *Metrostroy* was a *Comsomol* construction site and everyone was supposed to choose not the job he wanted but the one for which there was a demand. Three and a half thousand Communists, fifteen thousand *Comsomol* members in overalls, hard hats and *metrokhodkas*[4] were the vanguard of this remarkable construction effort. And this would ensure its success: in a short period – three years – the first stage of the underground was ready. The work was hard but no one was disheartened and the girls didn't want to lag behind the blokes in anything. The doctors didn't want to let us work underground but we kept getting permission for it anyway.

But so far, I kept studying at the *Metrostroy* FZU. We had four hours of practical work and four hours of theory daily. The study was not easy: for us new chums, wire-cutters that were a toy for an instructor would become heavy and fall out of our hands when we tried to twist wire or cut it. And it was even harder to understand blueprints! So as to live closer to the FZU I moved to a hostel located nearby. It was a whole township of barracks. There were four large rooms in a barracks with three rows of beds in each and a table in the middle. We did our lessons and drank tea at this big table. There were no breakfasts, lunches or dinners as such for us. You couldn't get up to much on the 28 roubles we were getting!

In 1928 the 'Three Prelates' Church near the Red Gate[5] was demolished. The No.21 shaft of the *Metrostroy* was sunk there and later on in 1934 the entrance hall of the 'Red Gate' Metro station was built. It was right there in the shaft precinct that we made the first slabs for the joists of the concrete 'sleeve' of the tunnel. All the slabs were lifted onto a gantry, from there loaded into a cage, and let down into the shaft. Back then during the first stage of the *Metrostroy* only loads were carried down the shaft and pulled up it, whereas the pit workers went up and down using a ladder. I will remember that ladder all my life – a narrow well or 'pit-shaft' and inside it an almost vertical ladder with narrow footholds. If someone was climbing up and another one down at the same time it was really hard to pass by each other. We had to take our gloves off for it was hard to hold on to the slippery rungs with them on. The light from our feeble lamps was quickly lost in the thick darkness. And the gumboots of other miners following you would step on your hands as you held the rungs. How afraid I was going down into the shaft for the first time in my life! But the further I got from the surface the warmer I got and the lighter it was, and now we were already at a depth of 40-50 metres. Our reinforcing rods lay to one side and trolleys of earth were coming into the pit one after another and the cager was rolling them into the cage and sending them upwards.

The cager is a pit worker who receives loads and sends them up and down. He's got a rubber jacket, gumboots and a wide-brimmed hat on and you can't tell straightaway if he's a man or a woman. He seems like a giant not only because of his dress but also because he so easily handles the trolleys loaded to the top with earth. But now the cage is gone and I see the cager, having taken off first his hat and then a small cap turned peak-backwards, straighten his bushy white hair ...

---

4   Translator's note – gumboots.
5   Translator's note – A historic site in Moscow.

We, yesterday's new brigade of pals, shouldered our reinforcing rods and, bent over by the weight, strode forward through a gallery towards the tunnel where they would have to be put together precisely according to the design drafts and every crossover tied with wire. Then carpenters would make a casing and the concrete workers would pour concrete into it … We walked through the gallery in single file. It was hard to walk for the load was heavy and we wanted to throw it down, straighten up and have a rest. But we carried on lugging it and someone began to sing quietly "Through the valleys and across the hills …"

Suddenly I felt a sharp push, a flash as bright as lightning and then, darkness, and in the darkness cries … I had received a heavy electric shock … I came to my senses in the shaft precinct: I was being carried somewhere. Noticing an ambulance I got scared, broke away from the hands carrying me and dashed off onto the piles of gravel …

I spent three weeks in the Botkinskaya hospital and when I got back to the pit I found out that Andrey Dikiy had died. He had snagged a bare electric cable with the hooks of the reinforcing rods. The death of our workmate shook us all …

After discharge from the hospital I wasn't allowed to work and the shaft committee[6] offered me a place in a floating holiday home. I refused and decided to see my mother in the village. I hadn't written her about my visit but when I got off the train at the Kouvshinovo station both my mother and my sister Maria – my godmother – were there to meet me.

"How did you find out that I'd be coming?" I asked my sister. Maria explained it simply, "Mum had some sort of dream, then she came over early in the morning and said: "Let's go to meet Annoushka[7]– she'll be coming today". And you know our mum – she's like a commander – if she gives an order you carry it out without arguing!"

Mother stopped Maria, addressing me: "My girl, why have you grown so thin? And you're so pale …"

"I'm trainsick", I explained, "you know how winding the railroad beyond Torzhok is, don't you?"

"Oh yes, God forbid", mum said. We got into a cart and went to Volodovo …

My holiday flashed past imperceptibly and now I was at the shaft again. From September I'd been studying at the *Metrostroy* workers' faculty – sometimes in the mornings, sometimes in the evenings – in shifts. We worked six hours a day, never sparing ourselves no matter what. Sometimes we stayed in the shaft for two shifts in a row. Once, having worked the evening shift, I stayed for the night. I remember that we were binding fittings in the tunnel. My arms grew terribly tired, lifted all the time holding up the wire-cutters. And it was muggy and hot in the tunnel and I was desperate for a sleep, especially by morning. Someone, curled into a ball, had fallen asleep on a step of the scaffolding. And suddenly, as if on purpose, the head of the shaft Gotseridze and the *Narkom*[8] for Railways came down underground. Noticing the sleeper they stopped.

"Why are there children in the shaft?" The *Narkom* asked sternly.

"They are *Comsomol* members", Gotseridze answered.

"Send them up top immediately!"

They would have too, had we not mutinied. Standing up by fair means or foul for our right to work in the shaft we added years to our age. It was harder for those who were

---

6   Translator's note – local trade union.
7   Editor's note – literally, 'Little Anna'.
8   People's commissar, or minister.

not tall enough. In a week it was all sorted out – we were tying fittings again but doing our best not to catch the bosses' eyes.

There was such an atmosphere on our shaft that everyone rushed to the pit-face with a kind of joy, with pleasure. It was a blessing – to go to work cheerfully and to consider yourself useful and necessary to the people. To be conscious of the fact that something done by you, by your hands, would remain in your dear land! Nowadays, so many years later, no matter how many times I ride through the 'Red Gate' Metro station it seems to me to be the most beautiful. And when they say there are better ones I get angry. My *Comsomol* youth is set firm in this station, in the cold stone …

What can I say, we, the youth, had amazingly high morale back then. We always wanted to do something, to learn something. In the beginning Tosya Ostrovskaya and I passed tests to get a "Ready for work and defence!" badge[9], a "Ready for medical work in defence!" one[10], then for the "Voroshilov marksman"[11] and even this wasn't enough. We joined a choir, and began to go to Sokolniki[12] for roller-skating. Tosya skated well but I had already smashed my elbows and knees but stubbornly kept getting up from the asphalt, kept practising and at long last – hurray! – I learned how.

---

9 Translator's note – a set of sports and fitness tests.
10 Translator's note – a set of tests on primary medical skills.
11 Translator's note – shooting skills award for civilians.
12 Translator's note – a recreation park in Moscow.

4

Out of the pit and into the sky

O nce in the shaft lunchroom I read a recruiting notice for the *Metrostroy* aeroclub glider and flying groups. Only recently the *Comsomol*'s IX Conference had put out the call: "*Comsomol* members – take to the air!" Once we were visited at the *Metrostroy* by some field editors from the *Comsomol'skaya Pravda* newspaper promoting it. At the same time our own paper – *Udarnik Metrostroya*[1] – reported that the *Metrostroy* aeroclub had been granted territory for an aerodrome not far from the Malye Vyazemy station, 4 U-2 biplanes and 3 gliders. Future airmen and parachutists were invited to pull up stumps and build a field aerodrome and hangars for the planes and gliders. Well, if they need stumping we'd do the stumping! To be honest, I'd secretly dreamed of flying for a long time, the way people dream about far countries, alluring but unattainable. And now, having read the recruitment notice I plucked up my courage and made the first step – I headed to the given address – 3, Kuibysheva Street.

I found the building I needed but was afraid to go in. I had already read all the posters, the wall newspaper, the notices hung in the corridor, but still couldn't find the guts to approach the door marked "Entrance examination".

"Who are you waiting for, young lady?" A serviceman in a flyer's uniform asked me.

I couldn't see his face: my eyes were fixed on a gold-embroidered badge on his sleeve – the Air Force emblem … Many years later POW airmen in the Kostrinskiy concentration camp would present me with exactly the same emblem. They braided a handbag from the straw they slept on and embroidered the Air Force emblem (an airplane propeller) on it with my initials: "A.E." – Anna Egorova – and passed it to me in secret … But back then I began to say, stammering, that I longed to join the aeroclub's flying school and had even brought an application.

"An application is not enough", the airman said. "You need references from the site, from the *Comsomol* organisation, a medical certificate, an education certificate and a birth record. When you collect all the papers, come with them to the credentials committee. The committee will decide whether you'll be accepted or not."

Having thanked the airman, and inspired by making a start, I dashed outside and running at full speed rushed towards the Red Gate, to the pit. The *Comsomol* committee approved my decision but in the brigade …

"What's got into you?" Vasya Grigoriev gloomily commented. "You're better off going to an institute to study – let blokes do the flying."

"And this weakling wants to be a flyer! She hasn't got over her electric shock yet!" Tosya Ostrovskaya declared.

And her my bosom friend! We even slept together, so to speak – our beds stood next to each other in the dormitory, we worked in the same brigade, studied together at the workers' faculty. Even our skirts and blouses were 'interchangeable': one piece for both

---

1   Translator's note – literally, "*Comsomol* Crack Worker".

of us. One day she wore skirt and blouse and I wore a dress, the next day it would be the other way around. Tosya dreamed of becoming a doctor but I hadn't decided yet what to do and we used to argue a lot because of this. Running ahead I'll say that Antonia Sergueevna Ostrovskaya would become a doctor and spend the whole war at the front as a surgeon. But back then she was keen for me to go to medical school together with her.

But our foreman settled the argument:

"She's wiry, she can take it. Let her join!" he concluded and gave me a reference.

Now I would have to go before a medical commission, and not just one but two. We had many qualms: we were spooked about certain twists and pitfalls supposedly invented by the doctors for those wanting to fly. But I was pleased to find no twists or pitfalls during the commission. Ordinary doctors in ordinary offices listened to our chests while tapping them, spun us in a special armchair to test our inner ears and if there were no shortcomings wrote: "Fit".

To tell the truth, only 12 out of 20 came for a second examination, but it all came out well for me. The doctors all wrote the one most wonderful word in the whole Russian language – "fit". Now only the credentials committee was left.

And then one day, having finished night shift in the shaft I had a shower, changed clothes, had breakfast in the shaft canteen and went to the credentials commission. It was situated in a former church in Yakovlevskiy Lane near the Kursk train station. Now there were classrooms and aeroclub offices here. They didn't call me up for quite a while and I (after all it was after night shift!) fell asleep sitting on a wooden bench. But as soon as I heard my surname I jumped up and not yet fully awake, rushed into the office. I was supposed to appear before the high commission in a military manner and report according to all regulations, but all I said was:

"It's me, Anya[2] Egorova, from shaft 21."

All those sitting at the large table burst out laughing together. The stream of questions was endlessly long: I was asked about my parents, brothers, sisters, my work, and on geography …

"Determine the longitude and latitude of the city of Moscow", I remember someone from the meticulous commission suggesting.

I approached a map hanging on the wall, then for quite a while I led my finger along the meridians and parallels and finally gave the answer. Everyone laughed again: it turned out that I had confused longitude and latitude.

"She's just flustered", a *Comsomol* representative put in. "She's a crack worker."

"Well, if she's a crack worker …" An airman drawled. "Tell us, girl, which group exactly do you wish to join?"

I understood I had to stop "bleating", and pull myself together, and start talking properly, sensibly – otherwise everything would be ruined: they'd throw me out and never call me back. I gave the deepest sigh and said "I want to be a pilot!"

"Ooh, what a smarty she is, and the *Comsomol* swore she was flustered. Not just anywhere, but straight to flying!"

Someone growled from behind the table "It's a bit soon, she's the wrong age, she should wait another year."

2   Translator's note – another diminutive for Anna.

How extraordinary: they wouldn't take me as a gold seamstress because of my age, wanted to kick me out of the shaft because of my age … And the same again when I fraudulently added two years to my age, again I wasn't good enough because of my age?

"For the time being you'll be on a glider …"

"And what's that?"

"You don't know? Strange … It's a flying machine. Well, how can I explain it to you more simply: it's a plane with no engine…"

"So that means that I've been dreaming of an engine in vain?" burst out from me. I approached the table and began to talk very fast, addressing really only the airman:

"Gliders are for gliding, a plane is what I need … Please understand – I long to fly …"

"This year gliders are what you'll fly, if you like it we'll transfer you to an airplane group. Next!"

Shutting the door behind me I collapsed on a chair kindly moved up by someone. Questions poured on me from all sides: "How was it in there?", "Where are they sending you?", "Are the questions hard?"

We studied theory all winter. It was hard to combine work and studying at the workers' faculty and in the aeroclub. But Tosya and I even managed to go to movies and sometimes even dancing. Our shaft was under the patronage of the Theatre of Operetta and we were often provided with tickets to shows. The actor Mikhail Kachalov was our idol and I even fell in love with him, trying to attend performances he acted in and to sit as close to the stage as possible.

In early spring we began to go to Kolomenskoye village for practice. It was said that this was where a serf called Nikitka, having made wings for himself, jumped from a high bell-tower. We would take off from a high bank of the Moscow river and hover on our gliders. Of course, by today's standards everything was done in a very primitive way. The US-4 glider was set up on the steep bank and anchored with a steel rod. The trainee would sit in the cockpit and the others would go down the slope, take hold of the ends of the elastic straps attached to the glider and at the instructor's command "Pu-u-ull!" stretch them out so as to shoot the one sitting in the glider cockpit as if from a slingshot.

In order to stay in the air for 2 or 3 minutes and spend the rest of time pulling on the gliders' elastic straps, having worked a shift in the shaft, all summer I would go to Kolomenskoye every day. By autumn in the pit, by now an inclined shaft, the congenial smell of warm moisture, paint and lacquer reached our nostrils. The smell of finishing works, a sure sign that the whole job was close to an end awoke a pleasant feeling in our breasts. The sensation of something festive and thrilling accompanied us when we walked on the almost ready station platform. But the walls were still bare and heavy crates with electric equipment were still being carried down one after another. We, yesterday's fitters, were now busy with revetment – it was a common practice for the Metro of that time. People wanted to build the Metro from start to finish and would master several interrelated trades …

In October 1934 a test train of two red wagons rode the Metro. What an exultation that was! We shouted "hurray!", sang songs, hugged, danced, ran after the wagons. My first ride in a Metro train left an indelible impression on me. It was such a big deal underground on 6 February 1935 when the builders did a 'fly-by' of all their 13 stations! And on 15 May 1935 the Metro was open for public use. The Moscow *Comsomol* organisation was awarded the highest Government decoration, the Order of Lenin, and a big group of the Metro builders was also awarded with orders and medals. For us the *Metrostroy* had become a great school of fortitude, character building and tempering.

5

Getting ready

"You've done enough digging in the ground, it's time to come to your senses. Go study if you want but in the meantime I've made an arrangement – you'll work in the editorial office of the *Trud*[1] newspaper. The position is nothing special but you'll be among clever and educated people. Hopefully they will influence your partisan personality."

So my brother declared, and took me to the Palace of Labour, to Solyanka Street, where the editorial office was located. And I began to read letters from *rabkors*[2] deciding to which department they should be delivered. The work was interesting but I missed the *Metrostroy's* enthusiastic people. That was why, after four months of 'torment' at the *Trud*, I fled to take part in the construction of the second stage of the *Metrostroy*, to the 'Dynamo' shaft 84-85. Now I started work as a rock-breaker and rock-drill repair mechanic, and at the same time as a voluntary librarian in the shaft's trade union committee. I had already graduated from the workers' faculty and the glider school – I had got my secondary education, becoming a gliding instructor.

In the flying club we studied flight theory, aerial navigation and meteorology, the 'Flight Operations Manual' and the equipment of the U-2 plane. By the springtime we had begun to go with an instructor to an aerodrome in Malye Vyazemy for aerial training. We would get on a steam train (there were no electric trains back then) at the Byelorusskiy train station and it would take us an hour and a half to get to Vyazemy. From there it was a kilometre's walk to the aerodrome through the woods along the Vyazemka river.

Our aerodrome! It was already waiting for us beyond the village of Malye Vyazemy where there was a large field surrounded by woods. Hangars, offices and residential quarters had been built there – and all by the hands of the *Metrostroy* students. We, the students, prepared ourselves for flying with a help of a small book in a blue cover. It was titled 'VVS RKKA[3] Flight Training Course", or simply KULP. It was sternly drilled into us that this book had been written in the blood of flyers. It contained directions for the flight student for studying and mastering flying skills, and "general advice".

Let's take, for example, clause 5: "Cultivate in yourself military discipline both on the ground and in the air, orderliness, politeness at work and in private life, constant attention even to small details, accuracy, punctuality, swiftness in action, and especially boldness within reason when resolving of a given problem". Very practical advice!

Back then we learned the pages of this book, remarkable from any point of view, almost by heart. Here if you please is another of its clauses: "Don't lose courage after temporary failures: on the contrary, after failures you have to show still more perseverance, persistence and will, to work still more to overcome difficulties, you should not become presumptuous

---

1   Translator's note – 'Labour'.
2   Translator's note – abbreviation of '*rabochiy* correspondent' or working correspondent – a correspondent who worked at industrial operations.
3   Translator's note – Russian abbreviation for the Air Force of the Workers' and Peasants' Red Army.

in case of success, nor allow yourself to slacken your attention, fall into laxity or ridicule your comrades. You should remember that during summer practice a serious and prudent approach to each sortie and exercise regardless of his personal qualities, flying skills and record, is required of every pilot. Infringement of this rule will inevitably eventuate in a breakdown or an accident, observance guarantees stable accident-free high-quality work".

We would re-read the pages of the KULP dozens of times before a flight, before implementation of another exercise, during preparation for exams. We also studied the 'Flight Operations Manual', the FOM. At the aerodrome first of all we took an examination before a mechanic on knowledge of the aircraft and the engine. Then, setting the plane up on a pivot post, we in turn entered the rear cockpit (an instructor sat in the front one) and, manipulating the levers, learned how to take off, turn around, and land on three points. An instructor patiently showed us how to work out the level for different flight configurations. To do this we would now lift the plane's tail, now lower it, now move it sideways.

At long last all the tests had been passed, the ground-based preparation had been completed and the next Sunday we should be flying. How slowly time drags when you are waiting … By now I was working at the shaft again – as a caulker. We caulked the tubing seals (this was to damp-proof the tunnels). It was really hard to caulk the arch of the tunnel – my arms raised up with a caulking hammer grew tired. On top of that when you do this work water pours from above directly into your sleeves and flows down all over your body, so you stand as if under a heavy shower of rain. When you are caulking the floor of the tunnel other difficulties arise. After a lot of preparation work done with a beading puncher you have to fill the seams with lead and tamp grout on top. Our work was considered unhealthy and a girl from the canteen would constantly bring us milk straight to the workplace and make us drink as much as we could! My duty was to prepare grout from cement, liquid glass, sand and other components according to the set proportions and fill the tubing seams with it. It was not a complicated job but it was difficult to do in gloves. Then I took them off and began to stuff the grout between the rough pig-iron tubing walls with my bare hands.

After the shift I washed my hands and looked at them: there was no skin on them, and they hurt terribly: "What about flying?" An anxious thought flashed through my mind. I ran to the medical unit and the doctor gave a gasp, "What have you done, you silly girl?"

"Will they skin over by Sunday?" I asked. "I have to go flying, you see."

"What do you mean, go flying!?" The doctor growled, smearing something on my hands and binding them up. She gave me a sick-leave certificate and forbade me to take off the dressings or wet my hands.

On the second day I nevertheless went to work but I couldn't stuff grout into the seams even with gloves on. Then I began carrying cement and sand in buckets. Trying to protect my sore palms, I would take the bucket like a ladies' handbag and carry it on my bent arm. Passing by with yet another bucket of cement I suddenly heard yelling. Blokes from the tunnelling crews were arguing. There was a lot of noise anyway – from rock breakers, from caulking hammers driven by compressed air, from hissing hoses, from trolleys. But the blokes were outshouting all the workplace noise.

"Anya! Anya!" I heard them calling me. "tell us which is right: opéra or òpera?"

Two huge blokes stood in front of me, with faces red from arguing, gripping colossal spanners in their hands. Just in case I stood between them and said in a conciliatory manner "In French it would be opéra but in Russian, òpera."

The blokes calmed down, sympathized with me because my hands were in dressings and one of them asked "Why do we never see you at dances?"

"No time, I'm studying at our aeroclub's flying school."

"Have you already flown?" The miners asked with one voice.

"Of course", I lied, blushed and, hanging the bucket on my arm strode to my workplace.

"What's wrong with your hands, Egorova? Why are you carrying the cement bucket on your hip and not in your hand?" the shift boss asked, coming towards me.

"It's comfortable like that." I answered and quickened my pace. At the beginning of the shift the brigade foreman had tried to ban me from working but I convinced him I would be assisting the brigade to meet the plan, and stayed.

By the end of the second *piatidnevka*[4] my hands had skinned over and I immediately headed to the aeroclub. Now we had to go to the aerodrome on a daily basis. The shaft was operating well but when I requested a transfer to work only day-shifts, for I would have to fly every day, our foreman Zaloev objected, "I won't let you! You have no right!"

The Ossetian[5] Zaloev was handsome. His eyes, black with dark blue, flashed with fires from under long bushy eyelashes, his eyebrows were like two wings, his curly hair poked out from under his miner's hat. He was tall and well-built. His ugly work clothes seemed to suit him! I was watching him carefully and he was running back and forth around the site brandishing his caulking hammer. "Here we go", I thought. "With his hot Caucasus blood what a whack he's gonna give me with the hammer!" but Zaloev, having calmed down, said reconciliatory "You no be angry ata me, me wanta good for you. Drop outta you flying, you may losa you head. Once we builda the station you willa join any institute you wanna. But now, Anya, you musta work."

"No, Georgiy, thanks for your advice but I'm not going to give up flying."

And here we are – having done a shift at the shaft we are heading off to our date with the skies as to a festival! It is noisy and cheery in our wagon our way to Malye Vyazemy. We sing songs – a beautiful blonde girl in a dark-blue velveteen dress with red buttons starts singing. She's got a blue silk kerchief the colour of her eyes on her neck. This is Anya Poleva – also a trainee flyer at the aeroclub. An hour and a half has flown by unnoticed and now we are walking towards the aerodrome. The lawns have become greener over the week we haven't been here and in some places the bird cherry trees have already blossomed as well. Victor Kroutov runs off the footpath, barges into the bushes and I am presented with the first bouquet of flowers in my life. I am still angry at him but accept the gift. The flowers from Victor are in my hands. I tear off a tiny petal and begin to tell my fortune, whispering to myself "I'll fly, I won't fly ..." instead of "He loves me, he loves me not ..." It comes out that I will fly and, rejoicing, I run lightly and freely towards my future ...

---

4   Translator's note – a five day period – in the 1930s in the USSR the normal seven-day week was replaced by a five-day week.

5   Translator's note – a national group in the Northern Caucasus.

6

My first flight

What greater thrill can there be in life than flight? I remember it thus: an airfield with skylarks and bluebells. Our planes are lined up, as are we in our brand new dark blue overalls and OSOAVIAHIM[1] helmets with goggles. Each group stood by its plane. Everyone stood to attention. A light breeze was blowing in our faces, we were breathing easily and freely. And it was so nice to live in this world, so joyful! I thought that there would be no end to our youth or to our lives …

"To your planes!" the head of the aeroclub orders.

Our instructor Georgiy Miroevskiy takes his seat in the front cockpit, a trainee pilot, Tougoushy, in the rear. We all envy our comrade: he is lucky to be the first to go up in the sky.

"Sta-art engines!" the head of flying gives the command.

"It's turned off!" Looking at the technician standing next to the plane's propeller, the instructor says "Inject fuel!"

"Yes sir, injecting fuel!" the technician shouts turning the propeller.

"Start up!"

"Yes sir, starting up!"

"Swing the prop!"

"Yes sir! Clear of the prop!" – And strongly jerking on a vane to vent the compression the technician runs away from the screw. The propeller began to spin, the engine started up, sneezing barely-seen smoke. The instructor threw his arms sideways, which meant "take the chocks from under the wheels". Then the plane smoothly taxied to the starting point.

We sit in the 'square' next to the tool kit bag, wheel blocks and slipcovers and watch the plane. The 'square' is a place where all the trainee pilots and technicians of the aeroclub free from flying are positioned. Each of us keeps his eyes on the plane. Now 'ours' has made several circles over the aerodrome and touches down. We all dart off to greet him but the technician pulls us up sternly, saying "Let just Egorova meet him."

Gripping the U-bow of a wing I run with long light strides trying not to lag behind the plane. Without turning off the engine the instructor orders the next one of us to get in, and we mob Tougoushy and bombard him with questions.

"How was it, good?"

"Good!" He replies smiling from ear to ear.

"How good?" I asked. "And not even a bit scary?"

"No, it wasn't scary."

"And what did you see?"

---

1 Editor's note – The Society of Assistance to Defence, Aviation and Chemical Construction. It was established in 1927 by the merging of the Voluntary Society of Friends of the Air Fleet, Chemical Defense and Industry of the USSR and the Society of the Assistance to Defence. In 1948 it was divided into three Societies – the Voluntary Society of Assistance to the Army, the Voluntary Society of Assistance to the Air Force, and the Voluntary Society of Assistance to the Navy.

Tougoushy becomes pensive, "The instructor's head, the rev counter in the mirror, the instructor's face in the mirror."

"And nothing else?"

"Nothing at all", Tougoushy answered seriously to our common laughter.

My turn has come. "May I board?" I asked the instructor. Miroevskiy gave permission with a nod, and I climbed into the cockpit, buckled up the belts, and attached the hose of the intercom.

"Ready?" The instructor asked me impatiently, watching me in the mirror.

Trying to shout down the engine's roar I yelled "Ready!"

I receive directions through the speaking device: the instructor will be doing everything himself during the flight and I will just hold the levers softly and memorise the turns.

"Try to take note of the flight heading, and the landmarks for turns. We're taking off!" I hear his order at last.

When we are in the air only the instructor talks, "The start is towards the south-west. On the right is Golitsyno, Bol'shie Vyazemy, on the left the Malye Vyazemy train station. We're making the first turn."

I am all attention. I do my best to remember what is below, lest I miss the turns …

"We're over the Malye Vyazemy station. Here is the second turn, memorize it", Miroevskiy continues insistently. When we were flying over ploughed fields the plane lurched heavily. Abandoning the levers I reached for the fuselage with both hands but it was as if the instructor hadn't noticed me move.

"Altitude is 300 metres, flying straight. Steer the plane!"

I had not expected that at all. But there was no choice – I began operating the pedals, the steering column, the throttle. And then the quietly horizontally flying plane began listing from one side to another, lifting its nose above the horizon or lowering it like a horse under a bad rider. The machine wouldn't obey my inexperienced hands! And it seemed to me that a whole eternity had gone by before the instructor took over the controls. The plane immediately calmed down and I gave way to despair: "My flying days are over! I am no good at it, and a coward to boot …" I wanted only one thing – that no-one find out about my disgrace: my inability to handle the plane even in straight flight! My hopes of becoming a pilot were dashed …

But the instructor Miroevskiy tells me about the third turn as if nothing has happened, asks me to keep my eye on the airstrip "T" point and whether we are flying parallel to the sign. Having finished the third turn he slows down and, descending, we approach the last, the fourth, turn. I hold the control levers but not so as to impede the instructor. Now he switches the craft to gliding, then hovers and lands on three points.

"That's it", I hear his voice in the headphones. "We've made it back! Now taxi to the parking lot."

And I interpret it my way: "My flying days are over. He'll cross me off as incapable". Having taxied the machine to the spot himself Miroevskiy turned off the engine and began to climb out of the cockpit. Having unfastened my seatbelts I clumsily got out onto the wing and jumped down on the ground.

"Ready to have my knuckles rapped" I said quietly, not raising my head.

"What's wrong with you, Egorova? You're not going to cry, are you?"

"I'm a failure!"

"But who succeeds on the first go?" Miroevskiy laughed. "Moscow too wasn't built in a day".

7

I'm a pilot!

The first Sunday of June was ordinary. A day like any other: bright, warm, summery. At dawn quaint palaces of white clouds were still hanging on the horizon but by the time flying started they had dissipated and the sky had cleared. The weather was just right – aviation weather. Truth to tell, the breeze was playing up a bit but not too much. The aerodrome woke up early from habit, and when the disc of the sun rose up above the treetops our tall and thin instructor Miroevskiy was already inspecting the line of trainee pilots. It was as always, like many a time before that, but for some reason today he was looking us over very carefully as if we were soldiers on parade, and checking our flying gear. And no less cordially, with his pleasant, unexpectedly low voice he announced "Egorova will be the first to fly with me if there are no objections."

The very idea! I took a step forward and my whole posture expressed full readiness.

"May I board?"

"You may …"

I deftly jumped up on a wing and then threw myself into the rear cockpit. That was how it should be. The front one was for the instructor.

"Taxi out!"

The obedient U-2, waddling from side to side like a duck, rolled towards the airstrip on the stiff grass. "Take the controls!" Miroevskiy ordered.

"Aye-aye, taking the controls …"

It was a routine dual training circle flight. As usual we took off, landed and taxied to the parking lot … Then the instructor's seat was occupied by the flight commander and we took off and landed again. And at this moment I was surprised by the inopportune appearance of the club Flying Service commander. The flight commander was already unbuckling his seatbelts and threw his leg overboard. It was time for me to get out too. But the flight commander made a sign with his hand as if to say: 'stay there'. There was a smile on Miroevskiy's kind long face. It meant that everything was alright – he was pleased.

In the meantime the aeroclub's Flying Service commander was already heading for the plane, doing up his helmet on the way and pulling on his leather gloves. Flying Service commander Lebedev was a simple, cordial and benevolent man. We, the trainee pilots, had never seen him blazing up, yelling at anyone, degrading anyone's human dignity even under stress. He always listened attentively to us, his subordinates, made his remarks tactfully, gave useful recommendations. When lecturing he would instil in us that a man in the sky doesn't learn just flying skills. He builds his character and his outlook on life in the skies. "For his success each pilot is obliged not so much to his natural disposition and abilities but rather to his diligence", he used to say. "All your flying days are still ahead of you. So gather all the best you have inside: courage; self-control; love for your trade, and work! That's the only way you will earn the gratitude of the people …"

And Lebedev was an excellent pilot too. They said that he had been awarded a Chinese medal for his excellent training of Chinese pilots in a combined aviation school in Urumchi. What skill must he have attained to train the Chinese pilots, illiterate, not knowing the Russian language, not having seen a plane in their lives?

All of us trainee pilots were eager to be examined by the flying unit commander himself and not by the head of the aeroclub. "Are they really going to let us fly on our own?" the presumptuous and thrilling thought flashed through my mind. However, I was ashamed of it straightaway: "How did that get into my head? No one has flown on his own yet …"

"Something's up!" I thought and the Flying Service commander climbed into the front cockpit.

"Fly a circle. Altitude's 300 metres, then land on the landing T on three points inside the boundary", I hear his voice through the speaking device. I repeat the order and ask for permission to taxi out.

"Taxi out and take off!" – The commander ostentatiously put his hands on the sides of the cockpit, thus showing that now I would have to do everything myself and he was almost an bystander here and was not going to interfere with the controls.

Well, if I have to, I will. I have been flying the plane for a long time, and the presence of an instructor has been somewhat soothing. After all, you know that if something happens he'll be sure to help. I gradually rev up and take off, doing everything the way we've been taught. Here is the last straight line of the 'box' – the most crucial one. I glide, set the levelling altitude, pull the lever to me with a barely perceptible movement – and the plane lands on three points near the T-point of the airstrip.

"Taxi in!" I hear the Flying Service commander's order.

When the plane stopped Lebedev ordered me to stay in the cockpit and headed towards Miroevskiy. The latter said something to him and then the instructor called for a sandbag to be put in the front cockpit. I immediately remembered that this used to be done to keep the plane aligned when a trainee flyer was flying on his own. And so it turned out. The instructor said, looking into my cockpit, "You'll be flying alone now. Do everything you just did with the Flying Service commander".

That's when my mouth went dry and my palms got sweaty! I wanted to thank the instructor for having me taught to fly, for letting me fly the first in my group, wanted to find many kind and good words but not saying anything, just sniffling I began to pull my goggles on. I did it too soon, paying no attention to the plane mechanic setting a sandbag on the seat. How many months I'd been waiting for those little words "fly alone", that sign of the highest faith in a young flyer. I'd been dreaming of them, saying them in different ways and thinking under what circumstances I would hear them. And now I heard them … Miroevskiy began to help the technician tie up the sand bag inside the front cockpit and was saying "This is for Egorova so that she doesn't get bored! It'll replace me! Well, don't hang back, flyer … Everything will be alright … Be calm."

"Contact!"

"Clear the prop!"

The propeller began to make its revolutions and the plane shuddered again. All my attention was concentrated on the instruments. Grasping the wing cantilever the instructor Miroevskiy walked alongside up till the start point, and confidence was passing from his strong skilful hands to me through the whole body of the plane as if by invisible impulses. Here were the control column, throttle lever, magneto lever … I had touched them hundreds of times, turned them, made the machine go through complicated manoeuvres. But that had all been done with an older comrade watching – and now I was responsible for each movement of mine and of the plane. Myself! Strange thing – whereas only several seconds ago the responsibility was pressing me down, now, at the starting line, there was nothing of the sort.

I turned the U-2 around during the take off. My heart was beating evenly, I was breathing easily, my mind was working sharply, my memory was prompting me to perform the well-programmed actions. The utmost concentration and determination! No, my dual training flights had not been in vain. The machine was gaining speed – one more second and the undercarriage left the ground. I am flying! Everything went well. The main thing now was to carry out all elements of the flight neatly and correctly …

Do many people know what a flight means? You will say: millions. Look how many of them dash from one city to another, from continent to continent. But how can you compare the open cockpit of a training plane with the hermetically sealed salon of a passenger liner? Everything in it is like in a bus: the walls, the windows, the ceiling. You can walk in it, move around paying no attention to any kind of atmospheric conditions. It's comfortable … But this is only the illusion of a flight: you do not fly, but you "travel by air". Being in a training plane is completely different, even if it's a U-2! Everything is open to the air: your head, shoulders, hands. Sink your palms into the rigid air waves and you will feel the strong chilling current. Turn around and you'll see – there is no one else in the whole world. There is only the sky, you and your plane obedient to your human will. It lifts you higher and higher: up to the stars, up to the sun. If you want to turn it sideward it'll do it, if you want to take it lower it'll do it. You're its master.

I was inundated by happiness. I wanted to sing, to yell into space. To shout that I was a pilot, that I could tell the plane what to do! I, a simple Russian girl, a girl from the Moscow *Metrostroy*! But the miracle that seemed to me an eternity lasted only a few minutes: just enough to manage to make a circle over the aerodrome. And now the U-2 was running on the grass again. Miroevskiy stood near the T-point. He raised his thumb and made some sign with a white signal flag. Initially I didn't understand what it was about but then guessed: permission had been given for a second flight. It meant I had done everything alright. And there was no limit to my joy during the second flight. I sang, then yelled something, finally, taking my feet off the pedals I tried to cut some capers, and I didn't notice I was approaching the fourth turn.

I am trying, trying very hard to land the plane as accurately as possible and I manage to do it: the U-2 touches down on three points at the T-point. Our *starshina*[1] Khatountsev meets the plane. He has grasped a wing with one hand and is holding the other one raised with the thumb stuck up. In revenge for him making me wash the plane's tail I stick out my tongue and rev up. The plane speeds up and Vanya runs with all his might accompanying me. And I am so cheerful, my soul rejoices so much, that it seems there is no person in the world happier than me! Having taxied to the parking lot I turn off the engine. Mobbing the plane, the guys ask me some questions, congratulate me, but I rush to report the mission accomplished to the club management. "Well done, Egorova. Keep flying like that", the flying unit commander said and shook my hand firmly.

That day three from our group flew on their own: Khatountsev, Petukhov and I. After the flight we went to work under the technician's command and again *starshina* Khatountsev 'entrusted' me with washing the tail unit. I was not angry at him – on the

---

1   Translator's note – Sergeant-Major.

contrary, I took a rag, soap and a bucket of water with pleasure … In the evening during debriefing the instructor declared his gratitude to us but Tougoushy gave us a scolding, "Why do you look only at the instrument board during the flight? Where's your field of attention? You can't fly like that! You will smash yourselves up and kill me. Just as I want to hand the controls over to you at landing I look in the mirror and see you looking not at the ground but at the instruments. We are not doing blind flights after all! And you have to act more freely in the air too, you mustn't tense up and get scared. The plane is reliable!" And he added, laughing, "History knows a case when a U-2 took off and landed with no pilot."

We all laugh and again Miroevskiy patiently tells us about flying a circle, shows the route on a mock-up, draws it on the blackboard and then asks Tougoushy to repeat everything. The trainee pilot repeats everything sensibly – after all, he's got degree in engineering – but during the next flight he watches the instruments again. The instructor makes him train on the ground, in the plane cockpit, and then finally the penny drops. Soon after that Tougoushy would catch up with us.

By the end of July when we had all begun flying on our own they suggested we take leave from work and go to camp, to an aerodrome. They made no obstacles for me at the shaft. On the contrary, our *Comsomol* leader Zhenya kept holding me up as an example at all the meetings, "These are dreadful, bleak times. The clouds of war are coming from the West. Imperialism, riding on a strengthened Fascism, is preparing an attack on our Soviet country!" he would say wrathfully and urging the guys to join the OSOAVIAHIM and pick up military skills. Many of the girls and guys answered the call. Alesha Ryazanov, a metalworker from our shaft's mechanical workshop, was among them. Running a bit ahead I'll say that Alesha would graduate from an aeroclub, then the Borisoglebsk military school for fighter pilots, and open his combat account of shot-down Fascist planes on the first day of the war. Ryazanov would defend the skies of Moscow, Stalingrad, Kuban'[2], the *Pribaltika*[3]. Our fellow *Metrostroy* worker would become Twice Hero of the Soviet Union …[4]

I quickly booked my vacation and, having received my holiday pay, sent almost everything to the village, for my mother, having written in my letter that I would be going to camp. I didn't explain what kind of camp it was.

They set up an army-like daily routine for us in the camps. It would be reveille, physical exercises, cleaning up the tents, breakfast if flights were planned for the second shift. If they were to be in the first shift, reveille would be before dawn and commencement of flying, at dawn. Soon we had all worked on our circle flying and started on the most interesting thing, aerobatics. Again we studied the 'Flight Operations Manual' which says the aim of learning aerial stunts is to teach the pilot to use the flying characteristics of a plane fully. This helps to master perfectly the art of manoeuvring the plane, necessary for a pilot in combat. But we were still doing our 'aerobatics' on the ground. The instructor Miroevskiy would hold a model plane in his hands and analyse with us all the elements of flying: where to look, what to see, how to operate the rudders and elevators, not just which way, but how fast and how far to move them. "Egorova", he asks me, "what kind of manouvre is a 'dead loop'?"

2   Translator's note – a province in Southern Russia.
3   Translator's note – a common Russian name for the Baltic countries.
4   Editor's note – with 31 or 32 personal and 16 shared victories.

"A 'loop'", I reply, "is a closed circle in the vertical plane."

"Good girl. Sit down", Miroevskiy encourages me and then jokingly addresses Petoukhov: "And what the hell is a 'spin'?"

Ivan gets up with dignity, tucks in his overalls behind the back, stands to attention, his grey eyes light up, and he begins, "A 'spin' is a quick rotation of the plane along a steep descending spiral. It occurs during loss of speed by a plane. The 'spin' as an aerial stunt has no independent significance but is mandatory for all flying personnel during training."

"Tougoushy! What do you know about the 'barrel-roll'?" Miroevskiy asks.

"It's a double flip over a wing in the horizontal plane. Exit is in the direction of entry", the student-pilot raps out in one breath, "but it's impossible to do a 'barrel-roll' on our U-2 – its speed is too low."

Tougoushy has changed since he'd learned how to fly. When his flying wasn't going well he walked gloomily, without a smile, and even his dark eyes seemed mud-coloured. But now Tougoushy shines, comes to the aerodrome in a white shirt and tie. His grey cloth OSOAVIAHIM suit is thoroughly ironed, the shoes are polished and not even the aerodrome dust settles on them. His face is clean-shaven, his eyes sparkling! We have begun to call him "Prince of Georgia" among ourselves.

"And how is the 'Immelman' carried out, Koutov?" The instructor questions solicitously.

Victor Koutov, a brown-eyed chap with a face as tender a girl's, demonstrates the order of implementation of this complicated manouevre. Victor works at a *Metrostroy* marble factory and studies at college in the evening. He is fond of reading, writes poetry and collects books. He usually buys them in two copies: one for himself and one for me. But I have no room to store books and I hand them over to the shaft library. Sometimes I come across hand-written verses in a book presented to me: they are written by Victor. I take the sheet of verses out of the book with care, and when there is no one around I read and re-read them and put into my hand-bag. Then, in the dormitory I hide them deep in my secret casket …

And that was theory, independent circle flying and ground drilling done. We have already been allowed into the 'zone', to practise aerobatics. Sharp turns, loops and spins, from fascinating terms in our textbooks, are becoming real indicators of our skills. And we fiercely strive further – strive to master aircraft navigation as well as possible. At this time Victor Koutov and Tougoushy became my permanent companions and tried to sit at the same table with me even in the dry mess. I liked Victor but didn't like Tougoushy although he was doing his best to win me over. He even tried flattering me: "Anya, it's as if you were born in a plane, I'm even jealous. First time you flew on your own, and you got no critical remarks. How could there be? – the plane in your hands is like a trained horse. But it doesn't obey me at all!" I said nothing, and what could I say? Now if Victor had told me that … We all were in good spirits and an elevated mood: every day we were discovering something new for ourselves. One would constantly hear, "You know, I nearly broke into a spin doing a loop!"

"You don't do sharp turns, you do 'pancakes'".

"What a dive Vitya[5] made today!"

Once we were coming back from the runway, marching as usual and singing our favourite at the tops of our voices:

---

5   Editor's note – a diminutive form of Victor.

Higher, higher and higher
We send our birds into flight ...

Suddenly one of the guys broke in, "Look, fellas, what's that showing red in the girls' tent?"

The song stopped. Everyone began to scrutinise from afar our tent with its sides raised, and coming up closer saw that my army bed was covered by a luxurious quilt. And there was a woman sitting on a stool next to it – my mother.

"Fellas, now that's devotion! All burst out laughing as one.

The *starshina* allowed me to leave the formation, and I hastily greeted my mother and blurted out, "What did you bring the blanket for? To make me a laughing stock?"

"My little girl, aren't you cold under army issue? My heart told me so!"

"I am not a bit cold, any more than all the others! And take it back, please or they'll laugh me to scorn ..."

But at this moment my instructor approached, introduced himself to my mother, admired the blanket and advised that I was a good flyer and soon would do parachute jumping.

"What do you mean, a flyer?" My mother exclaimed and stood up from the stool, letting her arms drop limply.

Miroevskiy was surprised too. "Why didn't you write your mother that you were learning to fly?"

I stood silent, and my instructor began to explain to mother as simply as possible what a U-2 plane was.

"Don't worry about your daughter! Our plane is absolutely safe, just like a cart. But a cart is drawn by a horse and the plane is driven by an engine of several horse-power. And it's good that you've brought the blanket. Everyone is cold at night: the forest is nearby, a river ..."

My mum calmed down and trustingly addressed the instructor. "Please keep an eye on her, sonny. She's kind of impulsive: first went to work underground, then climbed into the sky ..."

"Alright, alright, mamma. Everything will be fine. Don't worry about your daughter."

The same day mum left for Moscow. The blanket stayed with me but, to be honest, it began to disappear quite often. Once when it was raining I decided to seek it out and located it in the blokes' tent: Louka Muravitskiy, having wrapped himself in it as in a sleeping-bag, was sleeping soundly ...

... Time went by fast. The guys and I worked for the *Metrostroy*, flew in the aeroclub – we did aerobatics in the landing zones near the aerodrome, did routine flights. When the weather stopped us flying we studied parachutes and parachuting – how to pack one and the rules for jumping. We would have to learn it later and, possibly, it would stand us in good stead ... As expounded by the parachute trainer Vladimir Antonenko it was all very easy to do. But when the time came to jump I had barely managed to fall asleep the night before. In the morning the weather was fine – that meant we would be jumping. I remember putting on the parachute, primed it – in other words, pulled on the tight rubber bands and fastened them with strong hooks to the snap locks. The instructor checked the 'priming' and the nurse Ira Kashpirova my pulse, and at that moment something began to shake and ache in my chest! I walked to the plane like a bear, for the parachute hampered my movements. Clumsily climbing on a wing, I got into the front cockpit: the flyer Nikolay Lazarev was in the rear. We took off and gained about 800 metres altitude.

"Get ready!" I heard the pilot's voice.

"Aye-aye", I replied, scrambling onto a wing and looked down, grasping a console. Oh, God, how frightening! I wanted to get back in the cockpit and, probably, I would have done but the pilot slowed down and yelled "Go!" And gave me a slight shove forward!

"Aye-aye!" I yelled and jumped into the 'abyss'.

From then on I acted the way I was taught. I pull the ring but for some reason I feel that the cord hasn't come out and there will be no clap, and that means the parachute will not open! Suddenly I am jolted hard and the snow-white canopy opens up above me, and I am sitting on the straps as if in an armchair. I am surrounded by an amazing silence but an unrestrained joy grips me and I either sing something or shout. But the ground is already close. I tuck my legs a bit under myself and fall on my right side – everything according to the rules. Then I quickly get up, unfasten the parachute, furl the canopy and begin to pack it. At this moment the guys rush up, give me a hand and we unanimously agree to keep on and on jumping. It's a really great pleasure! After the jump the earth feels a bit special and so do I. A kind of confidence has appeared in me – "I can do anything!"…

In autumn, when the U-2 training program had been completed, a State Commission from the People's Commissar of Defence came to visit us. At first they examined us in all theoretical subjects and then began to test our flying technique. All of us performed aerobatics in the landing zone with excellent marks and the Commission was satisfied. It was time to say goodbye to the camp, to the aerodrome, to the instructors and to our comrades. We were happy and a little bit sad. We were happy that we had found our wings but sad because it's always sad to part …

I was working at the shaft and after work opening the library located in the shaft's dry mess. Instead of bookshelves there were sideboards and I sat next to them like a barmaid issuing 'brain food' – the books. The aeroclub graduation party would be in a month … We gathered together in the Malaya Bronnaya Theatre. All were dressed up – the guys even put ties on. The report was made by Guebner, the head of the aeroclub. He said most of the guys who had graduated from the club would be assigned to fighter pilot military schools. Mouravitskiy, Ryabov, Kharitonenko, Petoukhov, Vil'chiko, Khatountsev were among them. And suddenly, somewhat ceremoniously, raising his voice (or maybe, it just seemed to me?) Guebner announced, "And there is one "ladies'" ticket – to the Ulyanovsk OSOAVIAHIM pilot school. We've decided to give it to … Anna Egorova.

My breath caught from the unexpectedness and joy. Could it be the dream I'd been nurturing would come true? Everyone was congratulating me during break but I still didn't believe it, was afraid to believe it was going to happen. I believed it only when I had received a referral to the school and travel papers to Ulyanovsk. A beautiful girl with a red beret and red scarf, one end of which was jauntily thrown over one shoulder onto her back and the other fluttering on her chest, stood out of those who had come to see me off. She was dressed in a black overcoat and on her feet she had shoes with French heels. She was Anya Poleva – Louka's girlfriend – who along with me had undergone pilot training in our *Metrostroy* aeroclub. In an amicable way, Anya envied me leaving for pilots' school, and said she would go on with flying in the training detachment of the aeroclub and would secure for herself a referral to the Ulyanovsk school.

"And what about Louka?"

"What about him? He's gone to a flying school. I will keep studying too and when we get on in the world we will definitely get married … You know", Anya said, "I can't live without the skies now, without the aerodrome and its smell of petrol." And she added with a laugh "I am mad about flying and Loukashka[6]!"

She and I parted tenderly and I didn't know back then that within a year Anya would be no more. She fell to her death making a parachute jump from a plane. Her parachute didn't open …

We all knew that Anya and Louka were in love – they were not making a secret of it. Louka, a native of a small village lost in the Belorussian forests, having come to Moscow to live with his uncle, joined an FZU and soon he started working as a sinker in a *Metrostroy* shaft and studying in the aeroclub. Upon completion of our aeroclub's course he was assigned with Koutov and other guys to the Borisoglebsk Military Flying School. After graduation Junior Lieutenant Louka Zakharovich Mouravitskiy served in the Far East but the War found him in the Moscow Military District. He took part in aerial battles in his *yastrebok*[7] at the far approaches to Moscow, later near Leningrad. The flight commander Mouravitskiy distinguished himself not only by his sober-mindedness in calculations and his gallantry but also by his readiness to do anything to defeat the enemy. At the same time it seemed strange to everyone that Louka would write with white paint 'For Anya' on each one of his planes. The commanders kept ordering the flight commander Mouravitskiy to erase the inscription immediately, but before a combat flight the inscription 'For Anya' would appear again. Nobody knew who this Anya was, whom Louka remembered even going into battle … Once just before a combat sortie his regiment commander ordered Mouravitskiy to erase the inscription and said "Don't let it happen again!" And it was then that Louka told the commander about his lost bride: "Even though she didn't die in combat", Louka went on, "she was going to become an aerial fighter to defend our motherland". The regimental commander backed down …

In this very sortie Louka rammed a Heinkel He 111 bomber that was breaking through to a railway station defended by his lone plane. The enemy plane hit vacant ground beyond the railway and Louka barely managed to land his badly-damaged fighter near the station. After receiving medical treatment he returned to his regiment – and new battles several times a day followed … On 22 October 1941, four months after the War had broken out, Louka Zakharovich Mouravitskiy was awarded the Gold Star of a Hero of the Soviet Union for fortitude and valour during combat operations. And on the 30th of November 1941 Louka Mouravitskiy died a hero, defending the city of Leningrad.

---

6   Translator's note – diminutive for Louka.
7   Translator's note – literally, 'little hawk' – a common nickname for Soviet fighters.

8

Fate plays with human life

I had been banished from the sky in the Ulyanovsk flying school and my dream had been ruined. The rainbow had led me astray ... The Secretary of the City *Comsomol* Committee where I had applied, stood silent for a long while. Then he rubbed his hands, scratched his head, combed with his fingers his crew-cut of light brown hair and hotly exclaimed, "I've got it, Egorova! You will go to work as a Pioneer[1] leader in an NKVD labour colony for juvenile offenders.[2] You'll be there until the next draft to the flying school. Over that time all this will have settled down, your brother is sure to have been released and you will join again. The head of the colony is a good man – he'll understand. Anyway, let's go and see him ..."

Thus I settled at the colony in a small room of a wooden house. The colony occupied a large three-storey red-brick building located almost in the centre of Ulyanovsk in Bazarnaya Square. A large yard with shacks and workshops was adjacent to the building. All the kids studied in classes for four hours and for four hours they worked here in the yard in the workshops.

Of course, it was difficult to build a team from juvenile criminals. Each kid, aged from 8 to 16, already had a criminal record. Each group had its 'warlord' and I decided to start with him. But how would I pinpoint him? I began by simply walking around, watching and listening. I would come to a class, sit at the back, and observe how their life went on. The exercise books issued by the Russian teacher for dictation would instantly turn into playing cards and a real 'battle' would begin. Anything might be lost up to or including dinner. In the canteen you might see a scene such as one boy, stuffed, having eaten several dinners, and the losers drooling ...

My suggestion of joining hobby groups: shooting, aircraft modelling, sailing, got not so much as a nibble. But after watching closely a couple more times and consulting with the tutors and teachers I selected eight boys from different groups and walked them to the Pioneers' Palace, which was really splendid, in Ulyanovsk. And there, as I had arranged, we were received like dear old friends. Then I walked the boys to the tank and aerotechnical schools. We were received with interest everywhere: they showed us around, talked a lot and even became our sponsors. The tank cadets and the aircraftsmen began to spend time with us. It was they, I understand now, who lit a flame in the souls of these difficult kids. The ice was broken!

By the end of the third month of my work as a Pioneer leader the first detachment of Young Pioneers had been formed. For the first time a Pioneer's bugle resounded in the colony yard, a drum began to tap and 30 boys with red ties, a standard bearer and his assistants, marched past an improvised tribune, walked out through the gate and joined the columns the people of Ulyanovsk's May Day parade. But we had hardly gotten ourselves

---

1   Editor's note – a pro-Communist organisation for 9-14 year old children in the USSR, similar to the Scout movement.

2   Translator's note – a penal colony run by the NKVD – People's Commissariat of Internal Affairs.

organised when an order, forbidding any kind of Pioneer activities in the juvenile offender colonies, arrived. I was fired …

The flying school's supplementary intake hadn't started yet and I was still living in the colony. I started work at the Volodarskiy Munitions Plant, situated across the Volga. The manager of the human resources department asked me "What do you want to do here?"

I answered that I begged to be employed at any kind of work but my trade was construction – steel fixer, caulker …

"Will you go to Accounts as a clerk?"

"But I've never worked in accounting."

"Not a problem, you'll learn", the human resources officer said and added as if thinking it over: "If I send you to a workshop, they do shiftwork and for the first three months you'll be on an apprentice's wage. But in Accounts there's only one shift and a permanent salary. You'll just have to learn. When you see the chief accountant say you used to work as a clerk."

"I won't be able to work as a clerk", I kept repeating.

"You will, you will!" – And he registered me as an accounts clerk.

When I came to the chief accountant he asked me what kind of clerk I used to be.

"What d'you mean, what kind?" I was surprised.

"Well, was it bookkeeping or accounting?"

"Bookkeeping", I replied smartly, remembering the official's instructions.

"That's good. Go to the transport department and see the senior accountant."

I was immediately offered employment in the transport department accounts section and shown the desk I would sit at.

"Please tally up the statements" – the accountant handed me a stack of paper sheets covered with writing. But how to calculate, what with? There was an abacus in front of me and there was some kind of small machine. Everyone around me was smartly clicking their abacus beads, but of course I had no idea how to calculate that way! However, by lunchtime I had added up all the sheets but, to be honest, not with the abacus but on a sheet of paper. So that nobody could see how I was calculating I put it into a half-open drawer of the desk.

During lunch break everybody went to the canteen. They called me along but I declined and decided to talk to Maria Borek, – a bookkeeper sitting next to me. Maria would have her lunch an hour earlier than the rest so the section would not be unattended. As soon as everyone was gone I asked her "Maria Michaylovna[3], please explain to me how to calculate on an abacus, and what this machine in front of me is for."

Maria Mikhaylovna gave me a surprised look through her *pince-nez*, "That's an adding machine. But how are you going to work without special training?"

I stood silent, and what could I say?

"Well, we will practise during the lunch break and for an hour after work, and now I will explain adding and subtracting on the abacus to you …"

Many years have gone since then but I still remember Maria Mikhaylovna Borek, a Leningrader born and bred. She taught me bookkeeping, supported me in every possible way, looked out for me. She got me involved in the social life too. Nevertheless, when I

---

3   Editor's note – addressing a person using both their first and second (patronymic) name is a sign of respect in Russia.

heard about the additional draft to the flying school I immediately brought my application for the entrance examination. But I was rejected during the preliminary interview.

"During the last draft you concealed that your brother was an enemy of the people, and now you want to worm your way into the school again? You won't fool us – we're awake!"

And again I was riding the Ulyanovsk-Moscow train. The wagon was crowded and filled with tobacco smoke. Children were crying. Lying on the topmost bunk I was sighing for my dear brother and my ruined dream. But how could my brother be an enemy of the people? But my brother *was* the people! Our parents had had sixteen children – eight of them had died, eight had survived. Poverty had made my father take any work. He used to work sometimes as a truckdriver – he carried fish from Ostashkov, from Seliger, sometimes he used to go to Torzhok for cucumbers. There had been years when he worked at a dye-works in Petrograd. My father froze in the trenches of the Imperialist War[4], and defended Soviet rule during the Civil War. After all those battles he came home sick and died in 1925 at the age of forty nine. Vasya – the eldest of my brothers – wanted to study very much. But having done four years at the Sidorovskaya school he went by decision of a family council to work as a tailor's 'boy'.

Father said back then, "Mother, let's sell our sheep and I'll take Vas'ka[5] to Petrograd. I'll ask Egor Antonovich up there to put in a word for him with the boss. Very likely he'll be a tradesman. There's nothing here, is there? No place to study, and no way to keep him clad, shod and fed."

And then he addressed his son, "Maybe, son, you don't want to learn to be a tailor – then go and be a cobbler with Uncle Misha. He's your uncle, your mum's brother – he won't lead you astray … The choice is yours."

Vasya chose tailoring and studied right up until the October Revolution. The sixteen year old lad got himself a rifle during the days of the Revolution and went to war with it to fight against the Cadets[6]. Wounded, Vasya managed somehow to make his way to Aunt Agrafena's, a distant relative of our father. The Aunt panicked and sent a letter to the village, writing that only God knew if Vasya would live or die. On receiving this news my mother abandoned everything and rushed to save her son. She nursed him back to health and brought him home – tall, skinny and shaven-headed. But Vasya didn't stay at home long and soon found a job on the railways in Kouvshinovo. And some time later the workers put him forward for the position of salesman in their store. There was hunger and devastation in the country – back then they would choose as salesmen the most reliable men, the ones they trusted. Then Vasya was transferred to Rzhev, then to Moscow. It was a common biography of working class guys in those years: worked, studied on the job, became a Communist. Later he graduated from the Planning Academy, a *Komvuz*[7]. The workers of the *Moskvoshvey*[8] N5 factory elected him as their deputy to the *Mossovet*[9]. "Head of the Planning Department of the People's Commissariat of Internal Trade – what kind of enemy of the people is that?" I thought, turning over in my mind my dear brother's

---

4   Editor's note – a common name for the Great War in the USSR in the 1920s and 1930s.
5   Translator's note – another diminutive for Vasiliy.
6   Translator's note – a common nickname for the counter-revolutionary forces during the Civil war in Russia (1918-1922).
7   Translator's note – abbreviation of Communist University.
8   Translator's note – Moscow Garment.
9   Translator's note – Moscow City Council.

whole life. "Defamation! Slander!" And I remembered my mum praying to God, kneeling before the icons, as she firstly listed all our names, the names of her children, begging God for health and wisdom for us, and then at the end of each prayer repeating: "God save them from slander!" Back then, in my childhood, I didn't understand that word but now it was exposed before me in all its terrible nakedness ...

How slowly the train was going! But on the approach to Moscow I had become somehow indifferent to everything. Where was I going, what for, whom to? Here was Moscow, the city of my *Comsomol* youth. It was here where my fate had turned so suddenly binding a village girl to the city and the sky ... Moscow met me with an overcast and rainy day. This time no one was meeting me, nobody was waiting for me. I rang my brother Vasiliy's apartment from the train station. His wife Katya answered. Recognizing my voice she burst into sobs and couldn't say a word for a while. Having calmed down a bit Katya asked "Where are you now, Nyurochka[10]?"

"At the Kazanskiy train station."

"Wait for me near the main entrance, I'll come around shortly."

And there I was, standing and waiting. An hour went by, then another ... And suddenly I noticed a poorly dressed woman with a hangdog look.

"Katya?"

It turned out she had been looking for me dressed in military uniform and I was looking for her: a beautiful woman with splendid hair, sparkling eyes and proud carriage .. Again there were tears ... She grasped my hand and led me inside the station. We found a vacant bench and sat down, and Katya told me Vasya had been tried by a *troika*[11] that had sentenced him to ten years behind bars. Vasya had been accused of espionage and connections with British intelligence. His article in the 'Economy newspaper' had been allegedly reprinted by the British, and by this he had given away some sort of state secret ..

"Ten years! For what?" Katya said, sobbing. "Nyurochka, my dear, please don't ring me up or pop into my place anymore. Today I came by only to pick up Yurochka's gear We're roaming between friends' places at the moment although many of them are afraid of us ... And I'm afraid I may be arrested at home ... What will happen to Yurka[12] then?" Katya wept. I was in tears as well. We parted ...

Where was I to go? To Victor in his aviation unit? By no means, looking like this .. To the aeroclub? No. To the *Metrostroy*? To pitying looks, to let everything remind me of my happiest time, my daring dreams, to let every allusion to the past make my life miserable? No way! Maybe later, but what now?.. I'll follow my nose! Here in the timetable there is a train that will take me to my brother Alexey. So I'm off to that town ...

And now the train was dawdling, halting at each sub-station, drearily rattling its wheels ... I didn't find my brother in Sebezh – he had been transferred to a new post. I stayed overnight at the neighbours' place and in the morning I was on the road again. I had only 12 roubles left in my purse. I was just two roubles short of the fare to the town where my other brother Lesha[13] worked. Not a drama – I bought a ticket for all the money I had, and being one station short of the destination wouldn't be a big deal – I could walk it. Again I was riding in a passenger wagon on an upper bunk and nearly crying. Did

10   Translator's note – another diminutive for Anna.
11   Translator's note – a trio of judges – a typical court during Stalin's purges.
12   Editor's note – Yurka, Yurochka – diminutives for Yuri.
13   Translator's note – diminutive from Alexey.

I really have no willpower? And if I did why was I lying like this, flat on my back not wanting to make any effort? Why was I not fighting for my right to fly? I remembered the words of the First Secretary of the *Comsomol* Central Committee Sasha Kosyrev[14], loved by all young people: "Never deviate from your chosen course. Keep moving forward courageously and proudly ..."

"Keep advancing courageously and proudly!" I repeated these words aloud and at that moment the train, shuddering with all its long and clumsy body, stopped as if giving me a choice.

"Where are we?" I asked, my head hanging down.

"Must be Smolensk!" A man answered.

"How long are we stopping"

"Half an hour at least"

Unexpectedly for my neighbours in the wagon, I nimbly jumped down from my bunk, slipped my coat on, picked up my trunk and rushed for the exit.

---

14   Translator's note – died during Stalin's purges in 1937.

9

'Kokkinaky'

The train left. At the time it swung past the last traffic lights in Smolensk I was approaching the *obkom*[1] building. The winter dawn was only beginning to blue the white walls of the houses of the ancient city and the *obkom* doors were still locked. Having knocked a while at the entrance doors and feeling badly chilled, I set out jogging down the street. I ran up to the announcement board and back. And I did so several times until a pleasant warmth flowed through my whole body. Time went by and the day was beginning. Now right by me the first tram rumbled past, the first truck honked. And the door to my dreams opened ... I burst into the *obkom* together with the first visitors. I stuck my head into one room, then another – no, that wasn't it.

"Where will I find your Secretary?" I asked in a peremptory voice some weedy chap with spectacles proceeding importantly along the corridor with a brief case. He glanced at me in wide-eyed astonishment: who was this wanting "Himself"? But, detecting determination in my face and look, he asked no questions but said simply:

"Over there, around the corner there's a door padded with black leatherette ..."

A small chubby secretary blocked my way through this door with her chest but then either my appearance or look or my considerable height made her let me through to the door to my dreams. Seizing the opportunity I resolutely crossed the threshold and straight from the entrance, afraid of being stopped, blurted out in a rush "I need a job and accommodation. And as soon as possible!"

A young man sitting at a large desk raised his head a bit and looked at me through his spectacles in astonishment.

"What exactly is your problem, comrade?"

"My problem can't wait ..."

Terribly agitated, and confused because of it, I began to tell about myself: the underground, the aeroclub, the flying school, my brother ... I talked without concealing anything, like in the confessional. The secretary listened to me in silence and I saw a real concern and involvement in his look. It seemed to me that he understood he had before him a person who had been deprived of her life's work. Not just a girl but a *Comsomol* member who had mastered the complicated craft of flying. A major war was just round the corner, industry had been growing at an unprecedented pace, the army had re-armed and there was a desperate shortage of trained pilots. The *obkom* secretary knew all that perfectly. Listening to my confused story he was more and more surprised at how they could without any reason remove a student-pilot from flying at a time when flying personnel was so badly needed, when the OSOAVIAHIM had no time to train students for the flying schools. When the pre-army training program was strained to the limit!

"What kind of documents have you got on you?"

---

1   Translator's note – Provincial *Comsomol* Committee.

"Here you are", I laid my passport, *Comsomol* membership card, red certificate – the citation I had received from the Government for the construction of the first stage of the underground – and the certificate that I had completed gliding and flying training in the aeroclub.

Reading the documents, the secretary was questioning me, ringing someone, calling someone to come around, and I was sitting on a couch and... crying.

"Well, will you be able to train our guys in gliding?"

"Of course I will!"

"Excellent. You've got the right papers."

Even my breathing stopped!

"Well, cry-baby, let's go for lunch", I heard his mocking voice.

"Thanks, I'm not hungry."

"Let's go, let's go", he pulled me by the arm.

After lunch, seeing my empty purse, he lent me 25 roubles till my first pay.

"It seems you were interested in work and lodging?" There was craftiness in the secretary's voice. "Whilst you were crying here we recommended you to the Smolensk flax works as a bookkeeper. You'll be balancing the accounts. And you will organise a gliding school there. There is a go-ahead, youthful bunch there. Shoot off to the personnel department now. I have made all arrangements. As soon as you settle in go to the aeroclub and see the commissar – I've heard there is a training detachment for those who have already completed pilot preparation. How many brothers do you have?" the secretary asked suddenly.

"Five."

"Well now, how rich you are in brothers, and I have none! If you're gonna write about all your brothers you'll use up too much paper. Is that clear?"

"Thanks for your advice!"

"Show all your "credentials" at the aeroclub and request they accept you into the training detachment. Should any questions arise, don't be shy, come around ..."

"Thanks", sobbing through my nose, I muttered, and shot off to the flax works thanking my stars: what a lucky girl I was to come across good and kind-hearted people!

On the same day I was employed as a spinners' salary clerk, and by night-time I had been lodged in a dormitory in a room where the best shock worker, Antonina Sokolovskaya, lived. And I was accepted into the aeroclub's training detachment and I began to fly again. What a joy it was – to rush to the aeroclub after work. A lorry would be already waiting for us there and we would ride in it to an aerodrome located a fair way from the city ...

Well into autumn we sat exams on the theory and practice of flying before the State Board and were disbanded pending special orders. I had no hope of getting a referral to a flying school. After all there were five other girls in our detachment, hereditary natives of Smolensk, and I was a newcomer. Therefore I decided not to attend the aeroclub anymore and started getting ready for an aviation institute. An aviation one and nothing else. If I failed to become a pilot at least I'd be near the planes. Once upon a time my brother Vasiliy had insisted on my studying ... "Once upon a time"... And only a year and a half had passed since I bade farewell to Moscow, the *Metrostroy*, the aeroclub, my comrades, Victor, my brother. Somewhere up north Vasiliy was doing his term "incommunicado"...

Mama had written me that with the help of kind-hearted people she had done up a petition to our fellow-countryman Mikhail Ivanovich Kalinin[2] – trying to convince him of Vasen'ka's[3] innocence. Mama had had no response and then decided to come to Moscow herself. "Katya with my grandson Egoroushka walked me to the waiting room of the President's office and then left", my mum wrote. "There was a long queue, a lot of people had turned up. My turn came. I thought Mikhail Ivanovich would be there himself but looking at who met me I found no goatee. I expected the assistant would walk me to our countryman but he only said: 'The Chairman of the Supreme Soviet doesn't receive people on such questions …'"

I continued to work at the flax factory. Twice a week I trained glider pilots, attended courses in preparation for tertiary study. One evening on my day off I popped into a café, sat at a table and ordered an ice cream.

"Egorova!" Someone called from behind me. I turned to the voice and, seeing the aeroclub commissar, came up to his table. He introduced me to his wife and daughter and seated me next to them.

"Why aren't you attending the aeroclub?" The commissar asked me.

I expressed my concerns and he told me, "You should after all, yesterday we decided to grant you the only female assignment to the Kherson aviation school.

"Me?"

"Yes, you, 'Kokkinaky'[4]! And turning to his wife he explained with a laugh, "The guys gave Anya that nickname and I've been calling her that!"

"That's fine, call me that, I even like it", I replied frankly. "After all, the Kokkinaky brothers are famous test pilots and record-breakers!"

"Tomorrow take the referral from the aeroclub headquarters, resign from the factory and go to Kherson as fast as possible. Consider that you'll have to pass exams there on general secondary school subjects as well as special disciplines. The competition will be hot, get ready!"

Indeed in Kherson there was a great flood of graduates from the country's aeroclubs. They came from Moscow and Leningrad, Arkhangelsk and Baku, Komsomolsk-on-Amur and Minsk, Tashkent and Dushanbe. It was not a military school but OSOAVIAHIM one. Only girls were being accepted in the navigating division and mostly guys in the instructors'.

First of all we were sent for a medical examination. Those who passed would be divided into groups for the general subject exams. The oral exam on mathematics was run by an old lecturer from a teacher's training college. Convinced that he had poor hearing, we helped each other with prompts and most of us received 'fives'[5]…

Gradually our numbers were becoming lower and lower – but now we had passed the credentials committee. Following the advice of the Smolensk *Comsomol obkom* I had said nothing about my elder brother. At long last the lists of those accepted were posted up I read: "Egorova – to the navigating division". There was no such great boisterous joy in my heart as back in Ulyanovsk but nevertheless I ran to a post-office and sent my mum

2   Translator's note – the President of the USSR – a notable figure during Stalin's reign.
3   Translator's note – diminutive for Vasiliy.
4   Translator's note – surname of famous Soviet test-pilot brothers in the 1930s.
5   Editor's note – the highest mark of the five-point system still employed in Russia.

a telegram – I wanted to make her happy for a while. Yes, to make her happy by letting her know her daughter had been accepted into flying school!

When she got my telegram from Kherson my mum replied with a letter, which I have kept.

My dearest, greetings!

I got your telegram. I am happy for you. But I would be happier if you were not striving for the sky. Are there really no good occupations on the ground? Your friend Nastya Rasskazova graduated from veterinary college, lives at home, treats livestock in the *kolkhoz* and her mum has no trouble at all. But you – all of my kids – are somehow driven, always want to achieve something and strive for something.

There is no news from Vasen'ka. Ah, my girl, my heart's been tormented with suffering about him. Is he still alive, my dear boy? I remember coming to Moscow to see him and he'd already become a director and some kind of Deputy. He put his leather jacket on me, linked his arm in mine and walked me to a theatre. And there were mirrors all over the place in there and I actually thought, why are there people looking like us walking past – what a surprise! If you could only put in a good word for him …

But you do your studies, do your best. What can be done now if you have already fallen in love with your aviation and you are doing well in it. If you – my kids – are happy I am happy too. If you grieve – I – your mother – grieve too.

I've got eight of you – my children, and I am uneasy for all of you. All of you – my baby birds – have flown away. I've seen the last one – Kostya – off to the Army. I ordered him to serve faithfully and honestly but when the train had begun to disappear behind a turn I fell over onto the platform unconscious. What has happened to me – I am at a loss …

Oh, mama, mama! How could I explain to you what flying meant to me? It was my life, my song, my love! He who has flown into the sky – found his wings – will never betray it and will be faithful to it till the end, and if it happens that he can no longer fly he'll dream of flying even so …

I liked the way the teachers in our school conducted the lessons. The most interesting classes were run on meteorology by an old retired sea captain who had ploughed all the seas and oceans. He was the idol of us all! The captain would enter the lecture room with his head proudly raised in a peaked service cap with a very high crown. We would all stand up to greet the captain, and looking at his meticulously ironed and made-to-measure uniform I would want so much to look like him! But the captain was not tall at all, had deep-set eyes that looked at us kindly and respectfully. The captain would begin each lecture with an ancient superstition: "If the sun sets in a cloud, navigator beware a gale …" Or he would recall another proverb related to our future occupation.

For the first time I understood what a good teacher was: he loved his profession, was addicted to it, and would not only impart good knowledge but would also inculcate in his listeners a love of the subject. Studying was easy for me. After all I had already worked as an instructor! We studied the theory of flying and, of course, flew – on two-seat U-2, UT-1 and UT-2 trainers.

The war against Finland sped up our graduation. They abruptly shortened, 'rounded off' the training program and took us through to the exams, which we also sat in a hurry. They didn't even manage to tailor us uniforms and we graduated in the old blouses and skirts we'd worn as cadets.

After graduation I was transferred to the Kalinin City aeroclub to work as the aeroclub navigator. But it turned out on site that there already was a navigator in the aeroclub but they were short of a pilot-instructor. I really wanted to fly and happily agreed to take up that position. After a test of my flying techniques I was permitted to train student pilots and was assigned to a group of 12 men. The guys were different in their general level of training, physical development and character. They were united by one quality – their passion for aviation. Everyone was eager to complete ground training as fast as possible and to begin to fly. And I knew exactly how they felt!

The flight commander Senior Lieutenant Petr Chernigovets came to our classes often. He had been a fighter pilot in the Army and had been sent to the OSOAVIAHIM to "reinforce the training personnel". Chernigovets was really a skilled flyer, knew mathematics and physics well and easily explained cumbersome aerodynamics formulas. The students liked him for his respectful attitude towards them. Petr helped me a lot too. One flying day the senior pilot-instructor Gavrilov crashed. The trainee pilot was thrown out of the plane when it hit the ground, and in the heat of the moment he got up and ran. The surgeons examined him, auscultated him and suspended him from flying. And in five days he was no more … Flights stopped. The students walked around depressed. The flight commander Cherepovets ordered the whole fight to line up to analyse the accident.

"A plane, as you are aware", he began, "is a plane and no matter how slow and simple it may be, you have to treat it respectfully – in other words, carefully and seriously. The experienced pilot-instructor Gavrilov had relied on his student but the latter neglected the laws of aerodynamics or knew them poorly – and here is the result. During the last turn, as we all saw from the ground, the plane nosed up, lost speed and fell into a spin. There was not enough altitude to pull the machine out of its critical position and it hit the ground. The profession of pilot", Chernigovets continued, "is not only romantic but dangerous as you have seen for yourselves. But there is no point being down in the dumps, let's get down to business!"

And he began to draw right there, on the sand, various plane positions in the air simultaneously explaining and asking one or another student. It helped the guys get over it.

For an instructor the first independent flight of his student is an event just like his own. I remember that the student-pilot Chernov was the first one from my group to be sent by me into the air. The detachment commander had already approved it but I was uneasy and requested the squadron commander to fly with him once more. The *comesk*[6] made a circular flight with Chernov and yelled "Why waste plane resources, let him go!"

I took the signal flags with emotion as the instructor Miroevskiy had done long ago. Everyone was watching the trainee pilot as he sat in the cockpit, focused and serious, and waited for permission to take off. I raised the white flag and then swiftly stretched my arm out showing the direction along the airstrip with the flag.

---

6   Translator's note – abbreviation for 'squadron commander'.

The plane headed for take off and it seemed to me I had forgotten something, hadn't said something! I wanted to shout out some loud directions after him! Keeping my eye on the plane I walked to the finish point to meet my pupil at the landing T ...

A student called Zhoukov was the second to fly and he made it superbly too. But a student called Sedov gave me a lot of trouble. While everything had been coming easily to Chernov, Sedov had learned to fly slowly, if surely. I understood that later, when all twelve students were already flying independently, and I began to summarise the hours they had spent with me in the air. It turned out Sedov had flown with me less than the rest. "How did that happen?" I thought about it and understood: I had held up Chernov as an example all the time but had made Sedov do more ground training. As a result more fuel and plane and engine resources had been spent on Chernov. But both of then flew at the same level by the end of the program, and Sedov even did it a little bit more elegantly and confidently.

One day the State Commission came upon us unawares but by now I was confident – my guys flew well. Only one student got a 'four' for aerobatics, the rest got excellent marks.

There was a festival at our aerodrome on Aviation Day. We, the pilot instructors, had been preparing for it ahead of time. We had been flying in formation, practising individual flying, flying in pairs and sixes. We'd been flying gliders too. Parachutists had been preparing their own program but it was we, the flyers, who would have to drop them. And early in the morning the aerodrome was ready to receive guests. The space for spectators was marked off a thick rope. We checked our planes time and again, specified the program – and the festival began!

At last the announcer called out my flight. I carried out an aerobatics set over the aerodrome, landed and hadn't managed to taxi in when I was told: "Your mum is here". It appeared that having found out from a provincial newspaper that there would be a festival here she came to Kalinin and headed to the aerodrome straight from the train station. Of course, mum had brought with her a basket of gifts. She sat down on the grass behind the barrier and began to watch what was happening in the air, and she was sitting quietly until my surname was announced. Then she got anxious and when I began to do aerobatics, mum rushed to the centre of the airfield shouting "My girl, you'll fall down!" holding her festive lace apron as if she was setting it under me so in case I fell I would fall on it! Orderlies walked mum to headquarters. It was clarified who she was worried about – and then the head of the aeroclub offered her "a ride in an aeroplane". But mum refused categorically ...

After our students graduated we, the instructors, were awarded a river boat tour from Kalinin to Moscow to visit an agricultural exhibition. And soon we steamed down the Volga feasting our eyes upon the marvels on her banks. Then we sailed through the channel[7]: seeing the shipping locks for the first time, I was amazed and delighted. Then there was Moscow. We visited the exhibition, I also saw my family on the Arbat[8]. Now Katya worked as a knitter at a stockinet factory, Yurka was studying at school. We talked a lot. My brother took an opportunity to send a letter in which he wrote that they had sailed down the Yenisei river for a while on a barge with criminals. The 'mobsters' scoffed at the 'politicals' and took away their clothes and food, but the guards either noticed

---

7   Translator's note – between the Volga and Moscow rivers.
8   Translator's note – a Moscow street.

nothing, or didn't want to notice. In Igarka they were put ashore and marched into the tundra. Many of them caught cold and died. Less than half survived …

The second stage of the Moscow Metro was already in operation and I felt a longing to see my station, 'Dynamo'. Its columns were tiled with semi-precious onyx. There was a bench between the columns and behind it in a niche – a bas-relief of an athlete. It was beautiful!

In the *Metrostroy* I found out that nearly all my mates from the *Metrostroy* aeroclub had graduated from the flying schools and were now serving in the Air Force. Victor Koutov was a fighter pilot in an aviation regiment on the Western border. He'd been writing me letters in verse, asking a reply to each of them but as always I had had no time. After graduation from the school Victor had visited me in Kherson hoping to take me away with him but I didn't even want to listen to him.

"Once I graduate I'll come to you myself", I responded back then.

"You won't! I know you pretty well. You'll have to be dragged to the altar."

"You do that then!" I burst out angrily. Victor left, and I was very melancholy. I would walk to school in tears … maybe I had a premonition that I'd seen him for the last time in my life …

We spent five days in Moscow and when we got back home we set about work so intensely that there not even weekends any more. Through the whole pre-war winter we trained pilots drafted via a special call-up of pre-conscription-aged youth. They were fully exempted from work and studying in any institutions. The aeroclub paid them an allowance. By the spring we had trained all of them and all of them were recommended for accelerated transfer to flying schools. In fact back then we had guys from two call-ups – exempted from work and not exempted from work. The students who studied without exemption from work started flying in the summer – after the graduation of the guys from the special call-up. Day after day we helped them find their wings and not all of them had started to fly independently when the war broke out.

10

This is war, girls!

Flying had dragged on till evening and a June night comes late. I was already tired but couldn't go home: I still had to do debriefing with the trainee pilots, and write up paperwork. As soon as I had sat at the desk my friend Mashen'ka[1] Smirnova stuck her head in the door, "Don't sit up late, Anyuta[2], we're going to the forest in the morning. We'll have you up with the sun!" she said and flitted away.

"Of course", I recalled, "It's Saturday today!" So many weeks in a row we'd worked with no days off – we could afford one. The girls' idea was a good one – off to the forest. The weather was as if 'on demand'. And the area around Tver'[3] is crawling with inviting places. And there's no need to walk far – get on a tram and it'll take you right to the pine-forest, the one beyond the 'Proletarka' Textile Factory.

When the first tram left we left with it. The instructors were glad – after all this time we'd got together. The car was filled with laughter, jokes and songs … The conductor was outraged, "You're playing up like schoolkids – there's no keeping you in check!"

There were five of us girls there: two aircraft mechanics, two Marias (Nikonova and Piskounova), two volunteer pilot instructors (Tamara Konstantinova and Masha Smirnova) and the two of us, pilot instructors via the Kherson aviation school: Katya Piskounova and I. Later, during the war, at night the latter would drop ammunition and provisions from her defenceless Po-2 down to the marines of a landing party at Eltigen.[4]

… But for now we were walking, feasting our eyes on marvellous spaces … The fading lilies of the valley showed through the grass in places – like a gift of nature … We came out on the Volga river, chose a comfortable spot on her high right bank and sat down, admiring the passing steamships. But usually music was heard from them and it was uncommonly quiet. And suddenly we heard the distinct voice of a radio announcer echoing in the forest: "We are at war …"

All nature's colours faded then and there. Our cheerful mood had vanished somewhere. In a moment we became older than our years. All of us standing in that Sunday morning forest were certain: the country was rising to a mortal battle. And each of us who had mastered a military profession decided for herself not to stay out of it. Someone said briefly: "Time to go home", but in less than an hour we all encountered each other at the city military commissariat. Our little ruse against each other hadn't worked but our visit to the commissar's office turned out to be futile.

"Do your job, girls", the military commissar responded to our request to send us to the front. "You'll have enough work in the rear now."

---

1   Editor's note – a common diminutive for Maria.
2   Editor's note – yet another diminutive for Anna.
3   Translator's note – the pre-revolutionary name of the city of Kalinin – now Tver' again.
4   Translator's note – the scene of fierce beach fighting on the Black Sea coast in the Caucasus during WWII.

I had enough patience to stay at the aeroclub's peaceful aerodrome only for a month and a half. The alarming reports of the first days of war were stirring us up and at the same time we were informed that it had been ordered to evacuate the aeroclub into the deep rear. The day came when I walked to a train heading off to Moscow. Mousya Nikonova, my plane's technician, saw me off. Her husband, a tankman, had been badly wounded and was dying in one of the city hospitals. Mousya didn't cry but her beautiful face with brown almond-shaped eyes had become thin and dull. Another tanker who'd lost his arm lay in an adjacent ward. He was the husband of Tatyana Nikoulina, with whom we'd studied in the *Metrostroy* aeroclub. She'd come to him from Moscow, leaving her small daughter in the care of neighbours, and sat in the ward next to her maimed husband day and night, comforting and tending him as best she could. The war was already making itself felt – very brutally, sometimes irremediably …

At the train station Mousya Nikonova kissed me and putting a silver rouble into the left breast pocket of my blouse said quietly, "It's a talisman. You'll give it back to me when the Fascists are smashed." This talisman … It would be with me through the whole war. By some miracle I saved it but managed to return it to Mousya only many years later. She considered me dead and only through one item in a newspaper got to know my approximate address and found me. I remember standing near the house gate and seeing a woman with a vaguely familiar face coming towards me from the bus stop. She came up and began asking if I knew where to find … and then she fell silent and began to cry, having recognised me …

But all this was a long way off and at the moment I was on my way to Moscow to the OSOAVIAHIM Central Council. I found my way with difficulty to Three Stations Square[5], I noticed the camouflage on the buildings: they were covered with something like theatrical scenery. I was also astounded by the white paper crosses on the windows. The absence of the customary train station hustle and bustle was depressing. Men in military uniform walked about the station halls and words of command rang out loudly. When I was running across the square I nearly ran face first into a silvery gondola – soldiers were cautiously leading a balloon … I was also astonished by the flak guns in Krasnosel'skaya Street, these stood on the roofs of the many-storied buildings like cranes on long legs. And this was the atmosphere all along my way to Toushino: flak guns in parks, columns of troops, recruitment posters on the walls, a stern reserve in the behaviour of people in the streets. Not only the outskirts but the central thoroughfares of the capital were cluttered with lines of anti-tank hedgehogs[6] and barred with barricades. Moscow – now a frontline city – was becoming more and more austere day by day. Every day Levitan's[7] voice gave the Moscovites more and more alarming reports on the radio: "After stubborn and fierce fighting in the course of which …" The *Sovinformbureau*[8] communiqués reached people everywhere: at home, at work, in the street. It was impossible not to get sick of them …

I am slowly riding a frequently-stopping bus and, pressing my face to the window-glass, look at a girl in military uniform standing at an intersection with an energetically raised red signal flag. She's a traffic controller letting a troop column through. It was an ordinary tense day of war … I get to the building I need, a Colonel has a brief glance at

---

5   Translator's note – a square in Moscow with the three major train stations facing onto it.
6   Translator's note – large caltrop-like obstacles made of welded railway girders.
7   Translator's note – Yuri Levitan – a well-known radio announcer during WWII.
8   Translator's note – abbreviation of 'Soviet Information Bureau'.

the document I hold out to him and says in a hoarse and tired voice: "Egorova? And what do you, Egorova, want from me? What has happened back at your Kalinin? No petrol? Not enough planes? Please report quickly. You can see how many people are waiting."

Indeed the room, stained black with tobacco smoke, was crammed with airmen: old and young, in civilian clothes and in field uniform. All of them were talking, exchanging the latest news, awaiting here – in one of the offices of the Central Aeroclub – resolution of their issues and their fate. I had no intention of wasting their time.

"Actually, I have only one question. A personal one", I said loudly trying to talk over the noise.

The Colonel threw out his arms, "Is this the time to deal with personal issues?"

"Sorry, I've didn't express myself properly", I was embarrassed. "I'm only asking you to send me to the front."

"Oh, come on, 'only'"! The owner of the office unbuttoned the collar of his blouse. "You all repeat over and over again – to the front, to the front. If I do it your way OSOAVIAHIM's work will have to be wound down completely. And who, I ask you …", by the way the Colonel angrily looked around the whole office one could guess he was responding not only to me. "Who, I ask you, will train personnel for the front? No, sweetheart, go back to Kalinin and do what you're supposed to do! Who's next?"

But I was not going to back off. On the contrary I moved even closer to the desk.

"Our aeroclub is to be evacuated to the rear. I'm not going to the rear. I request a transfer to the front. You have to understand, I have a lot of flying experience. At the moment it is more important up there, over the battlefields …"

"You know what, Egorova? Allow us to be the judge of what and where is more important now …" The Colonel growled. However, he obviously understood it wouldn't be that easy to get rid of me. Becoming thoughtful for a minute, he turned over some piece of paper in his hands and, looking at me askance, said "Alright, whatever, we'll send you a bit closer to the fire, to the Stalino aeroclub" – that was the name of Donetsk back then.

"What, to Stalino? in 1938 that's where my brother …" I gulped but managed to say firmly: "Write the order!"

On the way to the train station I dropped in to my kinfolk's place on the Arbat. Katya was somewhere on defensive works, and the sixth-grader Yurka, having come home from school, was happy to see me and fussed about wanting to treat me to something. But in the sideboard there was nothing left but bread and a lump of sugar. He began to tell me that in his school the geography teacher had volunteered for the front but the director couldn't get permission to go.

"If I were him I would have run away to hit the Fascists long ago but he's still waiting for permission, a strange man …"

"Have you heard anything from your dad?" I interrupted my nephew.

He drooped a bit straightaway, then stood up, took some sheets of paper from a desk and handed them to me.

"Read this. Yesterday a Colonel came and said that he'd worked recently with dad somewhere far away in the North. It's night all day long up there in winter and in summer the sun doesn't set. Dad is building a beautiful city up there, like Leningrad, and a big mining and processing operation", Yurka said without pausing for breath. "The Colonel and many other former military men had been sent to the front. He'd managed to drop in to his home and also to our place and was very sorry not to find mum in."

I was reading the sheets of paper covered with my brother's writing. On one of them there was a letter to his wife and son, on another – his request to be sent to the front to defend his motherland from the Fascist invaders.

"Soon dad will go to the front", Yurka said confidently. – And I will ask to join him. If he doesn't take me I will go on my own. After all Vit'ka Timokhin and I decided long ago to go to the front. Vit'ka is not tall enough but they will let me do that for sure because I'm the tallest in my class! It's a pity you, Aunty Anya, aren't going to the front, otherwise I would be heading off there with you. It is never too late to study. Once we smash the Fascists you can study as much as you want …"

That night there was an air-raid warning in the city but we decided not to go to an air raid shelter – so we talked all night long. In the morning, sending Yurka to school and getting ready to go to the train station myself, I asked him to pledge his word not to make a step towards the front without my knowledge. Yurka promised but on one condition: if I managed to get to the front I would not fail to make arrangements for him to join me but in the meantime he would be studying at school and would do his best to master the rifle and the machine-gun. With that we parted.

Yuri waited in vain for my call to the front and his father's visit. He would see his father many years after the war when my brother received banishment after ten years of imprisonment. Vasya as well as many other 'political' prisoners survived thanks to the kindness of Zavenyagin, the director of construction and then director of the Norilsk mining and processing operation. To provide the construction works with high-level professionals, he recruited specialists from amongst the political prisoners, softening their regime. My brother was brought to Moscow under escort by plane more than once to get some plans approved. Of course, he wasn't allowed to visit his family on the Arbat or even ring them. He would stay in a NKVD hotel in the Mayakovskiy Square … I often called Katya, my brother's wife, a *dekabristka*[9]. When her husband received banishment, at her own risk she took Yurka with her and headed to faraway Norilsk by water: it was cheaper that way. It took them three months to get there – they barely survived. But the joy of the meeting instilled faith and hope into the family … In 1953 Vasya was fully rehabilitated but he stayed in Norilsk with his family. Now he worked as a deputy director of the Zavenyagin Mining and Processing Operation in Norilsk, and Katya in a tailoring shop. At the age of 75 my brother retired, but nowadays the third generation of the Egorovs works in Norilsk – my brother's grandchildren, Victor and Andrey. Life goes on …

---

9   Translator's note – a historical name for the wives of *Dekabrists* or 'Decembrists' – members of the Russian nobility who rebelled against the monarchy in 1825. Most of them went into exile to Siberia and some of their wives followed them.

11

Closer to the front

It was extremely sultry in the carriage. People sat pressed against each other. You don't stay silent long in such 'close unity' and I got into talking with my middle-aged neighbour, a military cadre all over. Of course, the conversation was about what was going on at the front – there was no other topic then. I was mostly asking questions – I was keen to find out everything from someone in the know – and the officer was answering. He asked only one question: "What are you, young lady, riding towards the front line for?" I showed him my orders.

"Strange people", the commander marveled, "what aeroclub could there be in Stalino now? The city's been evacuated …"

"It can't be!" I exclaimed.

My neighbour sighed heavily, "Nevertheless it can, my girl …"

Indeed, I found no one at the aeroclub: everyone had been evacuated. The officer was right. The wilful air of the steppe played through the empty premises of the aeroclub, resonantly banging the doors and windows. I was taken aback: what should I do, who should I turn to? I didn't have the fare back, or travel documents, or anything! I went outside, got my bearings and rushed downtown hoping to find there some office that would be useful, or simply to meet people capable of giving me sensible advice.

I didn't have the road to myself long. I hadn't walked even a block when someone grabbed me by a sleeve of my blouse. "What a fast walker you are!" A young sprightly voice said above my ear. "I barely managed to catch up with you …"

"Was it worth it?" I answered roughly, quickly turning on the stranger. I hated the street molesters, who were especially out of place in a frontline city.

"Now don't you take it the wrong way", the voice of the man, who turned out to be quite young, placated me. "I saw you go into the aeroclub. I thought it was no coincidence, some business must have brought you there. Let me introduce myself", the guy stretched out his hand, "local trainee pilot Petr Nechiporenko."

Not very willing, I returned his greeting all the same. But my caution had not passed yet and that didn't go unnoticed.

"You don't believe me, do you? Here are my papers. I am heading to the *voencomat*[1] and then to the front …"

"To the front?" I asked again, now with respect.

"Where else? But it's none of your concern – it's men's business. But I was trying to catch up with you because I noticed the 'birds' on your collar patches[2]. I wanted to say that I'd heard tomorrow some of the commanders would come. So don't miss out …"

"Tomorrow … And what am I supposed to do today?"

The guy smiled, "To the theatre, for example. An opera. The last show is on – *Carmen* – and then the theatre will be evacuated. It's here in the centre, just nearby."

---

1   Translator's note – military commissariat.
2   Editor's note – winged air force insignia.

I accompanied the guy to the city *voencomat*, wished him a victorious homecoming and felt some envy that he was already going to the war to defend the motherland. And I indeed went to the theatre then, but I remember that I was seeing the stage as if through frosted glass. Everything seemed vague and misty but after all I was sitting in the fifth row of a half-full auditorium. I didn't care much about the show: my thoughts were far, far away. Spain, toreadors, passion and love … It wasn't touching and stirring me. I watched indifferently as the beautiful Carmen began her famous *habanera* but at the highest note the orchestra suddenly broke off and an unexpected silence fell onto the hall. The singer froze with her mouth open in bewilderment. A small scrawny man walked across the stage, stopped just before the orchestra pit and rumbled into the silence, "Comrades, it's an air-raid warning! All of you are requested to go down into the air raid shelter. But please maintain order."

Such was the finale of that performance … From the air raid shelter I returned to the aeroclub premises and settled in for the night in one of the offices on a cushion upholstered with black leatherette.

In the morning someone knocked on the door and a broad-shouldered well-built man in Air Force uniform immediately appeared in the door. There were three cubes on his collar patches: hence he was a senior lieutenant. He didn't notice me straightaway for I was lying on a cushion behind a barricade of desks.

"What are you doing here?" He asked sternly.

"I am from Moscow, I have orders to report to the local aeroclub. And here I am, waiting for someone in charge."

The military man's face cleared: "Consider us here on the same business. I'm looking for someone in charge too. I've come to pick up pilots …" here the senior lieutenant made an expressive gesture with his hand – it was clear that our hosts had long left the palace of aviation …

"What shall we do then?" I asked him anxiously, and at that moment a sudden idea came to my mind. "So you've come to find pilots? Take me! Here are my papers. They are in complete order!"

The senior lieutenant read my orders from the Central Aeroclub attentively. "Well, your references are suitable. I'll take you, Egorova. But we have to make all the arrangements legally! Let's go to the *voencomat*."

A battered pickup drove us to the spot. Making our way through the dense crowd of mobilised men we presented ourselves to the commissar. But he, finding out what the matter was, just shook his head: "What's she got to do with us? She's come from Moscow – let her get back there".

"Now don't drag your feet, major! We need flyers badly", the senior lieutenant pressed.

"I can't, I have no right to spread anarchy", the military commissar persisted.

The argument went nowhere. We had to back down. Listarevich (the senior lieutenant had managed to introduce himself) calmed me down: "Forget about these bureaucrats. Let's go to our unit straightaway, we'll sort everything out on the spot."

We visited a military hospital on our way and it came out that the Senior Lieutenant Listarevich had picked up two pilots recovered from wounds, a mechanic who had lost his unit and a pilot from the OSOAVIAHIM. Now he cheered up, for he was not coming back to his unit empty-handed! We were rushing in our pickup to some of the 130th Detached Aviation Signals Squadron of the Southern Front. The senior lieutenant had been a pilot himself and was doing his best to prove it driving his pickup. He sped as if in a U-2, almost 100 kilometres an hour, without thinking much about the men sitting in back ...

At last, the aerodrome – or rather a landing area near Chaplino station in the village of Tikhiy. Covered with dust and pretty well exhausted from the bumpy ride we presented ourselves before the commanders' eyes straightaway.

"Not a lot of troops ..."

"The aeroclub was evacuated, Comrade Major", the senior lieutenant defended himself, "but I brought you some eagles."

"Eagles?" The Major asked again and gave me a somewhat suspicious and sidelong look.

Only now I did notice an Order of the Red Banner on the commanding officer's chest and rejoiced: it meant he was a combatant, so I couldn't afford to miss my chance. That was why I boldly reported "Former Kalinin aeroclub pilot instructor Anna Egorova reporting for duty."

"But there's been no order yet to draft women to the front."

"Do I really need an order to fight for the motherland?"

"That's true ..." The major looked at me narrowly.

"Have you got your papers, Egorova?" The Major's voice now sounded encouraging. "Absolutely!"

I quickly put on the desk my pilots' certificate, passport, *Comsomol* membership card and the orders to the Stalino aeroclub. Having thoroughly examined the papers the Major turned to a captain nearby: "Grishchenko! You'll fly off to Simferopol tomorrow. You have to fly anyway, and while you're at it you'll check Egorova's flying technique."

I intercepted Lisarevich's glance. My pleased 'recruiter' gave me a wink, "you see, everything is alright – you may consider yourself a pilot of the Southern Front's 130th Detached Aviation Signals Squadron".

The squadron commander was Major Boulkin and all the pilots were veterans who had flown the Polikarpov I-16 in Spain[3]. My eyes grew wide when I saw them all in brand-new uniforms and all with decorations. I thought – where am I? They fought in Spain – they are all heroes' heroes! And for some reason they'd been transferred to the Signals Squadron ... Grishchenko was deputy commander of the 130th Squadron and head of the flying service. For some reason he'd taken a great dislike to me (I didn't know why) but our flight from Tikhiy Village to Simferopol went safely and my position was approved. Later, when I had already settled down well in the Signals Squadron I was told that Petr Ivanovich Grishchenko used to be a fighter pilot who had been discharged from flying after an accident but after the war had broken out he'd obtained permission to become a pilot in the 130th Squadron. The deputy squadron commander flew courageously and he was entrusted with the most crucial tasks. Once in 1942 near Lisichansk Grishchenko's plane was intercepted by four Messerschmitts but Petr manoeuvred his defenceless *koukourouzniki*[4] so skilfully and deftly that the Fascists couldn't do anything to it and went home. Actually, in his riddled plane the lieutenant didn't make it to the aerodrome – he landed in a bog and nosed over. Our soldiers helped to drag the machine out, the pilot repaired it himself, completed his mission and returned to the squadron. When

---

3   Translator's note – during the Spanish Civil War 1936-1939 many Soviet pilots fought on the Republican side.

4   Translator's note – 'cropduster' – a somewhat contemptuous nickname for the U-2 biplane, that was used in agricultural operations.

reporting what had happened the former fighter pilot acknowledged: "It appears the U-2 is a plane too – nothing to shoot with but it's alright for ramming …"

Such was the plane I received on the third day of my time at the frontline. Not a high-speed fighter, not a dive-bomber, just a U-2. The plane I was attached to by my already long-term service, the plane that had undergone its second birth during the War and was redesignated the Po-2 after its designer Polikarpov. That was the plane that earned glory, the admiration of the frontline troops and the hatred of the enemy.

12

"Is it natural flair or is it all God-given?"

Frontline veterans remember this simple biplane getting the most unexpected, sometimes overblown, sometimes ironic but always favourable nicknames. For the infantry it was 'frontline *starshina*', the partisans nicknamed the U-2 'kitchen gardener' or 'cropduster' for its incredible ability to land on tiny patches of ground, and seasoned pilots respectfully called the nimble plane 'the duck'. But the nickname was not the point. The U-2 had won its glory by honest soldierly work: it transported wounded men, dispatched mail, flew reconnaissance flights, bombed the Hitlerites by night. Generals and Marshals, war correspondents and doctors considered it the best form of frontline transport. Its unusual maneuverability, simplicity of maintenance and ease of handling allowed it to conduct such operations as were for fast and heavy aircraft simply impossible.

It didn't seem a big deal to fly the U-2 carrying orders, searching for military units, reconnoitring roads, carrying couriers and signal officers. But this seemingly routine work was fraught with such the surprises and dangers! What kind of routine was it if all flights towards the frontline for fast communications with secret mail, and flights beyond the enemy lines were by rights considered combat sorties? It was not for nothing our squadron was recommended for Guards rank, but the unit was too small for that. Only in 1944 was the 130th Squadron given the honorific name 'Sevastopol' ...

But 1941 wasn't over and the front was moving east ... While putting up increasing resistance to the enemy, our troops were nevertheless giving up their positions. During the retreat communications between units were sometimes lost and there is nothing worse than loss of control when you're at war! The squadron's flyers were sent into the air to restore it or to despatch necessary information or a required order. They would take off in rain, in fog, in any weather.

... On 21 August I received orders to fly to the 18th Army Headquarters. I was advised of the approximate locality where this headquarters ought to be, but once there I would have to clarify its position. The squadron commander warned me that there would be many Hitlerite fighter planes en route. Blink and they will knock you off straight away. I remember the weather was superb, typical August, and at another time I would have been glad of that, but now ... In a clear sky a 'cropduster' was defenceless against Fascist fighters. You couldn't get away from them – you had no speed. And plywood is not armour, it doesn't stop bullets. And your only weapon was the revolver on your belt. The only escape was to dive towards the ground, spread your wings just above the grass and fly so low that you could hear your undercarriage mow the feather-like grass of the steppe.

And here I am hugging the ground. I have no navigator and I often look at the compass, the watch, the map, keep an eye on the ground: it's quite close, under my wings. I am happy that I can recognise the farmsteads flashing by under me – the time I pass over them coincides exactly with the calculations. Of course, the compass is a good thing but

51

I'm not much good with it. I prefer to compare the terrain I pass over with the map, and, to be honest, when working as a pilot instructor I rarely had to stick to a flight path, there were few 'blind' flights in the clouds or at night when you wholly rely on instruments. When farmsteads and gullies had stopped flashing under my wings and the barren steppe spread underneath, anxious thoughts crawled into my mind: what if this compass is off? Maybe they failed to get rid of the deviation? Now it seems to me that I shift course to the right … No, maybe, to the left! "Trust the compass, trust it … It'll lead you where you need to go …" I assure myself, "it won't let you down".

Suddenly I see two approaching dots. "Messerschmitts," I guess in a flash. Yes, that's them! And now they've swooped over my head, insolently showing off the spiders of their swastikas. They let off a burst, swept past somewhere but came back straightway. I remember them covering my U-2 with their shadows but they couldn't do anything else. So they left …

I sighed with relief: now I could concentrate on the ground rapidly flashing under my machine so as to get back my bearings. Here was the village where the headquarters of the 18th Army was. Noticing a small patch of ground with three U-2 planes – the Army Headquarters' Signals Flight – I landed. My passenger, a naval captain of the Dnieper Flotilla – went to Headquarters and I had to wait for him. In the meantime the pilots from the Army Signals Flight refuelled my plane, treated me to watermelon and told me about the situation on this sector of the front.

On my way back I lost concentration and was immediately punished for it: everything got mixed up and confused in my head. I began to swing wildly from one side to another looking for any noticeable landmark but only the deserted steppe lay silently beneath … Calming down a bit I headed eastward and flew by compass. I saw a railway station. I tried to read its name but couldn't. Then I decided to land and find out. There was a method of orientation called "questioning the local population". It turned out to be the village of Porovka. The Tikhiy farmstead was nearby and I returned to the aerodrome safely. There Squadron Commander Boulkin asked me, knitting his brows, "Why have you been in the air so long?"

"There was a delay with my departure from the Army headquarters", I weaseled.

It was the communications officer who told the major about our encounter with the Messerschmitts and about my desperate manoeuvres. I disliked Boulkin and I wasn't the only one.

"Get some rest!" Boulkin said. "You'll fly there again tomorrow."

But on the next day I had to fly to Kalarovka near Melitopol. There was the headquarters of the 9th Army and I'd been ordered to deliver a communications officer there with urgent orders. The weather that day was excellent, visibility limitless. So as not to come across the Fascist hawks, I flew hugging the ground. Here a village appeared, buried in verdure, and I lifted the plane a little: with this altitude I could have easily snagged a tree, a post or some chimney. As soon as I climbed up my field of view improved and I immediately noticed, not far away, white huts clustered around a wide gully. Turning back to the lieutenant-colonel I waved my hand down: to say 'that's it, we've arrived'. But while I was closing in for landing I noticed unusual, somehow convulsive movement, on the roads leaving Kalarovka. The troops were moving mixed up with cattle, carts loaded with goods and chattels milled around under the wheels of military trucks. Empty tonne-and-a-half[1] trucks were sweeping past on the sides of the roads, the infantry was marching not in columns but in small groups few in number. An uneasy disorder was everywhere apparent ...

I landed the plane near a windmill on a hillock, taxied right up against the mill and turned off the engine. "Something's wrong", the communications officer who had flown in with me muttered. "You stay here and wait for me to come." And he ran down a footpath towards the village.

I began to look for something to camouflage the plane with and, finding nothing, sat under a wing and began to wait. I waited an hour, twenty minutes more, thirty ... But the lieutenant-colonel still didn't come back. I began to feel somewhat alarmed. The crackle of gunfire was heard from the gully: there could be no doubt a battle was breaking out down there ...

I crawled out from under the wing and moved a bit forward to position myself better. There was hustle and bustle in the village: the cattle were bellowing, machines roaring, people running ... I had a full view of the village from the hillock: the gully divided it into two. And while the streets of the eastern side were crammed with troops its right half was empty. But right behind that emptiness lay the frontline. The sounds of fighting were coming from there – from the west. I understood: the Germans were just about to break through to the buildings about half a kilometre beyond the gully ... And that's what happened. Suddenly an explosion boomed in a deserted street, then another, then a third. The roof of one of the huts caught fire, a slender Lombardy poplar bent down in the middle, and frightened birds shot up into the sky. And suddenly in front of me, like on the movie screen, very close, the blunt snouts of German tanks came into sight. Their cannon muzzles were seemingly targeted directly at the hillock upon which the plane stood unmoving, an excellent target. Unfortunately it didn't just seem that way: a shell exploding by the mill made me run to the plane.

A good two hours had already gone by but the communications officer hadn't come back yet. Obviously, he'd forgotten about me. "What should I do? The Hitlerites will be here very shortly. I have to save the plane ..." – These thoughts got mixed up in my head. A second shell exploded next to my plane and tore the cladding of the fuselage and the wings with its fragments. I quickly jumped into the cockpit, tried to start the engine but failed, for I needed someone to turn the propeller. Then I saw a tonne-and-a-half truck rushing down the road. It was fishtailing for there was no tyre on one of the wheels. Running down to the road I tried to stop it but the driver (he looked like a boy to me) decided to drive around me. Without stopping to think I pulled my revolver from its holster and began shooting furiously at the intact tyres. He stopped and cursing began to pull out his rifle ...

"Drop that thing", I pointed at his weapon. "Help me start my engine instead."

The driver was taken, hearing a female voice. "Stop, I tell!" I said and put the revolver away.

"What are you up to? Don't you see: the Fascists are on us, the front's been broken through. I have to catch up with my unit."

"You'll still have time! My plane'll be lost here."

"The hell with it, jump in here while it's not too late."

---

1   Translator's note – a most typical truck in the USSR back then – a variety of Ford trucks were built under licence.

A new explosion made me turn my head towards the U-2. I saw shell fragments tearing apart the fuselage of my shuddering plane. "It'll be done for …" I jerked the door of the truck, "Come on out! Just for a minute."

"It's plain you're crazy!" the chap obeyed. "Where is the plane?"

I pointed up towards the mill. "You've gone mad! Don't you see them shooting? Your bird is about to catch fire! Jump in the cabin!"

I wouldn't, and so he gathered his nerve. With a quick look around the chap grabbed me by the arm and dragged me up the hillock. Now crawling, now dashing we reached the mill. It was already half-smashed by shells and its broken blades were hanging down. The wings of my plane had been holed too, and climbing up on one of them I got a real scare: an air-blast had torn away the seat of the rear cockpit and thrown it up on the dash-board of the front one. What if everything was destroyed? I got into the cockpit and was happy to see that there was apparently no serious damage.

"Take the propeller." But the chap had already grabbed it without an invitation.

"Turn the propeller a few times and jerk the blade, then jump away so it doesn't hit you!"

"Heave ho!" and the propeller began to spin. The driver was blown away as if by the blast – he disappeared straight away. I noticed only when the tonne-and-a-half truck scampered away behind the hillock. The Germans intensified their firing at my plane. I had to get out of the cockpit and turn the machine towards the take-off direction myself. And just where did I get the strength from? Most likely from fear – and the determination to escape the enemy at all costs and save the machine played its role too. Basically, I took off under the Fascists' very noses … There were no instruments, the dashboard was smashed, but the engine caught and I am alive …

I was flying east. The sun had already gone down and twilight had swallowed the ground. How would I land in the dark? I was circling, looking for my aerodrome, but below were only slag heaps[2], cables, the railways that led to each shaft. At last I saw a small light far away. Surely they hadn't set a fire for me? Fortunately they had!

It turned out that when all the deadlines for my return had passed they had decided in the squadron that I wasn't coming back. On top of that the pilots from the 6th Army Signals Flight had landed on our airstrip during their retreat and reported to Major Boulkin that my plane had supposedly been seen flying towards a village occupied by the enemy. In short they had they had given up on me in the squadron. Only my plane mechanic was stubbornly waiting and believing I would return. It was him who had set up the small fire on the airstrip.

After landing I didn't leave the cockpit for quite a while: I still couldn't believe I had broken free of the enemy's clutches. I took off the helmet, wiped my sweaty face with a sleeve of my overall, and stayed sitting in a kind of stupor. A routine day at the front had ended …

Dronov the mechanic, having looked over the planed noted, "You flew here on ambition, Comrade Commander. But no drama, we'll fix it up …"

In the morning the mechanic reported the machine ready to fly. My 'cropduster' looked brand-new. "Thank you, Kostya!" For the first time I called Dronov by his first name. He blushed, muttered something and for some reason began shifting the plane covers from place to place …

---

2   Translator's note – apparently from the coal shafts numerous in that part of the country.

"There's something God-given in you", the pilots were joking when I turned up to report to Boulkin the squadron commander, "Some natural flair! We had already said a few words for you at dinner ... You'd be sure to find your way even if all instruments were turned off and the maps were taken away from you."

"I would, I would for sure, especially if possessed by anger."

"Why would you be angry?"

"How could I not be! The communications officer ordered me to wait for him and didn't come back ..."

"Egorova!" the squadron commander called. "The Head of Frontline Communications General Korolev asked if you came back from the mission. The communications officer who flew with you sends his apologies for not warning you."

"Why did he desert me in Kalarovka?" I asked Boulkin angrily.

"He didn't desert you, he was trying to catch up with the Army Headquarters in a passing vehicle to give the Commander the Frontline HQ's order to retreat."

"What was the point over handing over the order to retreat if the Army had retreated long ago?.."

"He was doing his best to carry out his mission and was late ... But he returned to the Frontline headquarters. After all he sends you his apologies", the squadron commander repeated.

"Apologies to whom, if he doesn't even know if I'm alive or dead?"

I felt pain and anger. And my senior officer too! I was sure that abandoning me, a woman, to death, he had behaved in an unmanly manner.

13

See you after the victory

Quite often we had to fly to the South-Eastern Front HQ, located, back then, in Kharkov. There was complete confusion at the Kharkov aerodrome. Some planes were landing, others were taking off. Many 'horseless' flyers who had lost their planes in combat or even in non-combat situations roamed about the parking lot – the Germans had destroyed quite a few of our planes right on the aerodromes! .

A pilot from our squadron called Spirin flew to the Front headquarters with secret mail. When he came back after handing in the package his plane had disappeared from the parking lot. Spirin ran all over the aerodrome but the U-2 with number '7' on its tail had vanished. Spirin reported his plight to the squadron and the squadron commander sent me with navigator Irkoutskiy to search for the vanished plane. We flew to all the aerodromes and airstrips of the Southern and South-Western Fronts but couldn't find it. We arrived at the of Chougouyev aerodrome hungry and angry and decided to get hold of some food. Everyone was in the process of evacuation and there were enemy air raids over and over again. They wouldn't even give us bread in the aerodrome canteen without ration cards (we had none on us)! Irkoutskiy ran to see the local commanders and I got back to the plane and saw a major sitting in my cockpit and yelling: "Contact!" Another airman (also a major) pulled the propeller with his hands and yelled running away from the propeller: "Aye-aye!" I stood stunned, then jumped on a wing of my plane and began thrashing the major, sitting in the cockpit, with my fists!

"You thief! Thief! Shame on you!" I was yelling, but he turned his face to me and said quietly: "Why are you screaming like in the bazaar? Had you said civilly that it was yours we would have gone to look for another 'unclaimed' one. But you've started screaming instead and even hitting …" He climbed out of the cockpit and strode away from the parking lot and the second major minced after him. For some reason I felt sorry for them …

During the retreat we often shifted base and changed airstrips, choosing them beside some forest or village. Our airstrips were under fire time and again, and sometimes bombed. But despite the difficulties and deprivations related to the retreat the morale of Major Boulkin's squadron remained high.

"Fly a sortie and see whose troops are moving along the roads in this area", the squadron commander once ordered me, making a mark on a map. Flying in the daytime in a plane made of plywood and percale, which can be shot down by an ordinary rifle, wasn't a pleasant exercise. But an order is an order …

The troops on the roads turned out to be ours. "They are escaping encirclement", I guessed. Exhausted and worn out, they were carrying their weapons and their wounded. Noticing a red-starred plane they began to wave their hands, field caps and helmets. But what's this? Four Messerschmitts were diving on the column. For the first time I see the fiery thread of tracer. Soldiers were dropping, some ran away from the road …

Having made several passes on the column the Fascists pounced on my plane. A forest and a river winding between the trees saved me then. Nearly touching water with my undercarriage I followed all its curves and meanders. The manoeuvre was successful – the Germans fell back.

I returned to the aerodrome, landed and taxied to the parking lot. Dronov the mechanic greeted my return rapturously as always. And he had to patch up holes and fix up the plane and its engine after almost every one of my sorties! Nevertheless he had always managed to make my machine flight-ready for the next sortie.

There were many Moscovites in our squadron but that was no wonder: after all, it had been formed in Lyubertsy[1]. Every morning our radio-operators were asked:

"Guys, what's happening in the capital?"

Moscow was doing it hard: her most terrible days had arrived. The enemy stood at her gates, air-raid warnings were announced nearly every night. But the Moscovites faced the oncoming threat with fortitude. People of the most peaceful occupations: cooks and scientists, clerks and steel-makers, artists, engineers and confectioners were joining *opolchenie*[2] divisions. Moscow itself was turning into a fortress …

After capturing Mariupol and Taganrog the Fascists began to advance on our Southern Front. We flew to the Army Headquarters and to divisions several times a day. The Hitlerites aimed to penetrate into the Shakhty district and from there to Novocherkassk and Rostov. And indeed they managed to press our troops up against Novocherkassk but then the troops of Kharitonov's army, fighting to the bitter end, didn't allow the enemy to move forward even a metre. Abandoning the idea of capturing Rostov from the North and North-East, where our 9th Army had stopped them, the Hitlerites decided to deliver a frontal blow on Rostov. On 21 November the Fascists took Rostov. The very same day we relocated to the Lotikov Shaft airstrip near Voroshilovsk …

In the middle of the night a messenger woke the pilot Grishchenko and navigator Irkoutskiy. They were ordered by squadron headquarters to fly to the 37th Army with a top-secret package. We decided straightaway that it was obvious some operation by frontline and army troops was being planned. The nights are dark in autumn, especially in the South – and our planes were completely unadapted for night flights. In spite of this Grishchenko and Irkoutskiy flew the route safely and recognised the village where the headquarters of General Lopatin's 37th Army was located. They made several circles around the station but there was no sign of a landing strip – not even a lit torch. But no matter how long you are going to make circles there were orders to deliver the package at any cost and so Grishchenko slowed down, turned the ignition off and began to glide. They flew over a hut, then above something just as dark and at last the plane touched down and began taxiing. But the flyers were still sighing with relief when the plane at first abruptly rolled down, then suddenly up and at the same moment smashed into something. Grishchenko came back to his senses first and asked Irkoutskiy "Ivan, are you alright?"

"I am, but my hand hurts for some reason."

"And my foot's trapped, I can't pull it out …"

At last they made it out of the broken plane and went to look for the Army headquarters. It was still dark and quiet in the village – not even a single dog began to bark. However, they found the headquarters, handed in the package and told of their landing. The flyers were walked to a hut where wounded men lay on the floor on straw. Grishchenko's leg

---

1   Translator's note – a small town near Moscow.
2   Translator's note – volunteers, home guard.

was badly grazed and Irkoutskiy had broken fingers. They remembered there was a dying young female medic amongst the wounded, injured on her buttocks … In the morning the army communications commander Colonel Boborykin ordered the smashed plane burnt. The guys were not censured for that flight but were not commended either.

Our troops began to advance and now Rostov was liberated from the occupiers. An enemy attempt to consolidate his grip on positions prepared beforehand was frustrated and the Red Army troops kept pressing the enemy westward. Boulkin's squadron relocated to the Filippenko hamlet and the Front headquarters to the town of Kamensk on the Northern Donets river. I was very happy about that: all these months I'd been thinking with fear that my family might fall under occupation. My mum had written me that the Fascists were very close to our Kouvshinovskiy District. The Red Army liberated the city of Kalinin on 16 December. Torzhok hadn't been held by the Germans but they had destroyed it completely. "So many churches, ancient cathedrals – they razed it all to the ground, those antichrists", my mum wrote. She further advised that Konev's headquarters[3] had been located not far from our village and his officers were billeted at her place.

"They are so lovely and kind. I heat up the *samovar* for them, make tea from various herbs and they procure some sugar – we sit and drink tea with them, they tell me all sorts of news from all fronts. I used to question them about you, showed them your letter from the front. They said: "Your daughter is alright, Stepanida Vasilievna, there's a lull at that sector of the front now". They might be telling me untruths but it was so convincing and polite. You, my girl, don't worry about me, I'm fine, it's only you – my kids and grandchildren, my heart aches for. Nothing's been heard from Egoroushka for a long time, since the very beginning of the war, since he wrote me that he was going to hit the enemy, that was all. Kostya is somewhere at the Southern Front. Kolyushka's been badly wounded and he's in hospital now, Zina is in Leningrad, blockaded, working as a foreman at the 'Krasnyy Gvozdil'shik' plant. A death notice came about Vanyusha. Maria is in such a state from grief that she looks like death warmed up. I know nothing about Alexey – there's been nothing from him since he wrote me from Drogobych about his daughter Lilya's birth shortly before the war. Vasya keeps applying from Norilsk for permission go to the front but no one's answering. How are you, my girl? Take care of yourself, dress yourself warmly. I've knitted mittens for you with two fingers so you can shoot easier …"

In this letter my Mum prayed God to keep us, her children alive and to let the Red Army muster more strength and cleanse the Russian land of the evildoers …

The letters coming to the front were mostly encouraging. They wrote us from the home front that everything was going well with them, that they were provided with everything, that they were doing their best for victory over the bitterest enemy of humankind – Fascism. The most important message in the letters from the front was – one is alive, fit and giving the enemy hell. It was a sacred and just lie …

I received letters from Victor on the North-Western Front. Victor wrote that he was flying 'small ones' (that was what we called fighter planes during the war), that he had shot down nine German planes, that he had been awarded the Order of the Red Banner and two Orders of the Red Star. "When shall we meet again, Anya?" Victor asked, and answered himself, "After the Victory …"

---

3   Translator's note – Ivan Konev – one of the top Soviet commanders later in the war.

I remembered for the rest of my life how a young radio operator burst into the squadron headquarters and shouted from the door, "Guys! The Germans around Moscow have been smashed!"

We, the pilots, began spinning in some fantastic dance. Revelry broke out in all the units. Everyone was laughing, singing, hugging each other – and tears were gleaming in people's eyes … At last the Germans had stumbled! The victory near Moscow had not only military but also huge moral significance: all our spirits rose.

14

The Greenhorn

The winter campaign of 1942 was successful. The enemy was still very strong but the imperishable value of the first successes was that that they inspired us, instilling in us the spirit of belief in Victory. Those days this spirit was typical of all the troops on our Southern Front. Together with the troops of the South-Western Front they broke through the enemy defences at the Balakleya sector and formed the Barvenkovskiy Salient. Every frontline soldier was sweating on the success of the dashing raid by the two cavalry corps of Parkhomenko and Grechko on the Germans' rear. In the winter cold, on the ice-crusted ground they spread panic in the Hitlerites' camp with their sudden strikes. One encouraging dispatch after another was coming to Front headquarters via radio but suddenly the air waves fell silent. The commander needed to know exactly in which direction the corps could have moved after their last message had arrived. The commanders understood that the cavalry, exhausted in fierce combat and sleepless nights, needed rest. They had to be brought back, but how could it be done if the air waves were silent? "Let's send a U-2", The Southern Front Communications Commander General Korolev suggested.

A whirlwind was raging behind the misted windows but we – the Signals Squadron pilots – were up to the task ... On one of those days of February when a blizzard had swept banks of snow all over the streets of the Filippenko hamlet I was called up to the squadron headquarters. They told me about the situation on our sector of the Front and ordered me to fly to the Barvenkovo Region where I would have to find Parkhomenko and Grechko's cavalry corps and hand them over a package marked 'Top Secret'. The Southern Front Communications Chief was to fly with me as far as Barvenkovo, but from there I would have to operate independently.

An angry wind was battering the machine. The engine was shivering as if in a fever and sometimes the wail of the wind drowned it out. All this was not a problem but how to break through the solid curtain of snow? It was endless, it had swallowed my small plane and held me tightly in its hands. Snow was clogging my goggles and was hitting me in the face. There was practically no visibility: I had only my intuition and experience to rely on. But there are moments when even they are powerless – and that was exactly what I felt on that day. But at last we were here in Barvenkovo. I delivered the General not far away from the railway station and was about to fly on. Climbing out of the cockpit the General leaned towards me, looked at me with his sad eyes and kissed the helmet on my head ...

The snow was becoming thicker and thicker, the blizzard was getting stronger. In the cockpit I felt as if I were on a trapeze. All this taken together made it completely impossible to orient myself during the flight. What should I do? Return? But I had no right to take such a decision: I'd been ordered to keep flying and find the cavalry at any cost. Finding them would mean saving many thousands of lives... And I, finding any sign of a dwelling, would land my U-2 to learn who was there – friend or foe. Each time I had to land in extremely poor weather conditions. Airmen know what that's like. I landed three times and three times I took off despite the winds and snowfall. I flew very low examining every gully, every ravine. I noticed tanks on one farmstead but I had not got a good look at them when they opened fire on me. But it turned out alright – the snowstorm saved me …

No one knows how my flight would have ended up had I not noticed horses in a gully. "Those are ours!" I closed in for landing and as soon as I touched down two soldiers in cavalry uniform ran up to me. So I was right! "Which corps?" – I asked them.

"General Parkhomenko's 1st."

"I'm from the Front headquarters. Which of the commanders is here?"

"The Head of Intelligence."

An officer in a camouflage jacket was already walking towards me. He introduced himself as Head of Intelligence of General Parkhomenko's 1st Cavalry Corps, and immediately told me the current situation, and I plotted the position of the 1st and 5th Corps on my flight map with barely visible pencil marks.

"Well done, pilot! See, you found us on a day like this. Give me the package, I'll hand it over to the corps commander."

"No, I have to do it myself".

"Why 'have to'?" The intelligence officer took a short pause and then laughed loudly and resoundingly. – I took you for an aviator but you're an aviatrix! D'you want me to take you there?"

"No, I'll find my own way."

"Well, be careful", he warned. "You'll have to crawl for about a hundred metres up to that shed. The roundabout way through the ravine is too long and not safe: you can run into Germans …"

At last the package was handed over to a dog-tired General. He looked at the order and swore foully, not suspecting that standing before him in a flying suit and flying boots was a woman. A shell burst nearby. The explosion raised pillars of snow-dust, shaking the ground. Over our heads shrapnel whistled past, but the General continued to stand deep in thought. Then, turning to me, the General said decisively: "Here's what to do. Shoot over to Grehcko in the 5th Corps, deliver my message to him and then fly to Front headquarters – bring us a radio set. We'll do a bit more fighting here …"

"I won't be able to do it before dawn, Comrade General – the plane is not equipped to fly at night."

Another burst of cursing directed at the quartermasters who were lagging behind the Corps: the men and horses had nothing to eat. And on top of that the radio wasn't working, he had sent a cart yesterday to Barvenkovo but it had disappeared. Continuing to curse, the General waved his hand in despair and suddenly asked "Have you caught cold or something? Your voice is kind of weak."

"No …" I replied, took the envelope from his hands and asked: "What should I say at Front HQ?"

"What should you say?" The General said, still gritting his teeth. "Are you kidding, you greenhorn? Look what fire you've drawn down on us with your cropduster! You're staying here with us …"

"But you've ordered me to deliver the package to the 5th Corps. I request permission to carry out the order."

"Off you go then …"

It wasn't too difficult to find General Grechko's 5th Corps for I knew its location already from the Intelligence Commander of the 1st Corps. I landed my plane almost in the middle of the hamlet, handed the package in and took off straightaway. I remember that General Grechko was very polite. He told me, "Take off your flying suit, you're wet all over. I'll feed you and give you tea."

I said: "I have to head back."

"No, don't put on the wet flying suit!"

I was returning to my aerodrome by night: I made circles knowing I had definitely reached it but was afraid to land, lest I crash my plane. It was pitch-dark on the ground. I wished someone would think to light a match at least or have a cigarette! At last I noticed a light and descended for landing. I touched down safely and at that moment my mechanic came up and helped me find the parking lot. Dronov was waiting for me as usual, not leaving the aerodrome. It had been him who, on barely hearing the murmur of my engine, had rushed to the airfield with a blowtorch. It was its light I'd noticed from the air …

Chilled to the bone, dead tired, I entered the command post like a ghost, to report to the squadron commander that the mission had been completed. He listened to me in silence, silently went to the telephone and ordered he be connected to Front HQ. "Permission to go sleep?"

"Granted!" Boulkin casually waved his hand. I was offended. Passing by the canteen I walked towards the house I was billeted in. Despite the late hour my hostess wasn't asleep. Seeing me in such a state she began to bustle about, wailing "How did you manage to get so fagged out, darling? Have a drink, here's some warm milk …" She helped me to pull off my wet boots and the flying suit, gave me warm *valenki*. "May be you'd like to get up on the oven? It's lit …"

"The oven", I agreed weakly.

My hostess was the exact copy of my mum. All mothers seem to have something or other in common. Each time I came back to spend the night in her hut she would sit me at the table and start treating me to Ukrainian *borsch* and the most tasty pickled tomatoes. She used to put all this on the table, sit on the other side and begin to tell me yet again about her three little boys who were fighting somewhere in the North. She would recall how difficult it had been to raise them after her husband's death, regret that the sons hadn't managed to get married and present her with grandchildren – the war had started. At the mention of this the hostess would sigh bitterly, wiping with the ends of her apron the tears running down her cheeks and keep plying me with food: "Eat, eat, my girl. Maybe someone's mum will feel sorry for my little boys and feed them. Maybe even yours!"

After the hot milk I had drunk I got warm on the oven and dozed off. Around midnight someone knocked on the door. Grumbling, the hostess flipped aside the door hook and let in a man in a short army fur coat.

"Where is Egorova?" He asked.

I recognised Listarevich's voice and responded: "Here I am, Comrade Senior Lieutenant, on the oven."

"Hard as it may be you'll have to leave the warmth. You're called to Front Headquarters. I'm off for a vehicle …"

"I won't let her go", my benefactor wailed. "Have you ever heard of a girl tormented so! She's not had time to dry out, to get warm and you're getting her up again. Is there no bloke to get up at night? It's always her …"

I jumped down from the oven, quickly dressed, took my revolver and stuck a map in the leg of my flying boot as the vehicle came up. Senior Lieutenant Listarevich – executive officer of the squadron – deftly opened the door of the pick-up and said apologetically: 'Sorry that we haven't let you have a rest, Annoushka. You're urgently called to the Front headquarters to report on the cavalry corps you found today."

Listarevich was a very cheerful and joyful man by nature, liked to joke and laugh but over the last few days he had changed, as if into a different man. The Fascists had been committing atrocities in his native Byelorussia, in the Gomel Province: and his ancestral home was there – his old mother, a teacher and father, a postal worker. We could see Konstantin was worried but he wouldn't show it and seemed to have become even more energetic and was working with tenfold zeal.

Our squadron, although designated 'Communications' nevertheless carried out intelligence duties over the front, searches for units and groupings that Front HQ had no information about. The Chief of HQ often had to stand in for the Squadron Commander. He would have loved to fly missions himself – flying was more to his heart than HQ work – after all he was a former fighter pilot, having flown an I-16. But he couldn't: it was out of the question...

Our squadron was detached and it had its own kitchen, fuel, everything. We were fed well but you wouldn't always be on time for dinner. Later they began to issue us bags of sandwiches. Listarevich controlled many services: engineering, the PARM (field aircraft maintenance workshop), technical and provision supplies. But the executive officer kept up with everything. He also found time to talk to us, the pilots, the navigators, to ask what we needed or to say simply, smiling, before a sortie, "Good luck!"

Listarevich and I arrived in Kamensk-Shakhtinskiy, where the Southern Front headquarters was located, after midnight and an orderly walked us into a brightly lit room straightaway. I saw a group of generals around a large desk and stopped in confusion not knowing whom to report to.

"Was it you who flew to search for the cavalry corps?" At last someone asked me.

"Yes, it was me."

'Show me on the map where Parkhomenko's and Grechko's cavalry are."

I approached the desk seeing that two commanders had courteously made room for me. But unfortunately I couldn't recall all the settlements the cavalry were in. Feeling nervous I moved my finger for a long time over the operations map, marked all over by coloured pencils, but nevertheless failed to find the necessary area.

"Permission to show you on my map?" I asked timidly, knowing everything was plotted precisely on it, and pulled out of my flying-boot leg my old large-scale one with routes drafted along its length and breadth but still intelligible to me. Everyone laughed boomingly and amicably and I relaxed – the tension had disappeared.

"Down here ..." I pointed immediately.

Questions showered one after another and now I was answering clearly. I didn't have time to notice who was asking the questions but I was addressing only one General. His kind broad face with beautiful luxuriant moustache attracted me. Smiling, this man pointed with his thumb to another General, behind his back, as much as to say 'address him, he's the man in charge here'. But I was dragged as if by a magnet and giving my report, addressed again and again the moustachioed General with the gentle eyes.

When I had showed and told everything they thanked me and let me go. Leaving the room I came across the head of Frontline Communications. He inquired, "How was it?"

"I gave a full report, Comrade General."

"Well done …"

Korolev hesitated a bit and using the pause I decided to find out who the man was who was smiling at me. "Comrade General, who's the Commander? Is it the one with the moustache?"

"No, that was General Korniets from the War Council. Why, did you like him?"

"Yes, very much so …" I admitted.

Listarevich and I got back from Kamensk towards morning. But I hadn't managed to get warm properly and fall asleep when again an order came: "You, Egorova, will have to fly across the front line again to deliver a radio to the cavalry corps. You know the route, I hope you'll handle it successfully", Boulkin said.

But the route had got no easier for having been reconnoitred. There was the same blizzard, the same snow, the same almost blind flying. But to be honest, it was easy to position myself on the map knowing the precise location of the troops. However, I had to go quite a bit off track as there were no cavalry at the old location – they had already taken cover somewhere. Having lost hope of a successful search I decided to land the plane and question the locals. Landing near a small unremarkable hamlet and leaving the engine on, I ran across the snowdrifts to the nearest hut. I knocked on the window with frozen-through fingers and this made a kind of especially resonant and booming sound as if someone had tapped one icicle on another. An old man in an undershirt over his pants and in *valenki* came out at my knock A very old man but sturdy and upright .. "Grandfather, have our men passed through here?"

The old man hastily interrupted me: "Get out as fast as you can, sonny! The Germans are here, came last night!"

He pointed and turning around I saw Fascists by the next hut. I should have run straightaway but my legs had become as if paralysed, somehow numb and wouldn't move at all. The old man saved me, giving me a shove in the back and I rushed towards my salvation – to my faithful 'cropduster'. The rattle of a machine-gun burst rolled over me from behind, I turned back and saw the old man in the white shirt crashing down into the snow. And whilst I ran to the plane he kept looming up in front of me – that sturdy man who seemed to have stepped out of a fairy tale. But another machine-gun burst reminded me that this was no fairy-tale. Then I nimbly jumped into the cockpit and revved up. My U-2 shuddered and quickly slid across the snow field on its skis. It took off under a hail of bullets and not all of them missed. The mirror on the centre-section stanchion was smashed and the percale on the right wing was rattling … I was very hot but my teeth were chattering as if from cold …

Not till the end of the day did I had manage to locate the cavalry again. I came across the now familiar colonel – the head of Intelligence – in the school building where the corps headquarters was situated.

"Congratulations on your safe arrival", he greeted me and walked me to Parkhomenko immediately. "Comrade General, here is the messenger from Front headquarters", the Colonel reported and handed the package over to the Corps Commander.

"Call him over, let him in", the General ordered mixing Ukrainian words with Russian, without lifting his head up from the map and not noticing who had come. But then he raised his head and I saw a face lined by fatigue and sleepless nights. But the strain of field life did not seem to have affected the General's habits. He was carefully shaved, his hair was combed. He breathed neatness and true cavalry bearing. I stood to 'attention' without noticing, which didn't escape the General's eye.

"At ease, at ease", he ordered jokingly. "You bear good tidings, you eagle! Did you bring the radio?"

"Yes!"

At this moment claps from nearby shell bursts resounded from outside the windows. To all appearances the Fascists had intensified the barrage. The General pricked up his ears: "The Devil sent you, lad!" he said. "You've brought trouble down on us. You've disclosed our location. See what the Hitlerites are up to?"

The Corps Commander had not guessed there was not a 'lad' but a 'lass' before him. It didn't seem the right moment to explain what was what. The shells and mortar bombs were exploding closer and closer, shaking the building. Window glass jangled somewhere just nearby and I heard shrapnel rattle on the roof. Parkhomenko remained unruffled and sat at his desk as calmly as before, his chest, decorated with battle awards, spread wide. However I was unable to stay calm. I was seriously concerned about the fate of my machine. My mission was complete and I had to rush back – it would be dark soon.

"Comrade General, what should I tell Front HQ?" At last I dared to ask.

"What should you tell them?" Parkhomenko rumbled. "You're making fun, aren't you? Don't you see what kind of fire you've brought down with your 'cropduster'? It's too late to fly, lad. You're staying here with us. Let your bird damn well burn! We'll find you a horse and teach you to sabre".

But no, I couldn't burn my 'bird'. After all, I had been ordered to come back and was supposed to obey orders. Running from the General's office I rushed towards my plane along wicker fences and huts. It turned out to be a long way. Fire sometimes pinned me down to the ground but I kept running from one shell-hole to another, relying on an old frontline belief that a shell would never hit the same spot twice. Fortunately I reached the plane in one piece and alive, but when I tried to start the engine I found it had been damaged. What a disaster ... So it had been hit by shrapnel. I had to make my way back to Headquarters along the same route. Cavalrymen were dashing back and forth, soldiers were loading carts with their humble possessions: the headquarters was preparing for evacuation. Parkhomenko met me with the words, "So, lad, you've decided to stay with us?"

"No, Comrade General, I request assistance!"

"What kind of assistance?"

"I need a horse to tow the plane away ..."

"I have no spare horses, don't you see what position I'm in?"

But I managed to convince the Commander: he gave me a horse. Rope was found as well. I tied it to the undercarriage axle with two knots and made kind of a collar on the horse's neck. I had everything attached and I was just about to take the horse by the bridle and go when a rider came to give me a hand – a hefty bloke from the Kuban Cossacks. He grumbled, fixing up the traces: "What the hell do we need this plywood jalopy for? If we hang around at all Fritz will nail us."

"So hurry up if you don't want to get nailed", I hurried him.

"Hurry up, hurry up? A horse likes it when everything's done neatly. Each rope should be just right ... It's no good for a beast to have its withers or whatever rubbed raw. It'll die ..." At last the bloke took the horse by the bridle and yelled loudly:

"Well, darling, off you go!"

I took hold tightly on a wingtip so as to hold it on the bumpy road. Fortunately, a heavy snowfall began soon and then night fell – it hid us from the enemy shells. It was the first and only time in my life I 'flew' such an unusual horse-drawn carriage. The horse worn out during the raid pulled without haste, paying no attention to the road. The plane groaned sadly on the bumps. Something cracked alarmingly inside with every new rut. The wings, clumsy on the ground, now bent down to the very snow, now resiliently straightened, lifting me with them. This unnatural vibration didn't cheer me at all: it looked as if I was about to lose my wings. But, be that as it may, with the help of the horse and the gloomy rider I managed to drag the plane to a safe place. We stopped in some village and in the morning I had time to poke around the engine. I asked the lady of the hut we'd stopped in to warm up some water, drained the oil from the engine into a cast-iron pot and put it into the oven too. Then my helpers from the cavalry helped me pour the now-hot oil into the tank, splashed hot water over the carburettor and began to turn it over. To everyone's joy the engine sneezed a couple of times and then started.

More than once on that February day I thought kindly of my aeroclub teachers. No it hadn't been a waste of time to make the student pilots take apart and put together all the engine components, it hadn't been for nothing they'd made us stay after flying, to tinker with the machine along with the mechanic. If you want to fly well – know your plane perfectly! Such had been the rule. And now a thorough knowledge of the equipment had helped me to handle the repairs.

"Permission to head off, Comrade General?" I asked Parkhomenko.

"Granted! Take the package and a wounded man, and don't be angry at an old fellow like me. All sorts of things happen in war. I took you for a bloke, and you're .. Something gentle appeared in the General's eyes, he awkwardly waved his hand and gave a shy, boyish smile.

15

A fellow native

Everyone in the squadron already knew of my woes – a message had been sent by the radio operators of the cavalry corps that had set up communications. Coming back to my aerodrome I landed and taxied to the parking lot, but didn't find Lieutenant Alexeyev's plane. Everything was scattered around the place in some disorder.

"What's happened?" I asked Dronov the mechanic.

"Lieutenant Alexeyev died …"

"Who was he flying with?"

"His navigator was Lieutenant Grachev. Grachev is alive but badly crippled …" My heart began to ache, tears welled up, and barely shifting my feet I walked away from the parking lot.

"What are you doing, Egorova, dragging your feet instead of walking?" I heard the angry voice of Major Boulkin. "Where's the package from the cavalry corps commander? Look a bit lively!"

I pulled the package out of my map case, handed it over to the major and went off to look for the squadron commissar Ryabov and the Party organiser Irkoutskiy. "How can this be?" I thought. "Our comrade, a pilot, has died … People should be called together to commemorate him. How can this be?"

I found neither Ryabov nor Irkoutskiy in place. They'd flown off on a mission before noon. To be frank, we were not overfond of Boulkin for his arrogance, dryness and roughness. But Alexey Vasilievich Ryabov was his exact opposite. The commissar had often flown as a lay pilot but would find time for a heart-to-heart talk, or a reprimand if one deserved it. However, if Ryabov had given a scolding no one would have resented it. The Party organiser Ivan Iosifovich Irkoutskiy was a good match for our commissar – a tactful, kind and thoughtful man. Irkoutskiy was especially good at locating encircled units. And he was an excellent navigator. In the squadron they joked that "Ivan would find the Fritzes[1] if they were underground". Once, when searching for a cavalry detachment, Irkoutskiy and airman Kasatkin came across German tanks. The latter immediately opened fire on them but Irkoutskiy quickly noticed that in one village were some men with bales of hay, wandering between the houses. The navigator suggested Kasatkin land the plane. When they landed, it became clear that in the village was exactly the detachment they were looking for. In order to disguise themselves the cavalrymen had hidden the horses in sheds, outhouses and even dwellings. Thus the crew had carried out their mission this time too.

Irkoutskiy was regarded in the squadron as a 'lucky one'. Once with the pilot Kasatkin he even landed straight on a minefield and everything came out ok – both survived unscathed. And once Irkoutskiy took off with the pilot Sborshikov to reconnoitre the roads near Nikolayev. En route they encountered 10 Ju-87s escorted by Me-109 fighter

---

1   Editor's note – the most common nickname for German soldiers in Russian military slang.

planes. The fighters pounced on the defenceless U-2, Sborshchikov landed the plane directly and he and Irkoutskiy ran from it in different directions. The Hitlerites made several passes on the plane, strafed the running airmen as well, but without success. The whole U-2 was holed but it hadn't caught fire and the flyers, as the saying goes, 'got off lightly'. When they came back home it turned out that our aerodrome had been bombed yet again – the whole airfield was sown with mines as if with tulips. How to land? There was a cross on the ground to forbid them from landing but nevertheless Sborshchikov touched down, manoeuvring between shell craters and mines during the run like a true circus artiste. The crew received a citation from Front Headquarters. But Sborshchikov was put on a charge by the squadron commander for landing when the inhibitory sign was on the ground.

"Egorova! You and me are fellow natives – I was born near Torzhok too", once Irkoutskiy addressed me and asked: "Have you been getting letters from your mum?"

"Haven't heard from her for a long time. I'm afraid the Fascists are raging around our parts. I fear for mum very much …"

"I haven't heard from my mum for a long while either", bowing his head, the *partorg²* said quietly, and went on: "Our *comsorg*³ told me the *Comsomol* recommended you to the Communist Party. So, I am ready to vouch for you. After all, Egorova, I joined the Party in 1939 and had been in the *Comsomol* since 1928. You see how old I am!"

"What are you talking about? You're only 31", I pointed out. "Are you married, Ivan Iosifovich?"

"No, Egorova, I haven't got around to it. I haven't had time. I had a girlfriend but she got married, giving up on me leaving the Army … Well, Egorova, Commissar Ryabov will give you the second reference – he told me about it himself", our *partorg* added finally.

The Party meetings in our squadron had always been short, with minutes written in a condensed fashion – just the resolutions, and questions were discussed mostly in relation to admission of new members and candidates to the Party. The commissar had always been present at the meetings. The Battalion Commissar⁴ Alexey Vasilievich Ryabov wasn't a skilled public speaker or a theorist. He was just a good man. With all his heart, with all his deeds the commissar had always tried to inspire the squadron personnel to carry out the tasks set us. And we had the same task as the whole nation – to destroy the enemy …

During one of the Party meetings I was accepted as Party candidate. It was in April 1942. At that time we were based in the settlement of Voevodovka near Lisichansk and the candidacy card was handed to me in the Southern Front headquarters. An officer from the political section presenting me with the card suddenly asked me:

"Comrade Egorova, aren't you a sister of Vasiliy Alexandrovich Egorov?"

"No", I answered glibly.

Later I would suffer a lot from my treachery towards my brother. How could I disown so heedlessly my elder brother who had taken the place of my late father for me? The bitterness still stings my soul. How could I answer that way? Many years later when my brother had been 'rehabilitated' and he had come to Moscow, I told him about it. He thought a bit, then smiled and said: "You were probably afraid they wouldn't let you fight?

"I did."

---

2   Translator's note – Party organizer.
3   Translator's note – *Comsomol* organizer.
4   Translator's note – a military rank for political officers.

"Oh, you cowardy-custard!" And my brother gave me a big kiss, forgiving my forced disavowal of him ...

For the first time after my 'Barvenkovo epic' I managed to sleep my fill. A good sleep drove away the fatigue. Everything I had endured during the two most difficult flights was left somewhere behind and sunk in the depths of my memory. But at the same time it was clear to me that new ordeals were waiting for me. Sprightly, full of strength, I entered the squadron headquarters and the first thing that struck my eye was a large piece of paper fixed on the corridor wall. I was going to walk past but one of the airmen who chanced to be nearby said with a cunning smile: "Don't turn your nose up, Egorova, read it – it concerns you."

"Me?" I was surprised and went to the paper ... Some amateur artist had depicted on it a fairy of the air drifting through a snowstorm. Under the friendly caricature was a caption: "A woman flies but the men have a day off!"

"They've given the blokes a good stir, eh?" Asked Listarevich who had suddenly appeared. I blushed and muttered something indistinct. "What are you shy for? You've taught all airmen a good lesson", and offered me his hand. "Let me congratulate you: the commanders have put you up for an award for searching out the cavalry corps ..."

"Egorova, the commander's asking for you!" came the call.

"You're to fly to the 6th Army to pick up General Zhouk – the Front Artillery Commander", the squadron commander ordered.

"Yes sir!" I replied, repeated the order and began to plot the course on my flight map. I took off when the day was already declining. It was pleasant to fly. Everything was white and clean and the sky was clear as if there were no war. However, as the saying goes God helps those who help themselves"! And just in case, I was doing a contour flight, hiding myself in gullies and copses, trying to merge with the countryside. Immediately after landing a light vehicle rolled up to my plane. A General came out of the car and I delivered my report by the book. "For the Front artillery commander you couldn't find a bloke?" He asked discontentedly. I answered the question with a question: "Permission to ask where we're flying to?"

A colonel accompanying the General named the required place. Taking the map from its case I plotted the course there on a wing of the plane with chilled hands, and got into the front cockpit. The general in his astrakhan, muffled in a scarf almost right up to his eyes, settled behind me and we took off. I could see the tired face of my passenger in the mirror fixed on the left hand side to a centre-section stanchion. Our eyes met time and again, I was showing him with my hand sometimes the earth decked out in silvery winter apparel, sometimes the sun – but the General continued to frown. But suddenly a shadow fell on the plane. I looked around and a treacherous chill ran down my back. Two Messerschmitts were insolently and self-assuredly diving upon us! I began to throw my machine left and right just above the ground fleeing the machine-gun bursts. But the Germans were coming in to the attack again and again! The engine snorted, then did it again ... The impression was that it was choking like a man short of air. Below, as far as the eye could see, lay the steppe, densely covered with snow. No welcoming smoke, not a hut. The domain of the wolf. Suddenly the engine stalled ... I turned back to my passenger' showing him by hand that I was going to land. In reply he just shook his head but an open dissatisfaction showed in that movement. "Talk about gentry", I thought. He doesn't understand they can kill us ... Like we have to land just because I feel like it?"… Especially given I was carrying not just an officer but a "God of War"[5] commander There'll be no end of trouble now!"

The engine stalled and I was going straight for landing. And the Messers[6] kept shooting at us. All the time the strong and gusty wind strove to catch the plane's tail, to turn it upside down or at least break its wings. Generally speaking it was a simple task for a good *stepnyak*[7]. A U-2 was not a large machine – just plywood and percale. The wind was stubborn but I was not the complacent type either: I was the determined type too! I held the lever tightly and we landed safely. I jumped out of the cockpit to assist the General who was dressed so warmly that he couldn't climb out by himself. But the Messers blood was still up. Heart-chilling bursts of fire were thrusting into the snow right next to our plane. At last we stopped the plane and ran towards the forest. We were stumbling, falling over, getting up and running again. My General had already run completely out of breath forcing his way through the deep snow drifts – his clothes and age were definitely not suited to cross-country running. Suddenly everything fell silent … Hearing that, I asked the General to wait for me behind the trees.

"What are you saying, wait for you till the cows come home?" The artilleryman interrupted me angrily, catching up with me. "In this weather I'm not going to do that! We have to leave the machine and look for some dwelling before it's too late."

We again reached the plane, which shuddered convulsively at every squall of wind I looked at it anxiously, turning a deaf ear to my 'passenger's' words, and thought to myself: "If it blows a bit stronger it'll break the machine, carry it away. We have to tie it down immediately". And I climbed into the cockpit.

"What are you going to do?" The artilleryman was surprised.

"I'm going to get the hawser from the fuselage – we'll be tying the plane down."

"I'm sorry but this way we'll be tinkering with it till dark. And we'll be done for in the dark!"

"Till dark or not, I have no right to abandon my equipment in this condition."

"Well, you know …"

But glancing at my face, my 'passenger' understood I wouldn't back away from my decision, and took the rope from my hands. We managed to drag the plane, tail forward up to the forest with great difficulty. Only here did I examine it properly. Well, all in all the Fritz had crippled my U-2 pretty badly. The holes didn't matter, the main thing was that a propeller vane had been shot off, one cylinder of the engine was gone and the oil and petrol tanks were breached. Strange that it hadn't caught fire!

At last we had fastened the machine, tying it to the tree trunks, and disguised it with branches. Together we handled it quickly. Having finished, picked up the documents and plotted the necessary direction on the map, we went deep into the steppe. Oh, that night march was a hard one. We walked for an hour, then another, then a third … Snowy wool kept tumbling from the sky with no end as if from a torn sack. It was becoming harder and harder to walk. But the worst thing was that fatigue was accompanied by indifference. I hung my head low to hide my face from the tiresome snowflakes. Only they kept me aware of reality. "Or maybe it's a dream after all?" – importunate thoughts were crawling into my head. "That's the staccato thumping of rock breakers I hear, the faint

---

5   Translator's note – a common Russian nickname for artillery.

6   Translator's note – popular Russian nickname for Messerschmitt Me/Bf 109 fighters.

7   Translator's note – a steppe wind.

shouts of miners in the tunnel, the jokes of my girlfriends from the brigade. I hear Tosya Ostrovskaya whispering something into my ear. I can't understand what she wants and then Tosya begins shaking me by the shoulders. But I still can't understand … And why is there snow in the tunnel? It tickles my cheeks so tenderly, wraps my hands so warmly. I really don't want to free myself from its comfortable arms. And again Tosya shakes my shoulder … But this is not my girlfriend – she can't have this manly bass …"

"What's your name?"

"Anna."

"You have to get up, Comrade Anna, get up and walk now." Now I could discern the words clearly. "It won't take you long to freeze like this..." But I hadn't the strength for even a step, and I sat in the snow again.

"I'm not going any further. You go on your own …"

"Get up, get up, Anna," the General kept tugging at me. "You'll fall asleep and freeze to death!"

"Yes, yes, need to walk", I replied automatically. At last I understood what was dream and what was real." I'll get up soon, for sure …"

My mind knew what to do but my legs refused to obey me. How could I find the strength to stand upright, so as to walk across this hostile snow-clad steppe? But the artillery General stretched his hand to me and I walked, managing to overcome my deadly fatigue … I held on to him for the first several metres but then felt more and more confident with every pace. The dead point was behind me and I found my second wind. And the howling of the wind no longer seemed to me so ominous, and the bottomless darkness was no longer so scary.

By dawn, with frostbitten faces and hands, we had come across our soldiers. They were artillerymen from the unit to which I and Frontline Artillery Commander Zhouk were flying. They walked us into a hut wherein an iron stove was burning and soldiers were sleeping all over the floor. I fell asleep as soon as I sat down by the threshold. In the morning the signalmen reported my location to my squadron, and mentioned that the plane needed serious repairs. Soon after that Spirin, the pilot, flew over to me with Dronov the mechanic and on a second trip he brought all the stuff necessary for repairs to the engine and plane.

It had taken the whole day to find the plane in an unknown forest (fortunately, a big patch of spilled oil on the snow had helped out) and tow it by horse to a village. Konstantin Sergeevich swore for quite a while examining the damaged plane. He wished a thousand damnations on the German flyers and on Hitler himself, promising to bury the *Führer* on an aspen stake. But at the same time he went about his business, quickly installing something like a tent over the engine to protect himself from the wind.

When I saw that for ease of working he'd taken off his gloves I began to assist him.

"Comrade Commander, what are you trying to do with the engine with such a frostbitten face, eh? It'll get scared and won't start", my mechanic joked. Indeed my face was scary: it had turned black all over. I daubed it with grease and on top of that put on a mask of mole-fur. Such masks had been issued to all airmen but we didn't like to wear them – the furry skin on its lining with cutouts for the eyes and mouth made us look as if we were at a carnival.

To send me off to warm up Dronov was inventing various ruses but then he gave up and the whole business went faster. Aircraftsmen are an amazing lot! As a rule they are great masters of their craft or as it is said now, 'craftsman with golden hands'. They wouldn't go to eat or sleep until a plane was fully ready and then, having handed it over to a pilot wouldn't leave the aerodrome but would patiently wait for his return. He would begin to tidy up the parking lot – he would roll up the aircraft covers, carry brake shoes to the right place, then would simply smoke so the waiting time didn't drag on so long. And he would cast glances at the sky time and again – is he coming back yet? A mechanic would recognise the approach of his plane from afar – by a note in the engine's roar known only to him. And then he would run to meet it! How happy these modest aerodrome labourers were when their pilots came back to the ground alive and in one piece. And there would be no limit to their grief if their pilots had not come back from a mission ... No, I could not have become a plane mechanic – I wouldn't have had the strength to wait! Especially at war when all possible time for return is up and all hope rests on a miracle but the mechanic still waits, peers into the sky, listens, hopes ...

That time Dronov came back to the squadron with me and he showed his comrades the holes he had had to patch up in the frost.

"I counted 87 holes but Annoushka and the General weren't scratched! That's what it means to have the 'devil's dozen' as your tail number", Dronov chuckled. But I knew: apart from all the numbers, apart from luck, on those flights I'd been faithfully guarded by the hands of my mechanic. And by fate as well. I do believe in fate.

Generally speaking everything had turned out alright except that we'd got our fingers and cheeks frostbitten. But who would pay attention to that at the front? It was a trifle not worth remembering! But the Artillery Commander couldn't forget that night on the steppe and he remembered my personality. As soon as he'd flown back to Front headquarters he notified the signals commander Korolev: "I'm taking Egorova. I need combat pilots for the spotter planes ..."

When it became known in the squadron the airmen began 'making me see reason': "Have you gone crazy? You're a pilot, a human being, not a rubber balloon. You're meant to fly, not to hang like a sitting duck over the frontline!"

That was true – it's not too pleasant to serve as a target. But, word of honour, in what way were we, in our U-2s, not targets for the enemy's fighter planes? And I'd grown sick of being an aerial chauffeur ... I wanted to fight a real war. At least the spotter plane pilots helped to detect the enemy and wipe him out, but what about us? But nevertheless if I were to switch to another kind of aviation I would prefer to be a ground-attack pilot. I wasn't destined to become a spotter plane pilot ...

16

The *Katyushas*

issions, missions. There seemed to be no end of them. The squadron was manned by 'Spanish' pilots but they were shoving me – a girl – into the most difficult holes. It was an unpleasant sensation.

"Egorova, you will be flying in search of the *Katyushas*!"[1]

And again I would answer: "Yes sir, flying out!"

The *Katyushas* had just arrived at our Front and it had significantly raised our previously depressed spirits. I was given an approximate area and told that they were big trucks with installations for rockets. They would have slip-covers on top. I was also ordered to hand over to General Pushkin – a Corps Commander – a top secret package.

The thaw was on. It was raining in the area of our aerodrome. Visibility was at its lowest – about a hundred metres. When I had flown away from the aerodrome a wet snowfall began and fog overcast everything around – I couldn't see a thing! I decided to increase altitude: maybe up there it would be a bit clearer than near the ground. The altimeter was already indicating 900 metres and indeed the fog had thinned out – but what was that? The plane began to shudder. All its cross-braces began to vibrate. I glanced overboard and saw the wings, the fuselage, even the propeller covered with a smooth icy crust.

The engine was working, all rudders and elevators were functioning but the plane wouldn't obey them, it was losing altitude. I pushed the control column away to lose altitude faster but soon some instinct warned me that the ground was already close – somewhere very close. What's down there, below me? A house, a forest, a river, a gully or something else? I turned off the engine and slowly pulled the lever … Bang! The plane touched the ground and carried us off, dragged us somewhere. I did my best to slow down, to stop our movement. But there were no brakes on the U-2 and I was using the rudder.

At last the plane stopped and it became astonishingly quiet. Nothing could be seen two steps away – there was fog and I was afraid to walk away from the plane – I could get lost. I had to wait until the fog dispersed. In the meantime I cleaned the ice from my plane and determined my location approximately, based on the time and flight speed. And when it had grown lighter I saw a large haystack in front of the plane's nose. How had I managed not to run into it?

Having taken off I managed anyway to find General Pushkin's Corps with the *Katyushas*. But on my way back I ran into a heavy snowfall again. I landed the machine by now in pitch-darkness – not even the plane parking bays were visible, so after touch down I taxied 'on a wing and a prayer'. It was a good thing Dronov the mechanic had heard the 'voice' of his plane and run to meet me.

The squadron commander gave me a long dressing down then: "Tired of living, are you?" The pilots maintained a gloomy silence: it appeared that they had turned back half-way without completing their missions. The Southern Front Signals Commander General Korolev declared his gratitude to me and the political department presented me

---

1   Editor's note – here, a nickname for M-13 truck-mounted rocket missile launch systems.

with a gift – a parcel from the home front. The most interesting moment was that on opening the parcel I found a tobacco pouch on top. "To a dear soldier from Marousya Koudryavtseva – as a keepsake" was embroidered on the pouch and inside there was a photo of a pretty girl. In her letter Marousya asked the young combatant to give the Fascists a real good bashing and come back home soon and victorious. And there was so much in that parcel carefully laid out under the tobacco pouch! Tobacco in packages, a bottle of vodka wrapped in woolen socks and, wrapped in a towel with red embroidery, a small bag of dried fruits. At the very bottom of the box there was a school exercise-book and a dozen envelopes. Half of them bore the address: Town of Mary, Turkmenskaya SSR[2], Maria Koudryavsteva. I gave the pouch, the tobacco and the bottle of vodka to my aircraftsman, the towel to the hostess of the house I lived in, and kept the woollen socks and dried fruits for myself. I decided to pass the photo, the writing-book and the envelopes to Victor Kravtsov – a well-built Kuban Cossack who was 22 years old. I remember that in whatever place we were located all the local girls couldn't take their eyes off him, but the Cossack wouldn't pay attention to any of them … However, maybe he was only pretending that he was indifferent to them all?

"Victor", I addressed Kravtsov, "Have a look at the photo – what a wonderful girl! You write her a letter instead of me. Make her happy to know the parcel got to its destination – to a young soldier, to a pilot on top of that."

"Still up to your tricks", he growled but took the exercise-book …

Red Army Day came. Our squadron gathered for the festive assembly and executive officer Lisatrevich solemnly began reading a Decree on behalf of the Supreme Soviet of the USSR: Lieutenant Spirin was awarded with the Order of the Red Star, Junior Lieutenant Egorova – with the Order of the Red Banner (by now I'd been conferred officer's rank here in the signals squadron).

I had just flown back from a mission and being a bit late was sitting behind the rest. I still had the noise of a working engine in my ears and I didn't catch whom the awards had gone to. Suddenly they all clustered around me, began to congratulate me, but I was standing and not believing it: why me? One might say, I'd found myself at the Front by chance. I'd carried out all the missions I'd been given as a soldier should, from the heart. But there was no denying that although it had often been difficult I'd done my best. For some reason I recalled the road reconnaissance sortie – to find out which troops were on the march – ours or the enemy's … You couldn't say it was much fun to fly in the daytime in a defenceless plane whose only weapon was the pilot's revolver! Everyone knew the German aces chased our planes and it wasn't a big challenge for a Messerschmitt to down a U-2, but their reward for this would be the same as for a shot-down fighter plane.

"Comrade Commander, what's wrong with you? Are you alright?" I heard the voice of Dronov the mechanic. "You look awful …"

"I'm fine, what's up?"

"They're calling you to the presidium."

The Order was presented to me by a member of the Frontline Military Council Leonid Romanovich Korniets: the very same General who had shown me by mimicry and gestures that I had to report the location of the Cavalry Corps of Parkhomenko and Grechko not to him but to the Front Commander.

---

2   Translator's note – a Soviet Republic in Central Asia, now Turkmenistan.

17

A hooligan on the road

In May 1942 the South-Western Front troops began their advance in the direction of Kharkov. We, the airmen of the Southern Front Signals Squadron, were always abreast of events on the front line. We would be advised of the situation before a sortie and we would narrow it down, making flights either to this or that army, corps or division. The troops of the South-Western Front would have to destroy an enemy army grouping and liberate Kharkov. Two of our frontline armies – the 9th and the 57th – were supposed to work together with the South-Western Front. And on 20 May they ordered me to fly to the 9th Army with a top-secret package. I don't remember why I had to fly alone. Usually we would fly with navigators, signals officers, special messengers or with someone else but this time I had taken off alone. I remember that approaching the town of Izyum I saw on the roads and simply across fields the movement of our troops. Many fires showed themselves in the Severnyi Donets Valley, near Svyatogorskiy and in Izyum.

Fires had always aroused in me unreasoning alarm and anxiety since childhood. "A thief will leave the walls at least, but a fire will leave nothing!" the people of our village used to say. It had stuck in my memory for the rest of my life how the harvested corn had burned. Before threshing the corn was usually dried in barns. The sheaves would be stacked on grates in covered bays and a large stone oven – a *teplinka* – would be heated underneath. Heat would come up and dry the sheaves for threshing. Our corn barn caught fire from failing to watch the *teplinka*. A heart-rending cry resounded in the middle of the night: "Fire! We've got a fire!" Everyone jumped out of bed and began to rush about the house. My half-dressed brothers dashed out of the house, and mum couldn't even make it to the door, holding in her hands the first thing that had fallen into her hands – the *samovar* …

Now there was a war: whole cities, our whole land, were burning but still I couldn't get used to the fires. And now my heart thudded anxiously at the sight of the burning valley. And above me in the sky an aerial battle was raging. A couple of our I-16s were fighting against six Me-109s. The odds were not even but our pilots were skilfully avoiding the Messerschmitts' fire, closing in for head-on attacks, and the Fascists, fearfully keeping their distance, couldn't do much. Our guys obviously had the advantage. They shot down one Me-109: it crashed, and I must admit I was gloating and didn't notice when a German fighter pounced on me like a black kite. A fiery spurt cut the air in front of my eyes. I wished I could dive into a ravine or a gully but there were only flat fields with loose piles of last year's corn before me nearly up to the very horizon. On the right there was solid forest, on the left – the town. My machine caught fire: it immediately became hot and stuffy in the cockpit. The tail was burning – now it was going to reach me, the engine, the fuel tank and then … Having barely touched down I jumped out of the plane and tearing off the smoking rags of my overalls ran towards the woods. The German seemed to have gone berserk. He descended to contour level and turned the whole fire of his guns on me. In 1941 and also in 1942 the Hitlerites could afford this luxury – to chase a lone Russian soldier across the fields in a tank, to strafe someone with all cannons and machine-guns, diving from the sky … But I kept on running and falling over. At times I would fall down pretending to be dead and hiding my head under the corn stalks, arms and legs spread out. When the Messer went away to turn around I would jump up, clasp the secret package to my bosom and run again …

Having expended all his ammo the Fascist flew away. I was in a forest. It was quiet – there was no one around. And suddenly I wanted so much to lie in the glade, as in my childhood, to shut my eyes and switch off! Young foliage had already appeared on the trees – the spring was coming into its own. I had never been afraid of death but suddenly now I wanted to live so much! It would be bad to die in the spring. One's life is much, much dearer in the spring …

Whilst I was on the run my plane had burned to the ground. The bag of mail and my leather jacket that were in the fuselage had burned too. What could I do now? How to find the 9th Army headquarters? Looking around I saw a telephone cable hanging on some tree branches. I followed it, hoping it would lead me to some command post. I had barely walked thirty paces when I met two soldiers who were winding the cable onto a reel.

"Where's the CP?" I asked them.

"What do you mean the CP, the Germans are there!" they yelled without stopping. "It was evacuated long ago, everyone's gone."

"Where to?"

The soldiers didn't know – their business was to wind the cable. Coming out of the forest I ran towards the road across a field – but the road was empty. Lone soldiers and small groups of horsemen moved however they could, staying away from the road. A truck racing past rode around me as I stood in its path with my arms stretched out. Then an *Emka*[1] appeared – I tried to wave it down but in vain – the *Emka* dashed past me without slowing down. Then without stopping to think I pulled out my revolver and fired into the air. The driver reversed and stopped not far away from me. Then a front door opened and a dashing captain with a medal on his chest effortlessly leaped out of it. He deftly snatched the weapon from my hand, twisted my arms behind my back and then thrust his hand into a breast pocket of my blouse for my papers. I couldn't allow him to treat me this way! No less deftly I bowed my head and bit the captain, who screamed from pain, on the hand – the blood actually spurted! I saw a chubby General get out of the car. He began questioning me: who I was and by what right I was behaving outrageously on the road.

"And who are you?" I blurted out, but handed him my certificate. This certificate was quite impressive – issued personally to me it recommended all military units and civil organisations render all assistance to the presenter of this document in the performance of his duties.

"Where are you headed?" the General asked, more politely now.

"To the 9th Army headquarters."

"Get in the car," he offered and courteously enquired: "Where did you get burnt?"

I told him what had happened to me and suddenly … burst into tears – I don't know whether it was from resentment or from pain. My burnt hands hurt really badly and to top it off that captain had stripped off the skin when twisting my arms and now they were bleeding.

---

1   Translator's note – a Soviet-made light vehicle M-1.

"Don't cry, girl" the General began to calm me down, "otherwise your face will smart from the tears. We'll get you to 9th Army headquarters in a flash ..."

But the "now" and "in a flash" are quite imprecise concepts in war. Only after three hours did we find the Army headquarters where I handed the package over to the head of the operations department. They swabbed my face and dressed my hands in the medical post. They fed me in the canteen and by evening they had sent me off to the aerodrome.

I got a fraternal reception in the squadron. Narodetskiy the Quartermaster even brought me sweets instead of the hundred grams of vodka we were issued with for sorties. He knew that I wasn't drinking my ration and was giving it away to the mechanic or the pilots and he was trying to give me a treat for the occasion with sweets or something tasty. When we had been based near Voroshilovgrad and living in tents in the forest we didn't do much flying. Narodetskiy invited me to go on an excursion to Voroshilovgrad once. Having had a look around the city we dropped into a supermarket and there I saw a wide-brimmed hat with a splendid spray of artificial flowers. I stood for a long while admiring it and then the catering officer, catching my gaze fixed on the straw wonder, whispered something with the sales-girl and she handed it over to me ... The hat was hung on a nail in my tent. But once I was coming back from a mission and what did I see?... our pet Drouzhok[2] – a dog travelling with the squadron since we were at the Tikhiy farmstead – in that hat! My brothers in arms had cut holes in it for his ears, tied it on firmly with twine and the dog was rushing about in that stylish apparel, barking. Of course, the pilots were hiding from me in the tents ... Then they laughed and Kravtsov scolded me: "That's for taking presents from the Quartermaster!

Now, when I had returned alive, although with burns on my face and arms and in scorched boots, everyone was happy.

"Don't feel bad about the plane, Egorova. The main thing is that you are in one piece and you delivered the orders to the troops ..." Malikov the squadron engineer soothed me. "And you can always get another plane ..."

Of course you could always get another plane. But how bitter and hurtful it was to be shot down and unable to avenge it. The pilots were saying new equipment was coming to the front: Petlyakovs, Yaks, Lavochkins ... Every plane was a dream! But I had been greatly impressed by another machine. Only once or twice had I seen it in flight but remembered it always. A small monoplane of classic shape, its wings were slightly swept back. If you looked at it from aside it might seem a torpedo was flying. Legends were circulating about this plane ... It flew swiftly just above the very ground and climbed up to the sky like a hawk! The plane was manoeuvrable, with a good field of view, well-protected. There was a lot of talk about it. Once I heard a pilot describing it in glowing terms: "It doesn't break off into a spin during an uncoordinated turn, on the straight it flies steadily even hands-free. And landing? It almost lands by itself. In a word, it's as simple as a stool. It won't let you down in a dogfight and will knock a ground target for six. To cut a long story short – it's a *Sturmovik*[3]". Of course that was something to get dizzy about.

However, a dream is only a dream, but again I had to fly a U-2 to the 6th and 57th Armies surrounded by the Hitler's troops. Down there our troops were short of ammo, food and fuel, and there were a lot of wounded men. Attempts to break through the encirclement had come to nothing. The armies suffered heavy losses in men and matériel.

2　Editor's note – literally, 'little buddy'.
3　Translator's note – literally, a 'stormtrooper'.

Due to reverses in the Barvenkovo-Kharkov area the situation had become quite grave. We were flying a lot as always – and the Fascists pilot were hunting us as before. We were getting our share from the ground as well and we pilots were in trouble.

Having lost their machines, Serezha Spirin and Victor Kravstov returned to the squadron. A badly wounded Vanya Sorokin was sent to hospital. It had been five days since Sborshchikov with his navigator Cherkasov had flown on a mission and not returned …

Naum Sborshikov was a heaven-born pilot! Before the war he had worked as a pilot instructor and taught more than forty students to fly. I'd known him from the times of the Ulyanovsk aviation school where we studied in the same section of the class. Then our paths had diverged but when I arrived at the front and the squadron he welcomed me like one of the family. By nature he was a private, quiet man, but he protected me as much as he could and helped me with everything. When Sborshchikov didn't come back I couldn't accept his death for a long while and kept waiting. When five days had gone by everyone stopped waiting – even his plane's mechanic. I also had little hope for his return and when no one could see it tears would unexpectedly well up in my eyes. I felt sorry for Cherkasov too. An always joyful, smiling fair-haired man of no great height, in his faded blouse and then-fashionable canvas boots – looking at him it was hard to imagine how much suffering had fallen to his lot … He had volunteered to defend Republican Spain and flew in a bomber as navigator. During one of the combat sorties the plane was shot down. The pilot and the navigator were captured by the Fascists and after long interrogation and torture both of them were sentenced to death. But the Soviet Government managed to protect them and just before the War they both returned to the motherland.

"I was born in a shirt[4]", Cherkasov liked to repeat with a laugh.

How I wanted to believe that the one "born in a shirt" would soon join us with the latest joke he had thought up, at which even gloomy Sborshchikov would laugh. And they came back! They came back completely unexpectedly when we had all given up waiting. Naum's head was bandaged so that only his eyes were visible through the chinks. There was no boot on his right leg and it was wrapped in something as well, his blouse bore rusty blotches all over it. One of Cherkasov's arms was bandaged slung on a belt and he was leaning on a big stick with the other...

4　Translator's note – a Russian proverb identical to the English "to be born with a silver spoon in one's mouth".

18

Pandemonium

It was June 1942. The troops of the Southern Front were threatened with encirclement. The enemy had occupied the Donbass and entered the great curve of the Don River, by this move forming a threat to Stalingrad and the North Caucasus. Large masses of troops and materiel had concentrated before the Don river fords. Cattle and tractors were driven to the same crossings. Carts loaded with goods and chattels with children sitting on top waited for their turn as well. This was at night time. At dawn incessant raids by German aviation would begin. Our flak guns would fire near the fords but there were not enough of them. There were hardly any planes in the air with red stars on their wings, so the Hitlerites first bombed, and then with German pedantry strafed the crowds of people from low altitude. It is painful to recall what went on at those crossings. Women yelling, children crying, cattle bellowing ... Pandemonium!

We were in retreat with our troops. Falling back to the Don we kept changing airfields one after another. Everyone was getting extremely tired, literally dead on his feet: we were getting a lot of missions. There was no time for rest, no place to eat – and sometimes even nothing to eat. Lunch cooked at an old aerodrome would arrive at a new one, and sometimes would not find its way to us at all. We slept anywhere, in cockpits and on plane covers under the wings. The moment you dozed off they would yell: "Board your planes!"

One of those days Potanin – a pilot from our squadron – was ordered to fly reconnaissance: to determine where the enemy's mechanised columns had advanced to and what their strength was; to find out where the troop and materiel trains were and in which direction they were moving; to locate concentrations of Hitlerite troops and estimate their numbers. With Potanin went Belov as a navigator, a man straight out of architectural institute. Soon the pilot and the navigator noticed the Hitlerite tank and motorised columns moving south-east to the Don, towards its great bend. Our troops were in retreat and the German air force was on the rampage – bombing the roads crammed with refugees.

Having completed the reconnaissance Potanin and Belov turned back. They flew camouflaging themselves far away from roads and settlements. But the Fascists too were advancing sideways, in large and quite small detachments and groups. One such detachment attracted the attention of the crew by its strangeness – about 40-50 men in camouflage cloaks. Potanin thought they were our troops not knowing in which direction to move, and decided to show them the way. He made a steep turn above them, exiting it to the south-east, then another one – and suddenly the whole group shouldered their submachine-guns and opened fire at the plane with tracer bullets. "Anything can happen on the front", Potanin decided. "Our troops might have strafed us by mistake". But it turned out that it was German paratroopers who had fired at the U-2... The navigator fell silent and when Potanin glanced back Belov was pale and sitting with his head dropped lifelessly against the side of the cockpit. Anxiety for the life of his comrade prompted

Potanin to land as soon as possible and give him first aid. He landed his plane right there in a field but by then no assistance was needed. Belov was dead ...

During those hard days of our retreat, not far from Novocherkassk, we picked up a little kid of about three years of age. In nothing but a shirt, dirty, hungry, all covered with grazes, he couldn't say anything but the word "mum", whom he was calling incessantly, and his own name, Ilyusha[1]. Ilyusha was by now unable to cry and just sobbed. Approaching soldiers told us that recently a string of carts had been smashed by German aircraft and that they had seen this boy by his dead mother. And then when the Fascist vultures swooped again everyone had scattered in all directions. The boy had apparently run away too and so he had survived.

We didn't know what to do with him or whom to leave him with. We had to fly on but Ilyusha grabbed me by the neck and it seemed no force could tear him away from me. And then I decided to take the child with me. "Have you lost your mind? The kid needs care. What can you give him? Do you know where we're going to stop next?" the pilots shouted at me. But I clasped Ilyusha to myself even harder and ran to the village. Coming towards me I found an old woman with a walking stick. Shielding her eyes with her hand she looked long and closely at the child and then began crying and wailing, "Ilyushen'ka, my grandchild!" I handed the kid over to the old woman and rushed towards my plane in tears. And then suddenly everything became so unbearably painful and distressing! And for this orphaned Ilyushka too (how many of them were there on the wartime roads!), and for the misspent years, and for myself ... I loved kids so much, I wanted so much to have my own big family – many naughty little boys, mop-headed girls! The war had crossed out and ruined all such dreams ... I remembered Victor Kroutov often. I hadn't heard anything from him for five months already. He was fighting somewhere on the North-Western Front. During those minutes when I was alone with my reflections the thought "is he still alive?.." would weigh heavily on my soul. I kept trying to convince myself that letters not arriving were the fault of the field mail. But I'll be patient, I'll wait until they come ... At those moments I cursed myself amidst tears for being such a fool before the war: I had loved him to distraction for a long time, since the *Metrostroy* times and had never told him about it. Why?... "Do you love me?" he kept asking me during our dates and I would only laugh, and reply "What are you talking about? Of course not!" – "Kiss me goodbye!" – "Give me a break! Kiss me yourself if you want ..." – "She loves me! She loves me!" Victor would shout loudly and whirl me round and round holding me tightly by the hands ...

Everyone in the squadron – both pilots and mechanics – treated me well. Some 'suitors' appeared as well but I managed somehow to talk to them not tête-à-tête but in front of others – that way it was easier to fend off an 'attack' and let it be known that nothing was going to come of it. It wasn't easy, of course, to be a single woman in a group of men. Sometimes I wanted so much just to talk to someone heart to heart. But one stern word – War – held me back and cowed me ...

We flew over to an airfield previously prepared near Cherkassk but there was no headquarters, no canteen nor any fuel. Our land transport was a roundabout route via Maikop, Tuapse, Tbilisi and Ordzhonikidze because the straight road to Grozny had been cut by the enemy. Senior Lieutenant Listarevich had been appointed Land Transport

---

1   Editor's note – a diminutive form of Ilya.

Commander and Lieutenant Irkoutskiy Commissar. They left on 18 August 1942 – on Air Force Day itself – but we didn't feel like celebrating at this hard time of retreat. And our 'base' caught up with the squadron only on 30 October when the Front headquarters was already in Grozny. Thus when we had landed and turned off the engines, we gathered by the Deputy Squadron Commander Pen'kov's plane and began to think what to do next. We saw an ageing woman coming from the settlement we had landed near. She greeted us, looked us over and said "Do you have anything to eat, maybe you're hungry?" And without hearing an answer she suggested straightaway "I've cooked a bucket-size pot of *borsch*. As if I knew you would come around. My son is a pilot, after all, but I haven't heard from him for a long time …" and she began to sniffle, wiping her eyes with the lap of her broad blouse.

After a tasty lunch we decided to pour the left-over petrol into the tanks of one plane and fly to look for the rear services of our squadron. I happened to fly with Cherkasov. Again under our wings there was land enveloped by smoke, burning houses, burning unharvested wheat, corn, sunflowers. People were moving in carts and on foot, with parcels, with cows on leashes. It was painful to watch and even more painful to know that you couldn't help them.

Only five days later, somewhere near Pyatigorsk, at last we found our headquarters. Here they read out 'Order 227', a stern order whose meaning boiled down to: "Not a step back!" As a rule the order numbers were remembered only by staff officers. But even now this one, Order number 227, will be recalled by any war veteran if asked about it. It was said in this order that we had to defend every position, every single metre of our soil to the last drop of blood. Those who reckoned that the territory of the Soviet Union was big enough and we could retreat even deeper into it, to lines more suitable for defence, were condemned. The order obliged us to declare a resolute war on cowards, panic-mongers, infringers of discipline. To comply with this demand meant to save the motherland, to defeat the enemy.

Units raised from the troops to maintain order played a paramount role, but an 'amusing incident' took place as well. Between Pyatigorsk and Nal'chik the Fascists again shot down Serezha Spirin's plane, which was flying to locate the 17th Cossack Cavalry Corps. The August heat was on, and the pilot had taken off in just light overalls, leaving his uniform with his papers back at the aerodrome. He was shot down, the plane burned up, the pilot was injured too. Firing on the ground didn't give him a chance to lift his head. Spirin crawled. When he reached our lines he was immediately arrested as a deserter. No matter what he tried to say to vindicate himself nobody would believe him. Fortunately, a Front HQ liaison officer, with whom Spirin had flown to the fighting units many a time recognised him. The speedy court martial was postponed, and Commissar Ryabov flew off with confirmations and papers to pick him up.

The front line was changing several times a day. We had to fly all over the North Caucasus. The enemy Panzer units had already forced a crossing over the Kuban in the Armavir Region and captured Maikop and Krasnodar. The Germans had occupied nearly all the mountain passes, taken Mozdok and small bridgeheads on the right bank of the Terek River. It was difficult for us to understand the situation that had developed in the North Caucasus in August 1942. I remember getting an order to locate the headquarters of the 58th Army, again with the same navigator Cherkasov, whom I made a flight from Nal'chik to Grozny with. We found the Army and handed mail over to the Front headquarters but how much we went through during that flight!

I returned from the mission tired, despondent from all I'd seen, angry. I handed the plane over to Dronov and rushed to squadron headquarters. Now behind me I heard the mechanic's bitter words addressed to the engineer, "Again like a sieve! How I'm going to fix it and what with, I have no idea. There's no workshop yet …"

Calling in at the command post to report to the Commander of Task Implementation I saw the returned Kolya Potanin and Victor Kravtsov were already reporting. The quiet and sober-minded Potanin didn't look himself. Always well-kempt and tidy, now he was in a burnt uniform, his face smeared with oil and blood, hair scorched. He was reporting to the squadron commander Major Boulkin and to the executive officer Listarevich about what had happened and asking to be transferred to combat aviation. The following had happened to Potanin: he had been sent with important cargo to the Ardon area, to our units surrounded by the enemy. Many years later Chief Marshal of Aviation Konstantin Andreevich Vershinin – the former commander of our Aerial Army – wrote in his book "The 4th Aerial" about those flights: "Many brave men flew to encircled pockets in the daytime as well". It seems you couldn't say it clearer. At daytime, in a defenceless plane, into a surrounded area … The pilots despatched foodstuffs, ammo, medical supplies, other cargo to the troops … That day Potanin, having completed the mission, was transporting a badly wounded man out of the pocket. On the way back he found himself under ground fire and then under fire from Fascist fighters. No matter how well he manoeuvred, how he tried to escape the shells targeted at him, his plane was shot up, caught fire and fell into brush. Potanin managed to leap out under from the burning debris, then, rolling on the ground he put the fire on him down and rushed to save the wounded navigator, but he was already dead …

"I want to smash the bastards!" His eyes sparkling, clear and limpid as the sky, Nikolay was arguing with the squadron commander. "I can't do it this way any more. They hit us and we hide in the bushes! ."

The *Kubanets*[2] Kravtsov stood silent. Instead of reporting he, still silently, passed a paper of some sort to the squadron commander. I saw him, also soundless, reading it. With no hesitation he wrote something on it in bold letters, and passed the paper to the executive officer. Later we found out that Victor Kravtsov had refused to fly in U-2s and asked to be transferred to the ground-attack aviation. The squadron commander's reply was the same as many times before: "Denied"…

2　Translator's note – a man from Kuban, a Cossack-populated area in Southern Russia in the Kuban River basin.

19

"You want to go to a penal company?"

I t was a frightening and difficult time back then, in the autumn of 1942 in the North Caucasus. All fighting men from Private to Field Marshal seemed to be at breaking point. None of us had received any letters for a long time: the field mail had got lost somewhere. How was my mum, how was Victor, where were they? Were they alright? "Of course, they are alive and well!" I would reassure myself: "It's problems with communications!" In the left breast pocket of my blouse there were my Party membership card and two photographs – my mum's and Victor's, and a very tiny one of Yourka. Mum was as usual in a headscarf and looking at me with sorrow. But Victor, on the contrary, was laughing jauntily, slightly throwing back his curly head. He was in uniform. There were three cubes and 'birds' on his collar patches. Yourka was in a white shirt with a Pioneer scarf[1] on the photo. They hadn't wanted to accept him in the Pioneers because of his repressed father until the *zavouch*[2] stood up for him and for other similar unfortunate children. She said then: "If we don't accept our students in the Pioneers we won't form a single Pioneers group in the whole school. You all know that in our *Arbat* schools almost every second students' father has been repressed. Many were then accepted in the Pioneers but after that, true, the *zavouch* was fired …

In extremely difficult conditions, fighting fiercely, our troops retreated to the foothills of the Greater Caucasus Range. The enemy had occupied a vast territory: the Rostov district, the Kalmykia Republic, Krasnodar and Stavropol Provinces, penetrated into Kabardino-Balkaria, North Ossetia, Chechen-Ingushetia. On 25 October 1942 the Hitlerites threw up to 200 tanks into the battle and having broken through the lines of the 37th Army, they captured Nalchik on 28 October. Exploiting their success, in a week they approached Ordzhonikidze. But on 6 November the incoming reserves of our Army launched a counter-attack against the Fascist grouping and smashed it in six days of fighting. The Germans had gone on the defensive in the direction of Grozny too. The plan to conquer the Transcaucasus, Grozny and Baku oil-producing regions was frustrated.

It was in those very days when my last sortie in the communication squadron took place. I flew to the Alagir area and on the way I was attacked by German fighters. Manoeuvring literally between the treetops, I desperately tried to hide from them. The Messers were firing blindly but with long spiteful bursts. I threw my plane left and right … "When will they finally leave me alone?.." And suddenly … My machine smashed its wing into a tree. A heavy blow … A crack … Another blow! … When I came to my senses I couldn't understand at all where I was. My legs and arms were sore, my chest was constricted, it was hard to breath. Stirring a little I understood nothing was broken. But where was the plane? I looked around and saw it just nearby: it lay completely destroyed.

1   Translator's note – a red scarf – a sign of belonging to the Pioneer organization.
2   Translator's note – head of the teaching unit in USSR schools.

The engine was stuck into the ground, the propeller (more precisely, fragments of it) was scattered around, the ailerons were hanging on the trees with some other parts. In other words the plane was no more. I felt pain, vexation and bitterness deep inside. "What shall I do? What shall I do …?" I repeated over and over again hobbling towards the aerodrome. There was no proof that I had been attacked by the Germans. I thought: "What if I say I crashed the plane myself. It'll be a chance to get transferred to the ground-attack aviation!" After all, by that time I had already flown 130 combat flights in the U-2!

Only the day after, towards evening, did I find the village of Shali, beyond Grozny, and appear before the squadron commander. "I crashed my plane and am ready to bear responsibility for it according to the war time rules" I rattled off, standing at attention.

Major Boulkin, it seemed to me, was in a bad mood. Looking at me angrily he began to yell, "Do you wanna go to a penal company? You'll find out there what hard times are! Now look – they've started playing vandal to escape to combat aviation!"

Whom Major Boulkin had in mind I didn't know, but it hurt to listen to his abuse.

Alexey Ryabov stood up for me. "Look, Commander, let's transfer her to the UTAP[3] together with Potanin. Let her be retrained. After all, there've already been five requests to send her off to a women's regiment …"

This was the first time I had heard about that, but I didn't have a chance to say anything – Dronov appeared from nowhere: "Permission to speak? I'll fix up Egorova's plane. I promise!"

Many years later I found out Dronov had indeed restored my plane and handed it over to the squadron engineer, but then secured for himself a transfer to another unit and worked as a mechanic on an La-5 fighter plane till the end of the war. Nevertheless, Potanin and I were transferred to the town of Salyany on the Caspian sea to a training regiment. And the first obstacle on my way to a combat plane appeared immediately.

"So, a ground-attack pilot?" The Regimental Commander said with interest. "But do you know what a hellish job it is to attack ground targets? No woman has fought in a *Sturmovik* yet! Two cannons, two machine-guns, two batteries of rockets, various bombs – that's the Il's[4] armament. Trust my experience – not every good pilot can handle such a machine! Not everyone is capable steering a 'flying tank', of orienting himself in combat conditions while hedge-hopping, bombing, shooting the cannons and machine-guns, launching rockets at rapidly flashing targets, conducting group dog-fights, sending and receiving orders by radio – all at the same time. Think it over!" he reasoned with me.

"I've though it over already. I understand everything" I replied briefly but resolutely.

"God save us, what a stubborn one! Then do what makes sense to you!" And the Regimental Commander backed down.

I lived there in a two-room flat with the wife of one of the pilots, who had flown to there from Baku. There were plenty of planes in the training regiment but all of them were obsolete. We flew UT-2, UTI-4, SB, I-16, Su-2. You could choose any plane and I flew a lot in an I-16. People said the I-16 was a very difficult plane to handle but I had no problems – that made the guys envious. It was such a small, wonderful plane, so agile! But of the Il-2 *Sturmovik*, which the regiment commander had commented would be beyond my control, there was still no sign. Still, my new comrades and I were eager to master that very *Sturmovik*. Nevertheless, I enthusiastically set about studying the equipment

---

3   Translator's note – Air Force Training Regiment.
4   Translator's note – Ilyushin Il-2.

that was new to me. I learned to handle a fighter plane and to conduct a 'dog-fight'. I could confidently take off in a light Su-2 bomber. Finding that its take-off and landing speed were almost the same as the Il-2's, I took to this plane with a special zeal. Its engine worked on *castorka*, that is, castor oil. They would say then: "The *castorka* has arrived, hold onto your guts!"[5]

Training flights were undertaken almost daily. I remember we started a dog-fight there, I began to loop my I-16, then landed and began to climb out, my head spun and I fainted: I was hungry. Petrol was plentiful in the regiment – fly as you please, but the food in the dry mess was watery, to put it mildly. We had cash, for we were paid wages, but there was nothing to buy – everything was rationed. The guys would go to the Kura river to fish for lamprey and call me to go with them. These lampreys were like snakes and that was why I thought: "My God, I'd rather stay hungry!" But having fainted after the fighting drill in that *Ishak*[6] I told them; "Guys, I'm coming with you and I'll eat lampreys". They would set up a campfire, fry them a bit and eat them.

Once I heard that the head of the political section of the 230th Ground Attack Aviation Division Colonel Toupanov had arrived at the UTAP to select pilots for combat regiments. Well, I thought "You can't die twice, but we'll all die once" and rushed to headquarters! I asked everyone I met: "Where's Toupanov?" But they only shrugged in reply. At last I stopped a stumpy man in flying overalls and uniform peaked cap and asked again: "Do you know where Colonel Toupanov from the front is around here?"

The stranger looked at me attentively, smoothing out the wrinkles on his overalls under his officer's belt. "And what exactly do you need him for?"

"I'll tell as soon as I meet him"

"Let's assume I'm Toupanov."

"You?" My insolent tone frightened me. What a blunder I'd committed! But there was no room to retreat. And furthermore the colonel repeated: "So, what did you want to tell me?"

"My name is Egorova," I started from the beginning. "I graduated from the Kherson aviation school, worked as a pilot-instructor, have been at the front since the beginning of the war as a pilot in Boulkin's squadron, maybe you've heard of it …"

"Can you make it shorter?"

"I can … Take me into your division!"

Obviously the colonel had not expected such a turn of events. He looked at me narrowly once again: was I joking or not?… But there was no sign of levity on my face. "Alright, Egorova. Come around tomorrow for an interview …"

In the morning about thirty men were gathered by the headquarters. Among the agitated crowd of pilots there were invitees and volunteers. Everyone wanted to fly the *Sturmoviks* – such was the mood! Toupanov spoke to every man – questioned them about flying, home, family. Some were picked for the 230th Ground Attack Aviation Division, some were not. When it was my turn and I entered the office, Toupanov, not responding to my salutation, kept silent and at last said, "Do you understand what you're asking? To fight in a 'flying tank'! Two cannons, two machine-guns, rockets! And hedge-hopping height? Diving? Not all men can handle that …"

---

5   Translator's note – referring to the use of castor oil as a laxative.
6   Translator's note – a nickname for I-16, originating from the Russian pronunciation of *I-shestnadtsat* (I-16), literally, 'a donkey'.

"I understand," I replied quietly. "Of course the Il-2 is not a ladies' plane. But is the U-2? Dying is not ladies' business either! It's not the time for bearing children!" Here I got heated. "But I'm not a countess, I'm a *Metrostroy* girl. My hands are no weaker than a man's ..." And I stretched both hands forward. But the Colonel wasn't looking at them at all. Only now had he noticed the Order of the Red Banner on my chest.

"What were you decorated for?"

"For locating the Cavalry Corps and carrying out other missions for the Southern Front HQ", I replied.

"W-e-l-l," Toupanov drawled. "In the first year of the war they didn't give many of those ..." And he continued, "It seems to me you said you used to work as a pilot-instructor before the war?"

"I did, in the Kalinin aeroclub."

"And how many people did you teach to fly?"

"Forty two ..."

Toupanov remained silent, and then began to ask about my mother, then about my brothers. Of my brothers I said they were all at the front, but concealed again that my eldest brother had been repressed. I told him about my sister Zena as well – she was in the sieged Leningrad working as foreman at the Metal Plant.

Questions poured as from a horn of plenty, and I kept answering hanging my head lower and lower, ready to burst into tears. There was less and less hope left that I would fight on a *Sturmovik*. I even thought Toupanov was distracting me from the main topic intentionally and was sure to conclude at the end of the interview that I wasn't suitable: women, he would say, do not fly *Sturmoviks* ... But something quite unexpected happened. The head of the Aviation Division Political Section smiled at me as if apologizing, and asked: "Have I tired you out with my questions?" And then concluded: "We are taking you on. Consider yourself a pilot of the 805th Ground Attack Aviation Regiment of our 230th Division. In three days we're heading off to Derbent. Be ready."

How happy I was! I rushed outside and began to do cartwheels on my stretched arms, to the friendly laughter of my comrades: it was lucky I was in trousers!

Before departure I went to bid farewell to the commander of the training regiment. He sincerely congratulated me on my transfer to the *Sturmoviks* but, as if by the way, suggested: "After all, we've received 'Ils' too. You'd get your own room – you'd be more comfortable. On top of that there's no flak here. Stay with us."

"No!"

20

"Not a woman, a combat pilot"

The group of pilots headed off to Derbent by train before dark. I was amongst them – the first female pilot who had got admission to the *Sturmoviks* ... Since my childhood I'd been lucky enough to meet good people. Wherever I studied, wherever I worked I would meet loyal friends, kind-hearted tutors. I was trained at the factory school by the old craftsman Goubanov, I was assisted by the engineer Aliev, who was the shift boss, in my transfer to the most important sector of operations – the tunnel. I was trained by the superb instructor Miroevskiy in the aeroclub, the secretary of the Ulyanovsk District *Comsomol* Committee gave me a hand at a very hard moment of my life, then there was Maria Borek from Leningrad, the Secretary of the Smolensk District *Comsomol* Committee, the Commissar of the Smolensk aeroclub ... Was it really possible to count all those who had warmed my soul with their sympathy and human kindness and helped me to realize my dream!

But not everyone met me with sympathy in the ground attack regiment. There were some (for some reason, especially many of those belonged to the technical staff) who grumbled under their breath "What good is a woman in ground-attack aviation?" But the regiment navigator Petr Karev shushed them: "The Regiment's not getting a woman, it's getting a combat pilot ..."

So there I was in the ground attack regiment. The Battalion Commissar Ignashov – deputy commander for political affairs – summoned us, the newly arrived pilots, by turns for interview. I didn't know what he had spoken about with my comrades, but I was stunned by his very first question: "And what's the point of putting yourself in mortal danger?"

"Mortal all of a sudden?" I growled, displeased.

But Ignashov went on: "A *Sturmovik* is too hard for a woman. And take into account, our losses are rather great. I'll tell you confidentially that in the latest fighting over Gizel village we lost nearly all our airmen. Although our plane is armour-plated, more airmen die in it than in any other kind of plane. Think it over properly and go back to the training regiment. The *Sturmovik* isn't suitable for a woman!"

"And what is suitable for a woman at war, Comrade Commissar?" I asked challengingly. 'To be a medic? To drag a wounded man from the battlefield under enemy fire, strained beyond her strength? Or being a sniper? To stalk the enemy under cover for hours in all weathers, kill them, get killed herself? Or maybe, a surgeon would be easier? To receive the wounded, to operate under bombing and, seeing people suffer and die, suffer herself?"

Ignashov wanted to say something but I was already hard to stop. "Obviously it would be easier to be dropped off behind enemy lines with a radio transmitter? And maybe now women are better off on the home front? They smelt metal, grow corn and bring up kids at the same time, they get the death notices of their husbands, fathers, brothers, sons, daughters? It seems to me, Comrade Commissar", by now I had began to talk quieter, "now is no time to see any difference between a man and a woman until we cleanse our motherland of the Hitlerites ..."

I finished my impromptu 'performance', and then Ignashov smiled: "That's right, my daughter is as cranky as you. She used to work in a base hospital as a surgeon, but no way: she had to be at the frontline. Currently she's somewhere near Stalingrad … We haven't heard from her for a long while – neither my wife nor me. My wife suffers especially – she's alone at home … Do you write letters to your family?" Ignashov asked, taking some pills out of his pocket. Only now did I discern how ill he was. He had 'bags' under his eyes, blue lips, and a pale and puffy face.

"I do write letters but haven't had any from home for a long time. I feel very sad sometimes. Then I convince myself that it's the field mail's fault …"

"At your age you can convince yourself even of something pleasant", the Commissar said, addressing me with 'thou' for the first time. "Are you married?"

"No", I replied in one word, and suddenly, as if I had at long last found someone to speak my mind to, to disclose my innermost thoughts to, I burst out: "But I love very much one man, a pilot. He's a fighter pilot, in combat somewhere near Leningrad. We wanted to get married before the war but I kept postponing it. One time I said that we should graduate from the flying school, another time that I had to turn out one more group of cadets, and then the war came …"

The conversation with Ignashov clearly took too long but we parted like old friends.

"You can come to me with all your questions, joys and sorrows. We will sort everything out together", he said, sort of casually, in farewell, and stretched his hand out to me. Ignashov was popular in the regiment. As for the political commissar who had been his predecessor in the 805th, once they had even bashed him! According to the stories he used to just walk around giving orders. The regiment was in combat, men were dying, everyone was having a hard time, but he would just give orders … Ignashov was a completely different man.

We were given only two days to study the *Sturmovik* equipment and get ready for examination by the senior regimental engineer. All the newly-arrived men were distributed among the squadrons straightaway. The pilot Vakhramov and I were sent to the 3rd Squadron. Puny, short Valya[1] Vakhtramov looked like a boy. And when we'd found out that he was only about nineteen we were surprised: this little chap, with this height, had managed to put up his age so as to join an aviation school!

When we reached the Ogni aerodrome Vakhramov lagged behind the train. There were very few passenger trains back then and he had to catch up with us on a tanker of fuel oil. Of course he was stained badly and had also lost his papers. In short, when Valentin arrived at the regiment nobody would believe he was a pilot: my confirmation was required. The regiment commander himself met Vakhramov out and said just one thing: "Clean yourself up!"

The regimental chief-of-staff Captain Belov told us the regiment's war stories, told about the airmen who had distinguished themselves in combat. We found out that our 805th Ground-attack Regiment had been raised from the 138th High-speed Bombers. It had been in combat since the first day of the war. The airmen flew bombing missions against the columns of German troops advancing from the Western frontier towards Kiev and losses in the regiment were very heavy. When almost no fighting machines were left in it,

1   Translator's note – diminutive of Valentin.

the regiment moved by railroad to Makhachkala[2] and then across the sea to Astrakhan[3] where the pilots were going to learn to handle the new Pe-2 plane – a dive-bomber of Petlyakov's design. I disliked it – but I didn't fly it, just watched it.

However, before the regiment had time to get quartered a new order arrived – to set about studying the Il-2 *Sturmovik*. And we were on the road again – this time to pick up the combat aircraft. And here the regiment received the name "805th Ground-attack Aviation". The staff learned to handle the new equipment and the regiment relocated to the frontline where it joined the 230th Ground-attack Aviation Division. Thus the combat life of the regiment began with flying the famous Ilyushin *Sturmovik*.

The Regimental Engineer began the traditional examinations on knowledge of the plane's design, engine, aerodynamics. The engine of A. Mikoulin's design had 12 cylinders – one of the most powerful engines of that time, developed specially for the *Sturmovik*. I knew well all its technical characteristics. It was incomparable with the U-2 engine. The U-2 engine had 5 cylinders and the exhaust nipples were located in the collector. On the Il-2 all the nipples extended outside, and that was why when the engine worked it roared mightily.

The Armament Engineer Senior Lieutenant B.D.Sheiko – still quite a young chap – checked our knowledge of gunnery. Like us, he had apparently just found himself in the ground-attack regiment.

"So, how should we aim when shooting rockets?" We asked him almost with one voice.

"Well, you put the crosshair on the armour glass[4] over the target and get it roasted!"

"And how do you set the electric ejector for bomb delivery?"

"It depends on what you're bombing. You can set it on single, batch or salvo", he answered.

"Tell us, what's the flight trajectory of a rocket launched from a dive? And how do you set up the rocket ejector?"

Questions poured as if from a horn of plenty and the young engineer went mad. Who's the examiner? You or me?" he asked, turning the kicker handle left and right. Not finding the right position he cursed, climbed out of the cockpit and went away from the aerodrome.

New examiners were waiting for us at the parking bay. The head of the aerial gunnery service, later to be a regiment's deputy commander of flight training – Captain Koshkin – greeted us gloomily. He was a man of quite non-athletic appearance, in a uniform which hadn't undergone cleaning and ironing since pre-war times. The phlegmatic captain, with his sad green-grey eyes and dolefully downturned lips, seemingly harboured some undivined grief. But you had to see Alexey Koshkin in combat! We'd been told about his duel with some remarkable Fascist contrivance. The Germans had designed a devilish machine which could destroy 12-15 kilometres of railway in one hour. And how much time and materiel, how many hundreds of soldiers' labour it took to restore all that! It turned out this disguised steam-engine dragged behind it something like a huge plough-share that tore up everything in its way – both rails and sleepers. And once the Ground Troops Command asked the airmen to destroy the enemy's machine. Regiment Command ordered Koshkin to destroy the engine. But how to find it? Only yesterday they'd seen

---

2   Translator's note – a city on the west shore of the Caspian Sea.

3   Translator's note – a city on the north shore of Caspian in the mouth of the Volga.

4   Translator's note – of the cockpit windscreen.

the steel threads of rails and today there were none. Koshkin had flown many times and run himself ragged but couldn't find the steam engine. But one day Alexey noticed a shadow in the beams of the setting sun. It was the large, improbable and ugly shadow of a steam-engine. "But where was the smoke? Where was the engine itself?" – Koshkin depicted his perplexity later. Having descended to low level, at last he saw what he'd been looking for so long. The Germans had installed a platform coloured like trees and bushes on top of the engine. The disguise was superb. Alexey attacked this 'theatre': he closed in from aside, took aim at the engine and opened fire. All in vain – the engine-driver sharply sped up and the shells sent by Koshkin shot past. He attacked again, again with no result

The duel between the plane and the engine lasted for quite some time but when a shell hit the boiler a cloud of steam shot up and the engine stopped. However, Koshkin kept pounding it time and again: with the cannons, with the machine-guns – he launched rockets point-blank, so greatly had that German devilry vexed Alexey! The engine turned into a heap of metal. Having photographed the results of his work the captain made it home with not a single shell-hole, although the Germans had shot at our *Sturmovik* from the ground and from that very engine with everything they had.

That's the kind of people who ended up in our regiment. It was impossible not to marvel at them, but I have to admit I began to doubt myself a little bit: would I cope with it like them, would I be able to?

After we passed our tests all our group was assigned to fly the UIl-2 – a training plane with dual control. It became known to us that Captain Karev would accompany our flights. The regiment navigator Captain Karev appeared before us surprisingly elegantly He seemed to have on the same military uniform as Captain Koshkin – but his carefully ironed blouse with snow-white under-collar, breeches with enormous flaps, polished box calf jackboots cleaned to shining and gathered into a 'concertina', peaked cap with a star on the cap-band, all this fitted him somehow especially smartly without breaching the regulations. For some reason I remembered his mischievous laughing eyes and his hooked nose from the first introduction. Karev walked me to the desired machine and stepped aside – as if to say, 'let her get to know it on her own …'

And indeed I was looking at the plane and couldn't get my fill of it. In front of me there was a beauty with an elongated streamlined fuselage, a glass cockpit and a pointed engine cowling sticking out far forward. The blued barrels of two rapid-fire cannons and two machine-guns menacingly jutted out of the front edges of the wings. Eight metal slats were fixed under the wings – guides for the rockets. I had already known there were four bomb bays in the central section. In there as well as up on two clamps under the fuselage six one-hundred kilogram bombs could be hung. Basically it was a cruiser not a plane! I rubbed the cold panelling with my palm. Metal! Not like on the U-2. The engine, the fuel tanks, everything was covered by durable armour. And a bird like that was entrusted to me! Staying silent for as long as was proper for a first date Karev asked at last: "Do you like it?"

"Very much!" I replied with a kind of special emotion.

"Well, let's do some flying now and see if you like the *Ilyusha* in the air", and smiling gallantly, he invited: "Be my guest!"

I made two circles in the dual-control plane, and after landing the regimental navigator asked me via the intercom to taxi to the parking lot and turn off the engine. "Well, now he's going to rip into me!" I thought. "I didn't suit the captain for some reason!" He hadn't dropped a word during the flight and had only whistled tunes from some operettas.

"Permission to hear your remarks?" I said trying to look cheerful.

"But there aren't any" Karev replied. "Go to the combat plane, tail number '6' and make a circuit flight on your own. Altitude 300 metres, landing as normal."

But I hadn't expected such a rush in the transfer to a combat plane. The UIl-2 had seemed to be 'blind' and cramped to me and I asked Captain Karev in a hoarse voice:

"Comrade Captain, do one more flight with me in the dual-control."

"No point ironing the air for nothing! Nowadays every kilo of petrol is counted", the navigator cut me off.

"But, Comrade Captain", I begged. "All the guys from our group got several accompanied flights, and Kulushnikov, he got the whole twenty five. Why won't you at least let me fly once more on dual-control?"

"Double-quick to the plane!" the captain ordered, and at that I ran. The plane mechanic Vasya Rimskiy checked off to me the machine's readiness. Putting on the parachute I climbed into the cockpit, buckled on the belts, tuned up the two-way for reception, checked everything off as we'd been trained and turned the engine on.

The sensation of take-off, the disappearance of your firm foothold, is amazing. The plane is still running across the rough field gaining speed, one more instant – and it detaches from the ground and the pilot is now carried on two steel wings. During the first circular flight I'd noticed how much faster this traditional route of four turns was completed – the U-2's engine was no match for the Il-2's. I had estimated the landing run precisely and landed exactly by the 'T'-junction: as pilots say, 'on three points'.

You wouldn't wish a better one! I taxied out and saw the captain showing me with his arms: 'do one more flight'. So I rolled for another take-off. Our aerodrome was situated almost on the shore of the Azov Sea, so during flying most of the route was made over the water. I couldn't swim and was afraid of water. Once in my childhood I nearly drowned: my mum was rinsing the washing, I was with her and fell into the water. I still feared water and swam only close to the shore. And here, after take-off there was a turn over the waves, a second, a third, a fourth one – all over the sea, and then I would land on the aerodrome. And doing a turn over the water I heard a backfire resound, then another – and the engine stalled. The prop stopped, a sinister silence descended …

I automatically pushed the control column away and switched the plane to gliding – so as not to lose speed and not to fall into the sea with the *Sturmovik*. After that I continued doing everything according to instructions: I throttled back, turned off the ignition, closed the fuel emergency shutoff cock. In a word, I set everything in the cabin on 'economy'. The aerodrome was already right in front of me, and all would have been alright, but the speed and altitude were falling catastrophically fast. I quickly understood that I wouldn't make it to the aerodrome and would have to land right in front of my nose. But what was that? The whole terrain was pitted by deep ravines! If I landed on them I would be done for! And at the same time I heard the anxious voice of the regimental commander Kozin in the radio: "What's happened? What's happened? Receiving!" But I couldn't reply for I had no transmitter. And I had no time for replying – all my attention was fixed on the ground. I noticed a narrow strip of flat ground between two ravines and decided to land on it, opened up the cockpit for a better field of vision, then lowered the undercarriage …

Needless to say, the time dragged agonizingly slowly. Then the machine touched down, rolled forward and I did my best to hold her and not to let her fall into a ravine To achieve that I was energetically 'pumping' – pushing the brakes with my feet – and the speed began to fall bit by bit, the wings to lower steadily, and the plane slowed down and stopped. And when I, wet all over, leaped out of the cockpit onto a wing and looked down I saw with horror that my machine's wheels had stopped right on the edge of a ravine. Numerous skeletons of dead animals lay at the bottom …

I examined the plane – it seemed unscathed. Everything seemed to be in place, and in one piece, except a bail was cracked slightly and a wing was damaged. And there were many patches on the wings and the fuselage as well – the 'Il' was riddled all over. The poor Ilyushin had been through a lot during the recent fighting near Ordzhonikidze! It had put its life on the line defending the approaches to Transcaucasia, to the oil-rich districts of Grozny and Baku. The engine must have been through a lot as well – and now it had succumbed. I knew in combat a plane engine was supposed to experience heavy overload, overstrain, and begin to play up by the end of its lifetime. But what had actually happened to it? Why had it stalled? There still was fuel, and oil too. True, some of the devices controlling its work had conked out. But I didn't want to blame anyone and had nothing against anyone. I understood that during combat a pilot sometimes had to rev up sharply, boost and sharply decelerate, dive at high revs, gain altitude, without sparing the engine. But it had stalled now when I was flying straight, at the assigned altitude, at the defined speed and revolution rate, when I was watching the gauge readings maintaining the most suitable operating conditions for the engine. Basically, I wasn't overburdening her but she had still stalled … I knew that as soon as we – the young pilots – had mastered our Il-2s completely, they would be written off and we would go to a plant to receive new ones. But that didn't make me feel any better.

Standing on the spot and pondering it over, I suddenly noticed an ambulance rushing and the pilots running across the field towards me. "Well, – I thought, – I'll get it now!" And would you believe who was the first to run up to me? The very same trainer from school who had unfairly given me just a 'good' mark for a problem I'd been the first to solve! Then, having left the vehicle, out of breath, Doctor Kozlovskiy appeared with his first-aid kit on him. Finding me in one piece and unharmed he began to wail, wiping off sweat and tears from his wrinkled face, "My sweetheart, you're safe! I'm so glad!"

The regimental commander, who would also fly with us to get a plane (the whole regiment flew) then told me: "Anna Alexandrovna", now for the first time he called me by my name and patronymic, "you've done well, you saved the plane. Whatever is damaged the mechanics will fix up in no time, grease up the percale, put on a lick of paint and it'll be alright – we'll fly again!"

By evening the *Sturmovik's* engine had been examined, repaired and tested. They turned the plane away from the ravine towards the sea and Captain Karev (being the most experienced pilot of the regiment) took off and safely landed at the aerodrome. And the next day after these events all the personnel of our unit were lined up. No one knew for what reason it had been done but suddenly I heard the following: 'Junior Lieutenant Egorova, step forward!"

My new comrades moved aside letting me forward from the rear row. I hesitantly stepped out of the line and stood to attention: "What's going to happen? Will they ascribe the fault for the forced landing to me? I'm going to get it in the neck! They'll say, 'she can't handle the engine'. How will I prove it wasn't my fault?"

And suddenly the regiment commander said ceremoniously: "For the excellent sortie in the Il-2 plane and salvation of the fighting equipment entrusted to you I express my gratitude!"

"I serve the Soviet Union!" I responded with breaking voice after a long pause.

After this incident attitudes toward me in the regiment changed abruptly ...

21

Dropping bombs through a 'bast-shoe'

Now the training flights began: each time more and more complex and crucial – flying in the zone, bombing, shooting. We had our own firing range in the mountains in a desolate area. There were dummy tanks, guns, railway cars, planes with white-cross markings – they served us as targets for drill attacks. How many times having gained altitude, I threw the *Sturmovik* into a steep dive, pressed all the triggers and fiercely attacked the targets! Then our group set about flying in a pair, a flight, a squadron As I said before, Valentin Vakhramov and I had been assigned to the 3rd Squadron. Its commander, Lieutenant Andrianov, having listened to us report for duty, stood silent for quite a while, puffing on a pipe with a long stem. From the first encounter I remembered him like that: tall, dark-eyed, with weather-beaten face, in a black leather raglan, a red topped black *kubanka*[1] tilted onto his eyebrows. Andrianov's raglan was girdled by a wide officer's belt with a holster on it holding a pistol, and on another, narrow, belt slung across his shoulder, hung a map in a mapcase. And it didn't just hang – it hung with style nearly touching the ground. All his looks and bearing said: "I'm not a boy any more, I'm a seasoned *comesk* even if no older than you in years".

"So", at last the *comesk* delivered without pulling the pipe out of his mouth, "whichever of you masters the *Sturmovik* faster and better, learns to bomb and shoot accurately and keep in good formation will be taken on by me as wingman for the very first combat sortie …"

To become wingman to an experienced leader – what else could we dream of? A good leader knows how to assemble the planes that took off after him into a group, how to lead it precisely along the established route and close in on a target which is not that easy to locate on ground pitted by bombs and shells. He knows how to cunningly avoid the ack-ack guns and screens of enemy fighters, and to strike as the situation dictates. It was no accident that the Hitlerites tried hard to shoot down the leader first of all – both from the ground and from the air. If they shot him down the formation would scatter and there would be neither accurate bombing nor well-aimed shooting – and in fact the combat mission would not be carried out.

In order to learn the craft of a flight leader one had to have been a wingman and to have survived. A wingman repeated his leader's movements during the first combat sorties He had to keep in formation, and he had no time at all to glance at the dashboard, to notice Messers, to see flak shell bursts. He had no time even to orient himself and often he didn't even know where he was flying to. Most of the *Sturmovik* pilots who died, died in their first ten sorties.

---

1 Translator's note – a smaller variety of astrakhan – originally from the Kuban Cossack province.

Valentin Vakhramov was mastering the *Sturmovik* quickly and easily and we stubbornly competed with him: who of us after all would be the *comesk's* wingman? But once … Vakhramov had flown back from the firing range, landed the plane confidently and already on his run-in, accidentally confusing the levers, he retracted the undercarriage … The Il's undercarriage immediately folded back and the plane began to crawl on its belly … When we ran up Valentine was already climbing out of the cockpit, gloomily looking at the prop blades bent into 'ram's horns'. There were tears in his eyes. No one was scolding him then, nobody was reprimanding him, but he was suffering so badly that it was sad to look at him.

By nature Valentin was a reserved, outwardly rather a coarse man. But this put-on roughness originated from his desire to look more adult. There was nothing funny or mysterious in him but for some reason the pilots had nicknamed him 'the Fakir'. Just once, forgetting about his 'dignity of seniority', he had shown us tricks with cards and burning matchsticks – and the nickname had stuck to him! I knew Valentin was fond of poetry and wrote verses himself, not daring to show them to anyone. I also knew that his mum – a worker on a military production-plant – and a sister he loved tenderly, lived in Siberia. When he got letters from them he would go off somewhere well away where no-one would bother him, and read them several times. Once he had showed me photographs of his family. Eyes similar to his looked at me from them with sadness.

"You have a beautiful sister", I remarked once.

"Yes", Valentin agreed, "but she's badly ill. I doubt whether I'll see her again. And my mum too – tuberculosis …" Only then I understood from where the Vakhramov's inescapable sadness came from …

Travel orders to pick up new planes arrived unexpectedly. We thought it wouldn't hurt if we trained some more over the firing range and in formation as well, but the commanders knew better. And now we were on our way from Baku to Krasnovodsk across the Caspian Sea. From there we would have to make our way to the Volga Region by train via Ashkhabad, Mary and Tashkent.

The Caspian Sea raged so, that it made all the airmen seasick, that was why we got off the ship in Krasnovodsk pale, worn out, and staggering.

"Well, 'Stalin's falcons'[2], why are you in the dumps? It's not the ocean of the air!" one of us joked bitterly.

We reached the train station with difficulty, took seats in the wagons and the train carried us to the rear across the Kazakhstan steppes. The train moved so slowly that one could easily walk next to it without falling behind. Having recovered from the sea voyage we felt much more confident and calmer than at sea. Some read, some played dominos, and song lovers gathered around Zhenya Berdnikov, an aerial gunner – Zhenya was a good guitar-player.

During stopovers we would run out to buy milk. It seemed to Vakhramov that a half-litre can, with which a woman was ladling out milk from her bucket, was too dirty, and he was outraged: "How can you dip a dirty can into the common bucket?"

The farmer's wife silently lifted her skirt, wiped the can with the hem, and smiling sweetly measured out three times half a litre into Valentin's mess-tin. Valya paid for the

---

2   Translator's note – a common epithet for the Soviet airmen adopted by USSR propaganda bodies during WWII.

milk and with curses handed it over to someone in the queue. Everyone there burst into loud laughter ...

Training started on the third day of our trip. The head of the aerial-gunnery service Captain Koshkin was the first to come to our wagon. "We'll be talking today about targeted shooting and bombing from a *Sturmovik*," he proposed and pulled out the manual from his map-case. "We need to practise it and pass a test."

"Why a test?" Rzhevskiy asked. "Let's sign on the brochure that we've read it – that's all the labour we need for such a thing."

The special instruction on the use of factory markers and viewfinder pins necessary for correct determination of the plane's diving lead during bombing indeed deserved attention. In order to shoot there was a crosswire gun-sight on the plane: once you'd led the plane close enough to the ground, you pulled the triggers. The cannon, machine-gun and missile tracers might be corrected by one movement of the rudders, and the target would be knocked out. But there was no bomb-sight. Each flyer had worked out his own method of bomb delivery. We'd been bombing as if by eye – using a 'template' of 'bast shoe' or 'flying boot' size. Jokers suggested the following 'models': 'bomb-sight B-43' for a bast shoe size 43, or 'F-43' for a flying boot size 43. "And Egorova will have her own bomb-sight: BF-38 – box calf flying boot size 38!" the pilots laughed.

"Joking apart, how to handle it in reality?" I unwillingly wondered. Well, you could go into a dive using the mark on a wing, but then you had to determine the angle by eye and begin to count seconds: "twenty one, twenty two, twenty three"... At the same time you were not supposed to miss the right altitude – you had to watch the altimeter. But then you were under ack-ack fire, and on top of that you couldn't break away from your formation – then you would become easy prey for fighters. Generally speaking, although the instruction was just a nuisance to us, we practised it and passed that test before the captain. I have to admit that later our squadron bombed rather well. Either that instruction had helped or we all had the same size of flying boots ...

We stayed three days in Mary. Fortunately the news from the front was cheering – our advance in the Stalingrad area had begun. We found out during one of the numerous stopovers that the encircled German troops were in an exceptionally bad situation. They were being systematically bombed by our air force, harassed by the infantry and shelled by the artillery. However, our journey wasn't without its 'extraordinary incidents'. In the area we were traveling through were many evacuated families of our regimental comrades. Some had left Derbent earlier so they could catch up with us after seeing their families. One of those who caught up with us reported directly to the commanding officer: "Arrest me, Comrade Lieutenant-Colonel, I've killed a man ..."

It appeared that he had been in a hurry to see his wife and the daughter he had seen only on the day she was born. His wife had been writing him letters full of love and faithfulness and tracing on the paper sometimes the daughter's hand, sometimes her foot. And here he was turned up at home – his wife opened the door and gasped .. She didn't want to let him in but the pilot burst into the house – there was a rear-area serviceman nursing his daughter ... Turning into some kind of madness, our comrade shot him, grabbed his daughter and off he went to the train station. He made it to a big city, handed his daughter to an orphanage and rushed to catch up with his regiment. And here he was – come with cap in hand ...

Investigators would later find out the rear-area man had not been killed, only slightly wounded: the bullet had hit his leg. The girl would be returned to her mother, our comrade would be demoted in rank but he would be still in combat. But in the meantime our ride went on and on …

Here we were in Tashkent. We called in at the oriental bazaar, buying there the famous dried apricots that were allegedly a cure for all possible diseases. But the main point was, they were said to make one young and beautiful. Sure, we were young but everyone without exception also wanted to be beautiful and that was why everyone was buying dried apricots. If one had no money he would borrow from his mates. I also bought Tashkent sultanas but they turned out to be merely dried grapes with pits.

When approaching Kuibyshev at the Grachevka Station we heard a *Sovinformbureau* communiqué from the loud-speakers: "The Southern grouping of the German troops under command of General Field-Marshal Paulus has capitulated. The Northern group has capitulated too". This happened on 2 February 1943. It got noisy straightaway in our wagon: we rejoiced in the great success of our Army, shouted 'hurray'. And one more thing – we were outraged that they had been so slow taking us to pick up our new planes. We had missed out on the Stalingrad fighting …

22

Wingtip to wingtip

At last we arrived at the plant where we were to receive brand-new planes and fly them to the front. In expectation of the machines the pilots lodged in a huge dugout, as big as a *Metrostroy* tunnel, with two tiers of bunks. Here I received a letter from Raya Volkova, a *Metrostroy* girl. She wrote that the construction of the Moscow Metro was continuing, that the third-stage line with the stations 'Sverdlov Square', 'Novokuznetskaya', 'Paveletskaya', 'Avtozavodskaya', 'Semyonovskaya' would start operating soon. "At all stations", she wrote, "there will be bas-reliefs on the walls with the inscription: 'Constructed during the Great Patriotic War'. There's a war on but we are in peaceful construction work. It's true many *Metrostroy* men are building defensive installations as well. We've helped the men of Leningrad erect fortifications, laid out the Road of Life across Lake Ladoga ... The guys from our aeroclub are all at the front. Your instructor Miroevskiy and Serezha Feoktistov are fighting in *Sturmoviks*. Vanya Vishnyakov, Zhenya Minshoutin and Serezha Korolev, in fighter planes. Louka Mouravistkiy, Vanya Oparin, Sasha Lobanov, Arkadiy Chernyshev, Vasya Kochetkov and Victor Koutov have been killed ..."

"Victor who?.." I felt as if I had been struck by lightning – everything grew dark: there was neither sun, nor people, nor this war there ... It seemed there was nothing to breathe, my eyes couldn't see, my ears couldn't hear. When I had come to my senses I saw Doctor Kozlovskiy above me with a syringe in his hand. He kept saying:

"Have a cry now, sweetheart, have a cry. You'll feel better straightaway ..." But I couldn't cry. Something unbearably heavy lay on my heart and would not ease even for many long years after ...

A kind soul, our doctor! He looked after me and healed my soul back in that hard time of mine. And not only mine ... In the regiment there was no man more caring and attentive to us. Kozlovskiy literally looked after each airman: how and what he ate, how he slept, what his mood was. He always organised a Russian bath for us along with a change of underwear. He would pick some shack on a riverbank, skilful mechanics would put together a stove out of rocks, put on it a petrol drum, heat plenty of water – and the bathhouse was ready! Doctor Kozlovskiy always requested that a 'tub' be prepared for me – in other words a separate drum of hot water, and demanded insistently that I sit in it for no less than ten minutes. We airmen called our doctor 'Specially for You'. And here's why: when giving out to us chocolate or vitamins he would call each of us aside in turn, look around and say secretively: "Specially for you!" Wags among the pilots, catching sight of the Doctor, without pre-arrangement would pull chocolate out of their map-cases and yell all together: "Specially for you!" The doctor would take no offence and would do exactly the same at the next distribution of chocolates or vitamins. Kozlovskiy wouldn't refuse medical help to anyone where we were based. I remember in Timashevka near Krasnodar I ran up to him with a request to help my billet-hostess and her baby when it was born and snatching up everything necessary straightaway he rushed to save the mother and her baby. And this kind of thing happened many a time.

Our doctor once sent his wife a parcel along with a sergeant-major going via Moscow to Kuibyshev on service business. The sergeant-major found the hospital in which Kozlovskiy's spouse worked. Worn out by the heat, he unbuttoned the collar of his blouse, took off his field-cap and sat in a chair in the hospital ward. Then the woman he was waiting for turned up. The sergeant-major stood up, staggered up to the woman and said, "Hello! I bring you your husband's greetings from the front, and a present."

"Why are you out of uniform? What sort of way is this to talk to someone senior in rank?" he heard her squeaky voice turning to a screech. The sergeant-major was taken aback. He sharply turned around, put the parcel on a table, put on his field-cap and silently left the building. When he came back to the regiment he wouldn't upset the doctor, he just passed on greetings from his wife and added: "I handed the parcel over personally, don't you worry!" The sergeant-major was maligned and mocked in the regiment for quite some time after that but it had nothing to do with our doctor. Him we respected ...

There was always a long line in the plant canteen. When your turn came you would give them you ear-flapped hat and get an aluminium spoon. Our lunch would consist of three meals: 'hasty' soup, 'shrapnel' porridge and 'blancmange à la raspberry'. The guys would joke: "You can survive on it, but will not chase the girls".

Day in, day out we flew and pounded the ground – theoretically. We read whatever we could find about aerial and land battles, studied tactics: ours and the enemy's. We had already been issued with flight maps. We would match them up and stick them together. Whole bedsheets were the result: we had a longish flight route to the front ...

At Doctor Kozlovskiy's insistent request I was shifted from the ninety-person communal house-dugout with three-tier bunks, into a Finnish hut. A room had been vacated there and the commanders offered it to me – after all, I was the only woman. But right in this cosy hut was where I almost perished. Once I came from the aerodrome chilled and saw that the stove had been thoroughly heated and the coals hadn't gone out yet – they were playing beautifully with now blue, now red, now golden sparks. I feasted my eyes on them, warmed up, then swallowed some pill prescribed by our Doctor as a sedative, lay down on the bed, still dressed, and fell asleep. And here I was, asleep and I saw Victor, as if in reality, in a white shirt and tie. He has an embroidered Central Asian cap on his head. Then in a kind of mist I see myself in a pleated black skirt and a blue football jersey with white collar and laces. I have on a white beret, white plimsolls with blue edging, and white socks. The beret sits literally on the crown of my head and on my right ear – that was stylishness among us. All this magnificence had been acquired by me in the *Torgsin*[1] for an antique gold coin presented to me by my mum. And now, in dream as in waking, I saw in that *Torgsin* splendour not only myself but Victor too, with a tie he had never worn before. We were in the Sokolniki[2] among daisies on some vast meadow. Victor picked me one daisy and said: "Here, tell your fortune: who do you like more – me or 'Prince' Tougoushy?"

I felt easy and cheerful in the dream but suddenly I heard someone knocking on the door. I wanted to get up but couldn't. But they rapped on the door louder and louder repeating my name. I somehow got up and walked, holding onto the wall. I fell over, sat up,

---

1   Translator's note – abbreviation of the Russian words for 'Trade With Foreigners', a network of shops with luxury goods for foreigners and people possessing foreign currency and valuables in the pre-war USSR.

2   Translator's note – a recreation park in Moscow.

fell over again. I decided to crawl – nothing was working. At last I reached the door and turning the key slid to the floor … It turned out I had been poisoned by charcoal fumes the stoker had closed the stove damper too early. Fortunately our pilots were walking past my hut late in the evening. Noticing the light in the window they decided to drop in and began to knock on the door, but no one opened it. Then the guys understood – something had gone wrong … The guys carried me out to walk it off in the fresh air and walked me around outside all night long. By now crying, I begged them to let me go and have a rest but the pilots would have none of it: they had their own 'method of healing' – the aviation one. In the morning I turned up for studies run personally by the regiment commander He looked at me for a long time and then said briefly: "To the medical unit, immediately!

In the medical unit Doctor Kozlovskiy again began to wail over me: "My sweet girl what's this bad luck pouring over you as if from a horn of plenty? Where did you manage to hurt your forehead so?"

"I fell on the door key …" I told the doctor about my dream and added: "I wish I hadn't woken up …"

Kozlovskiy flung up his arms at me and began telling me off: "We'll all be there but not everyone manages to live his life with dignity. Only infirm, weak-willed people with fragile psyches die of their own free will … Keep that in mind, girl!"

On the second day after the incident I came to classes as if nothing had happened covering my grazes with powder. Those days everyone's mood was excellent – at long last after heavy defeats we were on the advance. We received brand-new silvery-painted planes each with a gunner's cockpit in which a large-calibre machine-gun half-ring mount was installed. This innovation cheered us up. From now on the *Sturmovik* would be securely protected from the rear against the enemy's fighters.

We were in a hurry to fly off to the front as soon as possible but the weather was holding up. It was March but the winter had gone mad and didn't want to give way to spring. But then a light frost came, the sky became clearer and the sun appeared. We took off and headed towards Saratov.

Nothing boded trouble, rather the reverse, everything was festively cheerful – the clear blue sky, comrades in arms flying wingtip to wingtip … Saratov came in sight – we were supposed to land at the Razboishina aerodrome. Due to the long flying distance we were running out of fuel and it would be dangerous to do a second circuit. Straight after landing one had to taxi out quickly to vacate the airstrip. But someone suddenly hesitated and the pilot next in line went for another circuit. The engine stalled, the plane hung in the air and crashed to the ground at an angle … Junior Lieutenant Pivovarov lost his life We all were shaken by our comrade's death and landed our planes at random. I'd seen many deaths at war but here, deep behind the frontline, when the war had been forgotten if only for a short time, it was hard to see a comrade's death …

Only this morning we had sat with him in the canteen having breakfast and he smoothing the fair hair hanging over his high forehead and casting a dark-blue eye towards me, said, addressing the pilot Sokolov: "Volodya, do you know who Egorova will be giving the hundred grams of vodka she gets for a combat sortie?"

"I will be putting my cup at the aerodrome by the landing T so that you and the other Bacchus worshippers will come home drawn by the smell, instead of going astray and landing wherever you feel like", I had rudely replied then.

"What was I talking to him so rudely for?" I cursed myself now. "What for?" Some kind of alter ego sits inside me. This alter ego doesn't listen to me. The first ego often keeps silent but the other one often asks for trouble. Once upon a time my brother told me that I had a 'partisan personality'. He may have been right: although I try to make myself quiet I don't always manage it. I'd snapped today again and now I was scourging myself …

The second part of our route was Saratov-Borisoglebsk. It was shorter than the first one and we flew it quickly. But what was that? My plane's left undercarriage didn't want to come down! The whole regiment had landed but I was still circling over the aerodrome trying to drop the jammed landing gear at different flight settings but couldn't do it. I cast glances at the fuel gauge: I would run out of fuel soon. For the last time I tried to unfold the undercarriage by energetic aerobatics but all in vain. They were already ordering me from the ground to go for a belly-landing. But I felt sorry for the brand-new plane and took a decision to land on the right wheel only.

Closing in for landing, right before touchdown I carefully tilt the machine towards the unfolded undercarriage. The plane softly touches the ground and runs down the airstrip listing to the right. I do my best to hold the *Sturmovik* in this position for as long as possible. But the speed drops, the plane doesn't obey the controls anymore, the list gradually disappears and now, having drawn a half-circle on the ground with the left wing and propeller my Il stops – there's no more fuel …

People mobbed the plane but I was still sitting in the cockpit with its closed canopy, in a kind of stupor. Sweat poured down my face, my back and hands were wet … Captain Karev jumped up on a wing. "Climb out, why are you still sitting? I wanted to welcome you with flowers but there aren't even any florist shops in Borisoglebsk. You may count on a bouquet from me!"

I got down on the ground and the first man I saw was the teacher of aerodynamics from the Kherson aviation school. It appeared that my *alma mater* had been evacuated to Borisoglebsk and merged with the local fighter pilot school where Victor Koutov, Louka Mouravistkiy and other *Metrostroy* guys had studied before the war … That same day the mechanics replaced the prop, fixed up and painted the wing and my Il-2 took its place in line with all the regiment's planes, looking no different from the others.

In the morning we were on our way to the front. We topped up the fuel tanks in Tikhoretskaya and headed towards the end point of our route, Timashevskaya, for service in the 230th Ground Attack Aviation Division of the 4th Aerial Army. The *stanitsa*[3] of Timashevskaya was called in Kuban 'that one': it was right there, where a woman lived seeing off nine of her sons to the front: Alexander, Nikolay, Vasiliy, Filipp, Fedor, Ivan, Ilya, Pavel and the youngest, Sasha who was born in 1923 and would become a Hero of the Soviet Union in 1943, posthumously. None of her sons came back home …

Our regimental staff had already arrived at the spot and quickly prepared us lodgings in a school. All the rest of us were looked after by the BAO (Aerodrome Services Battalion). Me they billeted in a hut not far away from the school where the flyers lived, hosted by a lovely young woman whose husband was at the front. Doctor Kozlovskiy as usual did his best to organise a Russian bath for us. But this time it was not in some hovel. A large panel truck arrived, parked near the river, pumped up some water, heated it up, and those who wished went there to steam, strictly observing a schedule set up by the regimental Chief-of-Staff and the Doctor.

3   Translator's note – a large Cossack settlement.

23

The skies over Taman

It didn't take long to get us into operation. We studied the operations area, familiarised ourselves with the intelligence data and, as the deputy *comesk* of the 2nd Squadron Pasha Usov liked to say, "we were off". The newly-appointed Chief-of-Staff of the regiment Captain Leonid Yashkin, appointed to our unit in place of the departed Captain Belov, summoned all the flying personnel to the headquarters dugout for a briefing on the operational situation in our sector of the front.

To start with he advised that he had arrived from the Academy without graduating from it, and before that he had been Deputy Chief-of-Staff of the 366th High-speed Bomber Regiment. Before the war Yashkin had served as a junior commander, and had a Leningrad working-class background. His father used to work at the 'Red Nailmaker' plant and perished during the Blockade of Leningrad. Telling us about it Yashkin began to run the fingers of one hand through his unruly fair hair and wiped a tear off his cheek with the other … Leonid himself had been a worker at the 'Red Nailmaker' in the past, and his sister Anastasia was a medic at the front.

Getting up from the table Captain Yashkin pulled down his blouse as if shaking off the hard memories, straightened his belt and the loaded holster on it, put on a businesslike look and began his report: "Developing the advance in the South our troops have cleared the Soviet land of Fascist vermin. They have advanced hundreds of kilometres and liberated many areas of the North Caucasus, the Rostov District, part of the Ukraine and reached the Azov Sea … Their plans to capture the Caucasus oil and conquer the Black Sea coast and its ports have led the Hitlerites to complete destruction and a retreat from the North Caucasus in the direction of Rostov and the Taman Peninsula. Now, fearing a breakthrough of Soviet troops, the enemy has built a heavy defence line from Novorossisk to Temryuk. There are concrete pillboxes, dug-out weapon emplacements, anti-tank and anti-personnel fortifications, trenches with communication lines, dense landmine fields, a large amount of field and flak artillery. Because of the numerous water obstacles the Germans have called this strongly fortified position 'The Blue Line'. According to their plan, it is supposed to cover their retreat to the Crimea."

The Captain went on with his report but I became pensive … Suddenly I recalled Lermontov's story *Taman*. I was fond of Lermontov[1]. Before the war Victor Koutov had presented me with a book of his verses, and currently it was striding with me down the roads of war …

"… In order to create a threat against their flanks", the voice of the Chief-of-Staff was coming from somewhere distant, returning me to reality, "and to prevent the German Fleet using Tsemesskaya Bay, on the night of 4 February troops sent from Gelendzhik landed there. They captured a bridgehead called 'Lesser Land'. The Germans have been trying all possible ways to annihilate the bridgehead. So, fighting doesn't die down there

---

1   Editor's note – M.Lermontov (1814-1841) is one of the most recognized Russian poets.

day or night. Thus, we will be helping our landing party to wipe out the Fascist scum on the Taman Peninsula …"

Straining my memory I recalled our history teacher telling us that Taman was colonised by the Greeks a thousand and a half years ago, then settled by the Khazars, Mongols, Genoese, Turks … Suvorov had built a fort there.[2]

"We have a mission. The squadron commanders are to stay for the briefing", Regiment Commander Kozin entered the room with these words and unfolded a map on the desk.

We left the cramped quarters but stayed together, waiting for the decision: what if any of us went on a combat mission? "Maybe I will be included in the fighting group?", I thought shyly. Everyone was excited – both novices and 'oldies', but tried to conceal it. Pilot Rzhevskiy told us a joke about a daughter who asked her father to tell her all he knew about steam engines, which had just come to existence. Her father talked a long time, showed her a picture, and then asked his daughter: "Well, do you understand everything?" "Everything, Daddy! Just show me please, where they harness the horses …" The airmen laughed. A short brawny fellow from Rybinsk, Volodya Sokolov ran up to me and, putting on a serious face with difficulty, said:

"Anyuta, let's swap heights!"

"Let's do it, Volodya. I love high-heeled shoes so much but feel shy of wearing them because of being tall. But how shall we do it? And what will I get for the difference – after all I am 170 centimetres tall and you're only 160?"

"Sokolov, Egorova, Vakhramov, Tasets, Rzevskiy, up to the commanders!" This was an order from the Chief-of-Staff. Everyone forgot all about jokes and ran into the dugout.

We were proffered not a straight flight route but a kind of zigzag one. "We'll avoid the enemy's flak guns. It'll be better that way. Stay in the formation, do what I do", the navigator Karev, our leader, said and showed us on the map who was to fly where. My position was wingman to the right of Petr Karev.

What I was thinking about before my first combat sortie in a *Sturmovik*, it's hard to say. There was no fear. There was a kind of satisfaction: look, they've included me in the first flight group, now I must not disgrace myself – after all, I am the only woman amongst so many men, and what men – *Sturmovik* pilots!

A quartet of LaGG-3s from a fraternal fighter regiment based on the same aerodrome as we were, was to escort us. There were five regiments in our 230th Ground Attack Aviation Division: four ground-attack and one of fighters. The Division was under the command of a Hero of the Soviet Union Colonel Semyon Grigorievich Getman.

Here we were sitting in the cockpits of our combat planes and waiting for the signal – a green flare. My eyes slid over the instruments, my fingers ran over (as if to get the feel of them) the numerous switches and handles – I was checking the correct setting of their positions. My mechanic Rumskiy was here, next to the plane. He had made the plane ready for a combat sortie long before but now he wipes clean the long ago cleansed and shiny reinforced glass of the cockpit, then sets straight a parachute strap on my shoulder and looks at me as if to ask: "What else can I do for you?.."

"Thanks, friend. I need to be alone for a little while and concentrate, to collect my thoughts", I thanked my mechanic, and looked at Karev's *Sturmovik* standing ahead of me to the left. The group leader was quiet. He put his hand on the cockpit sides and seemed

---

2   Editor's note – A.Suvorov (1729-1800) – a famed military commander of the pre-Napoleonic era.

to be singing. "Doesn't the coming mission really worry him in the least?" I thought with astonishment. But my thoughts were interrupted by a green flare soaring above the Command Post. Hissing nastily it rose above the field and began to fall very slowly and burn out. Time we take off! Our course – to 'Lesser Land'.

During the flight I did my best to stick close to Karev: I was afraid of falling behind. Here was our target. The leader swung his plane in a manoeuvre – I did the same, he dived almost to the very ground – so did I, he shot – I shot too. I dropped my bombs after him as well. But after the fourth pass on the target I fell behind nevertheless. And I didn't just fall behind but lost the whole group. What should I do now? Now I was flying on my own among dense shell bursts. I manoeuvred desperately, looked for the group but didn't see it … Near Myskhako I turned onto our territory and became a witness to dozens of our planes and the enemy's fighting an aerial battle over Tsemesskaya Bay. Fighter planes were falling into the sea, pilots were descending on parachutes, motorboats were rushing towards them from both sides. I was observing such a battle for the first time in my life …

It was not easy for a novice to make sense of the melee taking place over the Taman Peninsula. Two fighters dashed towards me like black vultures. For some reason I took them for our 'Yaks' but when a machine-gun tracer passed ahead of me to the right and they began to turn for a second pass I clearly saw white crosses on their fuselages. The Germans behaved extremely insolently, taking no care for their own defence, and attacked from different directions but without result. The *Sturmovik*'s speed was lower than the Messerschmitt's, and during one of their attacks they skipped forward and appeared in my gun-sight. I pressed all the triggers simultaneously but, alas, no discharge followed: all my ammunition had been spent over the target. That time I was saved by our fighters. They drove the Fascist vultures away from my plane and even shot one down – and so I made it home safely.

During debriefing Captain Karev harshly reprimanded me for falling behind the group. I couldn't disagree with him and I humbly admitted my negligence. During this flight the pilots Sokolov and Vakhramov were shot down by flak but several days later they returned to the regiment. Vakhramov and his aerial gunner were picked up in the sea by our motorboat, whilst Sokolov, having made it to our territory on his shot-up *Sturmovik*, landed on the Kuban river floodplain.

Fighter planes gave us *Sturmoviks* a reliable cover from the air. I still remember the names of many fighter pilots who became famous over Kuban: G.A.Rechkalov[3], V.I.Fadeev, N.F.Smirnov, G.G. Goloubev, V.G.Semenishin, V.I.Istrashkin. The callsigns of the Glinka brothers – Boris Borisovich and Dmitriy Borisovich – were 'BB' and 'DB'[4]… But it seems to me that the dashing fighter pilots didn't much like flying escort to us *Sturmovik* pilots, being our 'nannies'. It was another thing to get a combat mission to go 'free hunting'! You found a target, engaged the enemy without looking back at the *Sturmoviks*, shot a Fascist down and came back to your aerodrome victorious. But flying escort, your chance of shooting down an enemy plane was quite low …

3   Editor's note – ranked fourth in the list of top-scoring Soviet aces of WWII, with 56 personal and 5 or 6 shared air kills.

4   Editor's note – junior brother, Dmitriy Glinka is ranked seventh in the list of top-scoring Soviet aces of WWII, with 50 personal air kills; elder brother, Boris Glinka, scored 30 personal and 1 shared aerial victories.

We had our dogfights against the Hitlerite planes too. I remember our battle in which the pilot Rykhlin distinguished himself, his glory roaring all over Kuban. Rykhlin had joined the regiment with no military rank – in his OSOAVIAKhIM blouse with 'birds' on the collar patches and a magnificent sleeve insignia – the Air Force emblem. Rykhlin had used to work as a pilot-instructor in an aeroclub, had accumulated a lot of flying hours, and was put into operations quickly. By his second combat sortie yesterday's instructor was flying in the group of *Sturmoviks* led by the Hero of the Soviet Union Captain Mkrtumov. I was in the same sixer too …

…The greyish strip of the Kuban river flashed past. Mountains were sometimes seen through the shroud of low clouds. We were supposed to approach the target unseen, coming from the seaside, and the leader began to descend steadily carrying us behind him towards the ground. I saw Mkrtumov's intent profile through the open pane of my cockpit. The helmet tightly covered his handsome head with its Oriental profile, the throat-mikes fastened to the last button were visible on his neck, and from under his helmet a white strip of lining was visible – that was why his face seemed even darker and more sun-tanned.

Now the *stanitsa* Krymskaya was gone under my wing on the right, and that was when our leader again changed course, at the same time gaining altitude. So as not to fall behind I energetically revved up and gained speed. We crossed the frontline and the blue of the sea appeared through the risen mist. Far below gun flashes began to sparkle - we were under flak fire. Small grey puffs of shell bursts began to leap about the plane. I saw a large splinter hit the right wing of Mkrtumov's *Sturmovik* but his machine kept flying obediently.

The last seconds before an attack place an especially strong strain on one. It seems nothing else exists in the world for you – all your attention is concentrated on the leader and the target. In that flight, tanks with white crosses on the armour were our target. Our tankers and artillerymen were holding off pressure from the enemy with their last strength, and assistance from the air arrived in the nick of time. The bombs covered the target accurately, the ground attack followed. Attacking tanks is a complicated business involving a lot of risk. Tank cannon had enviable precision and more than once hasty pilots had paid for their errors with their lives. You had to watch your altitude really carefully. Our Goldy (that was what we called Rykhlin among ourselves, after his fiery-red hair) got a little carried away, forgot about his altitude in the heat of battle, and one of the Hitlerite tanks instantly pulled up the barrel of his cannon and opened fire at the plane! Rykhlin's damaged machine, barely pulling out of the attack, turned away towards Gelendzhik. But four Messerschmitts pounced upon it like a bolt from the blue. The pilot had no choice but to accept the fight with them.

Knowing the power of the forward fire of our *Sturmoviks*, the German fighters feared to attack from the front. In the current situation the high speed of the Messerschmitt was a nuisance for them and Rykhlin decided to capitalise on it. When two vultures, having put down their undercarriages to reduce their speed, sneaked up to the *Sturmovik* and began to shoot at it point-blank, Rykhlin abruptly turned his plane around towards the enemy and went on the attack himself. One of the Messerschmitts found itself in the Il's gun-sight with its yellow belly exposed. The pilot pressed all the triggers and the yellow-belly began to smoke, tilted on one wing and fell into the sea. The second Hitlerite met the same end. The aerial gunner Vanya Efremenko, already wounded in the arm, shot up a third one; a fourth Messer exhaled smoke as well. Quitting the dogfight it turned towards his aerodrome.

On his own, badly damaged, our *Sturmovik* had faced four Fascist fighters and got the upper hand! And this miraculous victory was made by a pilot flying only his second combat sortie. Rykhlin managed to make it to a narrow strip of land by the Black Sea in his bullet-riddled plane. Many of our troops saw the scene of the aerial battle from the ground, and when the pilot had landed his machine, sailors who happened to be nearby were ready to carry the fearless hero in their arms.

The Military Council of the 4th Aerial Army highly appreciated the feat of the gallant warriors. N.V. Rykhlin was appointed a flight commander and promoted to the rank of Senior Lieutenant, and Sergeant I.S. Efremenko became a Junior Lieutenant. By Decree of the Presidium of the Supreme Council of the Soviet Union on the 24th of May 1943 N.V. Rykhlin and I.S. Efremenko were awarded the ranks of Heroes of the Soviet Union

Then Rykhlin went on a course to improve his qualifications. Running a bit ahead I will say that many years after the war I suddenly received a letter from Rykhlin in which he advised that he was in hospital and asked to see me. By that time I was the only living person from of all our regiment, and I went. He was so happy to see me when I came to the hospital! It turned out that after the war he had married a woman with a son. The latter took a great dislike to him, wrote some kind of complaints against him, some kind of cock-and-bull stories – and they believed him: Rykhlin was arrested and stripped of his rank of Hero ... And his wife didn't stand up for him. It was a somewhat strange story ... After all, he was a kind and good man!

24

Tit, Petr and the rest

Sorties, sorties ... We were all were by now exhausted but there was no let-up. The losses were mounting. The weather was frequently bad, clouds pressed down to the ground, the planes came back after sorties literally riddled with bullets and the technicians barely had time to patch them up. We kept flying to the Choushka Spit and the Blue Line: we raided aerodromes, railway junctions, trains of enemy troops and materiel, attacked and bombed enemy ships on the Black Sea. This kind of work required meticulous preparation and we painstakingly prepared ourselves for each mission.

On one day of combat, awaiting the order to fly, the pilots lying back on the ground in the 'sun' pattern (a circle, head to head), were just about to tell each other funny stories in turn. If it was not funny the unlucky author would get a flick on the nose. This was in its way a psychological relaxation. Everybody grew hungry because of idleness but lunch was late, and we were casting our eyes to the road leading to the village from which the catering service girls were supposed to bring us lunch.

"They're coming!" Vasya Kosterov, a sturdily built Moscovite yelled, being the first to notice the battalion's ton-and-a-half truck. But at the same moment a messenger ran up from the CP and announced: "Combat crews, to the regiment commander!"

Forgetting about food we rushed to the headquarters dugout. Lieutenant-Colonel Kozin in his blouse with decorations on it, his head bare, stood at the table. His fair wavy hair was combed perfectly and it seemed he had just come from the barber's shop: a light wind blew us the smell of cologne. This time his faithful pipe lay on an ash-tray - a flattened shellcase. And Michael Nikolaevich began to explain us unhurriedly the oncoming combat mission: "Many trains of enemy troops and materiel have concentrated at the Salyn railroad station on the Kerch Peninsula. Your task is to bomb and strafe them so as not to let the Hitlerites shift them across the Kerch Strait to Taman. I appoint pilot Usov the leader. Let's think over and plot the route of your flight together. It seems to me we ought to do a low-level flight over the Azov Sea, dart out over the station and make a sudden strike ..."

We discussed the oncoming sortie, and when the flare soared above the aerodrome we taxied out to the start point and took off one after another. The escort fighters – a sixer of LaGG-3 type – took off after us. Approaching the Azov Sea we began to descend, and at this moment the Hitlerites opened fire at us with the shore batteries. Captain Pokrovskiy's plane flared up before my eyes and crashed into the sea in flames. It seemed to me that for an instant our group even slowed down, but then the wingmen caught up with the leader and we rushed forward, towards the target.

"My God! Why him?.." The appeal to God, learned by heart in childhood, burst out of me.

Tit Kirillovich Pokrovskiy ... A fearless pilot, an honest and gallant man! He joined our regiment as an established combat flyer, with three Orders of the Red Banner. He had got his first Order for fighting near Lake Khasan[1], his second, in Spain, the third at the very beginning of the Great Patriotic War. Everyone had been surprised by the appointment of the captain as a flight commander. "A pilot like that, and only a flight commander?" his brother-officers grumbled. Pokrovskiy was older than all of us, born in 1910, and we began to call him just 'Kirillych'[2] as a sign of respect. Sometimes he would relax and tell the airmen funny stories that ostensibly happened to him, and we would laugh. But more often he was tight-lipped and would shrink into his shell for long periods. Once after dinner at an aerodrome near the Popovichevskaya station we organized a dance. Pokrovskiy was sitting very sadly and wouldn't talk to anyone. Then I approached him and invited him for a waltz.

"Thanks, Egorushka[3]. Let's go for a walk instead", Kirillych said. I agreed, and we walked off. The evening was warm, the moon was shining. We headed along the *stanitsa* and then the captain told me his story. When he was shot down for the ninth time at the end of 1941, there were no more planes in his regiment. Five or six pilots remained, and they were sent to a training regiment (UTAP) to learn to operate new planes. However no new planes were found there either.

All the 'horseless' pilots without exception were eager to get back to the front. They didn't want to be idle during such a hard time for the motherland, and Tit Pokrovskiy tried harder than the rest to be sent to the front (to any combat arm!). He approached the commissar of the UTAP and had his say about this sore point that was eating at many of them. The pilot, of course, lost his temper, and the commissar immediately sent him to the *osobyi otdel*[4] to sort him out …

The *osobist*[5] gave Pokrovskiy a good talking-to, like an interrogation, for minutes arrogantly, rudely. And then Kirillych called the *osobist* "a parasite sniffing for easy 'prey' among the airmen" – "You earn decorations during interrogations and hide from the front!" the pilot said furiously. The *osobist* silently closed his folder with the unsigned minutes and left. Pokrovskiy was arrested, then he was court-martialled and sentenced to be shot for "shunning frontline service and for anti-Soviet propaganda". There was indignation and outcry in the regiment. Immediately after his arrest his pilot comrades went to a post office straightaway where they talked a young telegraph-girl to send an urgent telegram to the Chairman of the Supreme Council of the USSR himself. The telegram arrived in time and at its destination. Pokrovskiy was rehabilitated with the return of his rank, Party membership card and decorations. After all this horror Kirillych was assigned to our 805th Ground Attack Aviation Regiment.

And now Tit Kirillovich was no more … After his death we lost the escort fighters too: apparently an aerial battle had broken out somewhere high up. Some time later our group crossed the coastline and darted out not over the Salyn train station but over the enemy's Bagerovo airfield. About thirty or more twin-engine bombers with crosses were

---

1   Translator's note – a lake in the Far East of Russia; in the summer of 1938 there was a border clash between the Soviet and the Japanese armies there.
2   Translator's note – a colloquial form of Kirillovich, his patronym.
3   Editor's note – a diminutive made by transforming the author's last name to male first name.
4   Translator's note – a special political section in the Soviet Army's units largely involved in political control over the servicemen.
5   Translator's note – *osobyi otdel* officer.

lined up down there refuelling. Messerschmitts were already taking off along the airstrip towards us. The group leader Pavel Usov opened fire at them without hesitation.

"Smash the bastards!" Pasha[6] was yelling into the air. And we, his wingmen, struck at the Fritzes with everything we had. Usov set ablaze two Messerschmitts that hadn't managed to get into the air, and we kept strafing the bombers' parking bays with long bursts. After raking the aerodrome we gained altitude, and shot over to the Salyn Station straightaway. We dropped bombs on the trains of materiel and enemy troops and headed home across the Kerch Straits.

Several days later reconnaissance reported we had done a great job at the Bagerovo airfield and the Salyn station. We had indeed done well, but we had lost five crews ...

I remember the mechanics rolling up the covers of the planes that had not made it home – as if they were shrouds. And before my eyes my comrades were still falling into the sea and onto the ground ... I climbed out of the cockpit without taking off my parachute and helmet with its earphones, jumped down on the ground and ran away from the parking bay. Unable to contain myself any more I fell on the ground and burst into tears.

"You're really tired, Egorova, aren't you?" I heard the regimental commander's voice above me. "Have a rest, calm down. I haven't included you in the next combat sortie group."

"No, I'm flying!" I jumped to my feet. "And, please, don't make any exceptions, don't insult me!"

And here we were – my plane was refuelled, bombs and rockets fixed, cannon and machine-guns charged. I saw a flare soar into the air and again I hastily climbed into the cockpit, wiping my tear-stained face on the run ... This time our leader was Petr Timofeevich Karev – a Moscovite from Zamoskvorechie[7]. I liked flying with him: from my point of view there was no better leader in our regiment. It was somehow uncomplicated flying with him: he would tell a joke, then drop a catchphrase – and all that right before an attack! Look, we've done three or four passes on a target and haven't noticed the pressure! More than once fate forgave him his bold and openly reckless escapades in the air ...

I remember Karev once, having drunk up to 300 grams of vodka at dinner (that day he had made three sorties, and 100 grams were allowed after each sortie), leaving to tell the flak gunners defending our aerodrome what was what. "My old pals, you send far too many shells into the blue sky when the bast shoe-bearers appear"[8], Karev said. "I'll take off in my Il now and you shoot at me. I'll be shooting at you. Let's see who gets who!"

Of course, Karev failed to bring off that experiment but all the pilots – witnesses to that argument – were as confident of Karev as of themselves: of his infallibility and invulnerability. Everybody in the regiment loved him for his straightforwardness and approachability. He was always together with his comrades, lived their joy and problems, and during a hard moment he was more capable than anyone in his ability to raise spirits. The captain didn't disdain rough work, and one could often see him shoulder a bomb that was a bit heavy and quickly carry it to the plane. The young girls from the armoury worshipped such a voluntary helper and would vie with each other in offering to wash his clothes and handkerchiefs ... Petr would decline, thank them and sing in reply: "How many sweet girls, how many tender names ..."

---

6   Translator's note – a diminutive for Pavel.

7   Translator's note – a suburb of Moscow.

8   Editor's note – a nickname for German Junkers Ju 87 dive-bombers in Russian military slang.

Pilots, mechanics, technicians, aerial gunners would always gather round Karev in a tight circle, and then a confidential discourse would begin, usually ending in a burst of laughter – this would be Petr telling his 'abracadabra', as he liked to call his anecdotes.

Karev could be sent on the most complicated flight with confidence that he would carry out his mission completely. He fought bravely and boldly. Scornful of death, he would fly to a target through a wall of fire of Fascist flak and attacks by enemy fighter planes. During debriefing the regimental navigator set various tactical tasks before the pilots. All together we analysed how to attack a train or a tank column most successfully, or to bomb a bridge or river crossing, and why it would be better to approach such narrow elongated targets not perfectly parallel to the course but at a narrow angle. We talked about speed, wind direction near the ground and at intermediate altitudes, taking into account how in that case the dissipation ellipse would look when bombing or shooting. Karev's idea to manoeuvre inside a group of *Sturmoviks* became a common practice in the regiment. Initially, the pilots had been required to stick strictly to their positions in a formation. But Karev had got the tactics changed and required pilots to manoeuvre within certain limits: to fly above or below the leader, to change the distance between planes … All this improved alertness, impeded attacks by Fascist fighters and hindered their ack-ack from directing accurate fire at the *Sturmoviks*.

At Taman Karev was the idol of the young pilots. We all remembered Petr Timofeevich when he was Acting Regimental Commander, finding at a very difficult moment a courageous, clever and expert solution to a problem. During one sortie a bomb tore away from its clamps and exploded during a plane's take-off run. The surviving pilot and gunner managed to run aside and lie down but there still were five 100-kilogram bombs on the plane. The group's take-off was stopped then, but the combat mission couldn't be cut off! Karev ordered the start realigned by about thirty degrees. The planes began to take off again. Despite the realignment of the start the departing planes were passing close the burning machine on which there were still bombs, ammunition and rockets. Everyone could probably expect an explosion, but the plane blew up when the last Il-2, flown by Karev, was already in the air.

But from that sortie made by a sixer, when a bomb exploded on one of the Ils during the take-off, only two crews returned – Karev's and mine – his wingman's. We had found the target and dropped our bombs, then strafed everything in three or four passes, and retired with not a single loss. Although battered we got away. But we shot over a German aerodrome, and it was full of German planes – they were landing and taking off. Flak guns held us as if in a ring! We were over the Kerch Straits when somehow we broke out of that ring, but only Karev and I: all the other crews perished over the German aerodrome. I didn't even see who smashed them – either the planes taking off, or the flak. Now we had broken out into the Kerch Straits, and we had to go to the other side. Down below us white domes, the parachutes of our comrades, shot-down airmen, hung in the air like giant mushrooms … I still had two bombs unreleased, but behind us there were Messsers ready to make short work of our pair. Suddenly I noticed a loaded barge right underneath me, moving from Kerch – the temptation was great. I wasn't supposed to land with bombs, but I would have been told off had I dropped them just anywhere. So I fell behind Karev a little, turned the *Sturmovik* towards the target and jerked the lever of the emergency bombload release. I wobbled in the air a bit, the plane shook, wavered and became uncontrollable for a while – yet I kept watching the barge: how was it feeling down there? I hadn't missed: the barge listed and went down. But suddenly doubts pricked me like a pin: whose barge had it been – ours or the Germans'?.. I'd seen no markings on it. I had been moving away from Kerch busy with the enemy and besides, our men would have spread out canvas as a distinguishing mark, but this time I'd seen nothing. But you never can tell! That was why I decided to say nothing about it, and when reporting to the regiment commander on the sortie said not a word about the sunken barge …

The secret, however, had already been disclosed: prior to the landing my leader and our fighters had reported by radio the destruction of a vessel recognised by them as German, and Karev added "Egorova sank a barge full of materiel, there were tanks on it". And soon the Division Commander General Get'man pinned to my blouse a large silver medal 'For Valour'.

25

The Blue Line

At the end of May 1943 the Regimental Commander Kozin lined up all the flying personnel at the aerodrome and said with emotion: "Comrade Pilots! Whoever is ready to carry out a special mission from the North-Caucasus Front Command – I ask you to step out forward."

All the pilots stepped forward as one.

"No, that won't work!" Kozin smiled. "I'll have to pick. Major Kerov – three steps forward." Pavel Kerov, the 1st Squadron commander, veteran of the regiment, master of ground attack, stepped forward …

We youngsters had always marvelled at the major's enviable calmness and kindness. He was more like a schoolteacher than a fearless ground attack expert. He had never raised his voice at anyone, and if anyone was at fault Kerov would look at him with sad grey glazed eyes, shake his head and walk away, rolling like a sailor, leaving his subordinate to think over his behaviour.

I'd been told that once when only 6 operable machines were left in the regiment, an order had arrived to destroy a river crossing near the *stanitsa* Nikolayevskaya on the Don. They had to send all machines into the air and Major Kerov led them on the combat mission. The crossing was protected so well that there was hardly any chance of the group returning successfully. However, Kerov managed to cheat the enemy: he came at the target from the rear, smashed it and made it home with his whole group. His plane was towed from the airstrip by a tractor. They told me that Kerov walked alongside the *Sturmovik* riddled with shell splinters and supported it by a wing console as if it were a wounded friend.

"Soukhoroukov, Pashkov, Frolov …" The regiment commander called the pilots' surnames looking along the line. "Egorova", I heard my surname. "Strakhov, Tishchenko, Groudnyak, Sokolov, Zinoviev, Podynenogin …" And each of us took three steps forward from the line.

The regimental commander Kozin included just 19 pilots in the group – three squadron commanders, all the flight commanders and the senior pilots with combat experience. Soon after that we were met by the Front Commander I.E.Petrov and the commander of the 4th Aerial Army General K.A. Vershinin.

"You, comrades, have a task simple in terms of planning but very hard in terms of implementation", the Front Commander addressed us, adjusting his *pince-nez* and stuttering slightly. "Our troops are to break through the Fascist defence's Blue Line. But first of all we have to camouflage the advancing troops – to set up a smoke screen. You will do that." General Petrov looked at me carefully and I actually clenched my shoulders – I thought he was going to ask: "What's a woman doing here?" But the commander's gaze slipped onto other pilots standing by the scale model of the Blue Line – and my spirits lifted.

The General went on to say the smoke screen would have to be set up on time and accurately so as to blind the enemy, to close his eyes for the time our infantry needed in order to capture the main defensive line's trenches. The General clearly defined the direction and time for converging on the target, and then General Vershinin told us how to carry out the mission. We were to fly without aerial gunners, just above the ground and besides that without bombs, rockets or machine-guns in the rear cockpit, and the cannons and machine-guns were not to be loaded at all! Instead of bombs we would have cylinders of 'smoke gas' on the bomb racks. This gas, reacting with air, would form the smoke screen.

"The most complicated thing is that you are not allowed to manoeuvre", General Vershinin leaned over the map. "Look here, 7 kilometres in a straight line with no manoeuvring, and at an extremely low altitude. Do you understand why you're not allowed to manoeuvre?"

"We'll get a discontinuous screen instead of a solid one", one of the flyers said.

"A discontinuous one will mean the attack will break down somewhere", Petrov commented, stroking his rust-coloured moustache. "That's why the screen must be such that no searchlight beam breaks through it – solid, straight as a ruler!"

"This is what you'll do", Vershinin went on. "Once you see that the one flying ahead of you has put smoke out, count three seconds and press the triggers. Manoeuvring will mean wrecking the mission. But you'll be flying over fire, under fire, amidst fire ... It remains only to wish you good luck and a happy return ..."

Bidding farewell General Vershinin invited: "If any of you has changed his mind – feel free to refuse. It's your right. We want those to make this flight, who firmly believe that they will complete the mission and definitely make it home."

None of us responded to the General's invitation ...

On 26 May, when the Eastern sky had just begun to grow pink, we headed to the aerodrome in a ton-and-a-half truck. Michael Nikolaevich Kozin, always joyful and affable, was very gloomy. He was either angry that they hadn't allowed him to fly, or was worried about us. And the pilots? What kind of mood were we in before such an important take-off? I looked at them and saw Grisha Rzhevskiy romping with a kitten – his new mascot-playmate who didn't want to sit in his bosom under the leather fur-lined jacket. My brother Egor was fond of animals too. Mum used to find, hidden under the kitchen table or barricaded under beds, kittens and puppies with saucers of milk. Having eaten they would begin to mew or bark desperately, and mum would become angry and threaten to belt Egor, but could never bring herself to. The lad had grown up, joined the armed forces and war had broken out. My brother Egor didn't come back home. He was killed in action ...

Kolya Pakhomov was singing his favourite song:
"You, young Cossack girl, stand by the wicker fence,
Before the sunrise see me off to the war ..."

Tolya Yugrov excitedly said something to Valentin Vakhramov, and both laughed like children, holding on each other: as if nobody would have to throw himself into a firestorm in just a minute or two ... Misha Berdashkevich's blue eyes smiled at something. There were so many scorch scars on his naturally handsome face! Maybe he was recalling his escape from a hospital to his regiment in a hospital gown? Tasets, an ethnic Greek, stood pensively. Most likely he was thinking over again how to approach a target, is it efficient to do a circle and shift towards your own territory if Fascist fighters attack? Tasets is our 'great theorist' but also a good practical man as well.

Our 3rd Squadron commander Semyon Andrianov was hugging a colleague – a squadron commander – with one arm, and Boris Strakhov with the other one. All three were silently staring at the expanse of the Kuban Steppe, revived after the long winter. The twenty-year-old *comesks* always tried to seem respectable, putting on strict airs. Adrianov even procured a pipe and walked without taking it out of his mouth. He would move it a little to the corner of his mouth during a conversation, but in his eyes there was so much youthful fervour in his eyes, so many sparks ready to spray those around him! We knew that Semyon Andrianov was born in a steel worker's family in Nizhniy Tagil. There he graduated from school and the aeroclub and from there he joined the Perm pilot school. An ordinary biography for a pilot … We knew that Semyon had wife and a daughter. He'd been in our regiment since April 1941 and now he was a squadron commander. His deputy was Philipp Pashkov. He was a gentleman, and at the moment he was carefully protecting me from the jolts of the bumps in the road while the truck carried us to our fighting machines. He would often tell me about his native town of Penza, his mother, sisters and father – a disabled war veteran who died when Philipp was only three years old.

"When the war is over, let's go to Penza, *stanishnitsa*[1]. I'll show you the museum estates of Radishev and Belinskiy[2], Lermontov's famous Tarkhany estate. You know, Alexander Ivanovich Kouprin[3] is one of us Penza people too, from Narovchatov. And what forests we have! So many mushrooms and berries!" Filipp drawled rocking from side to side. Like any dedicated mushroom-picker he exaggerated: "You can come across glades in our forest where you can mow the saffron milk caps with a scythe. My mum cooks them so well! You'll come, won't you?"

For some reason Pashkov never called by my first name or surname, nor by my rank or position. He called me simply stanishnitsa. "Well, *stanishnitsa*, how are things?"

"Not bad, thanks."

Once (how many of those 'onces' there were!) Pashkov flew into the enemy's rear to undertake reconnaissance and aerodrome photography. He was escorted by fighters, but on the way back, when the mission had already been carried out, they were attacked by Messerschmitts. Six of them were up against our two LaGG-3 fighters and one *Sturmovik*. The leader of the pair of fighters told Pashkov to "tramp it" home and that they would engage the skinnies. Our pilots had nicknamed the Me-109s so for their narrow fuselage … But shortly after that the first LaGG caught fire and began to fall …

"You bastards!" Filipp cursed and flew his *Sturmovik* towards the dogfight. Well, naturally he shouldn't have done that, for he had to deliver the reconnaissance data and the film to the aerodrome. However, Pashkov managed to shoot down one Hitlerite, and another, shot up by him, retired from the fight, while the third one was cut down by our fighter. Upon returning to the aerodrome Filipp was strongly reprimanded, but when the film was developed the regiment commander hugged the pilot and congratulated him with an award – the Order of the Red Star. A week later Pashkov didn't come back from a sortie, and we counted him as dead. The war … How much grief, unforeseeable surprises, and sometimes just miracles it brought each day … Five days later Filipp came back to the regiment with his aerial gunner – unshaven, ragged and dirty but cheerful.

---

1   Translator's note – a common Cossack address to a female from the same *stanitsa*.
2   Translator's note – prominent Russian 19th Century democrats.
3   Translator's note – a famous Russian writer in the late 19th–early 20th centuries.

Upon his return Filipp addressed me by my first name for the first time, saying: "They say you cried bitterly for me? Thank you. But you'd have done better to believe in my life, to believe I would definitely come back ..."

And Pashkov perished anyway. It happened north of Novorossiysk, near Verkhnekabanskiy. That time I waited a long time for him, trying not to believe in his death, but never saw him again. I wrote about his death to his mum and sister in Penza, to the city where Filipp had invited me after the war.

...But for now we were all still alive and riding to the aerodrome. My thoughts were suddenly interrupted by some loud banging – it was pilots drumming on the truck cab, several yelling to the driver: "Stop, stop, what's the rush?" The driver slowed down and they ordered him: "Backwards fast!" It turned out a cat had crossed the road in front of us. That was trouble ... A second time the guys stopped the vehicle and made the driver reverse when they came across a woman with empty buckets on her yoke. It can't be denied that airmen are a superstitious mob.

...Our regiment surgeon Kozlovskiy was talking someone into having this blood pressure measured before a sortie. "Doc, you'd be better doing my kitten – he's acting nervous today for some reason", Rzhevskiy stopped him to the common laughter of all. "It looks like you've forgotten, Grisha, how you fed him five rissoles at dinnertime?" "Is your chest dry?"

The jokes were starting. We couldn't get by without them. From outside it might seem these happy guys were riding tipsy ... But here we were at the aerodrome. Technicians, mechanics, motorists, instrument specialists, armourers – all of them were by the planes. It was always like that: in frost, in heat, in the open air our workmen, descendants of wonderful Russian craftsmen, prepared the planes for combat. There had been no case in the regiment of anything that failed or broke down being the fault of these tireless workers of the aerodrome.

Tyutyunnik – the mechanic of my Il-2 – wiping his hardened, work-weary hands as he walked, reported the plane ready. Then he helped me put on the parachute, adjusted something in the cockpit, and when the engine had started he shoved a pickled apple he had procured somewhere into my hand and yelled in my ear:

"If you get a dry mouth, bite the apple!" and he rolled off the plane's wing like a ball, blown away by the spurt from the spinning prop.

I turned on the two-way and heard the voice of the group leader Major Kerov giving permission to taxi out. Pavel Usov's *Sturmovik* was ahead of me, the pilot Ivan Stepochkin taxiing right next to him. Stepochkin and Usov were two inseparable friends although very different in character and looks. Usov was a short stocky *rousak*[4] with chubby cheeks as if puffed up from laughing – an ever-smiling joker. Even Pavel's gait seems merry, hopping as if constantly looking for someone for another joke. Stepochkin was tall, with dark eyes and curly hair – a handsome guy with Gypsy looks. He was usually silent and pensive. Once, when walking about Timashevskaya, the friends went into a church where a service was on. The priest was preaching the benefits of fasting. Usov lingered there and doubting the usefulness of such a thing, began to ask questions, and then started an argument with the priest. When Stepochkin tried to drag his friend away from the church, Usov resisted.

4   Editor's note – literally, 'grey hare'; a nickname for someone with typically Russian looks.

It is interesting that the priest finally managed to prove his case to Pavel, and leaving the church the latter firmly declared to Ivan: "I'm going to fast!"

"And I will raise the issue of expelling the Communist Usov from the ranks of the VKP(b)[5] for his religious connections", – Stepochkin cut him off and walked away from his friend to the opposite side of the street. In the evening Pavel told all of us about the benefits of fasting with his characteristic humor and fervor. "Only", he said, "don't eat too much afterwards like we used do during Easter, that's no good. But to fast, eating Lenten foods, to give your stomach a rest, is quite good for you."

"So why have you just ordered another steak, Pasha?" Someone asked him. And a fighter pilot, Volodya Istrashkin, came up to Usov's table and put on it in front of him a half-litre jar of the sour local grape-wine.

"This is for you, matey, to help your digestion. It seems to me, the priest said today: "Permission is given for wine and oil"...

The pilot Vanya Soukhoroukov – a guy from Ivanovo – flew in my pair. Vanya was a quiet man on the ground – like a fair maiden – but you wouldn't recognise him in the air! It was him who in November of 1942 led a group of *Sturmoviks* to the Gizel area near Ordzhonikidze where in one of the hollows surrounding the Voenno-Gruzinskaya Road[6] he destroyed the enemy's tanks and vehicles. Later Vanya Soukhoroukov would win the title of Hero of the Soviet Union.

Major Kerov was the first to take off. We quickly joined the leader and took up combat formation. Glancing back I saw the huge sun rising in the east and the sky illuminated by its bright beams. But in the west, ahead of us, the sky was dark and smoke and fog floated over the ground ...

The Blue Line met us with multi-layered flak fire. Shell bursts stood like a wall, blocking our way. Our group broke through this screen at minimum speed and emerged over the *stanitsa* Kievskaya. Again the ominous tracers crossed the sky. Oerlikon shells were painting the sky with red balls, the splinters of burst shells were banging on the plane's armour. Now enemy mortars and heavy machine guns had opened on us too. We were flying through pandemonium but we could change neither course nor altitude – we had to go only straight forward. A sea of fire raged around us and I involuntarily pressed myself against the armoured seat back. The seconds seemed an eternity and I wanted so much to shut my eyes so as not to see all this hell!

Suddenly smoke burst from under the fuselage of the plane flying ahead of me. "Twenty one, twenty two, twenty three"... I count off three seconds. Oh, God how long they are! At last I press the trigger. Now come what may, I and the pilot ahead of me have done our job precisely. We haven't turned off course and haven't changed altitude. I want so much to see what's happening down there on the ground, how the smoke screen is spread and if it has a gap anywhere but I can't divert my attention. At last Kerov has turned right, to the east, and all the *Sturmoviks* are following him, and begin to climb up. Mission accomplished ...

We were flying over the escort fighter's aerodrome. In the headphones I heard Kerov's voice – deep, smooth as his temper: "Thanks, little ones! You've done a excellent job!" he thanked the fighter pilots for escorting us.

---

5   Translator's note – abbreviation for the All-Union Communist Party (of the Bolsheviks).
6   Translator's note – leading from Vladikavkaz to Tbilisi.

My heart is rejoicing: we're all coming back – all nineteen. Again there is a voice in the headphones: "Attention Hunchbacks!"

'Hunchbacks' meant us – it was a frontline nickname for the *Sturmoviks*, given for their cockpits standing out from the fuselage. I pricked up my ears.

"For successful completion of the mission", we hear on the air, "and the fortitude shown, all the airmen who took part in setting the smoke-screen are awarded the Order of the Red Banner ..."

Now it was quiet on the air. The Il's engine was running smoothly. Here was our aerodrome. The one whose machine was most damaged was the first to close in for landing – this was our rule. Then all the others, including me, landed. Having taxied to the parking bay I turned the engine off and only then felt the deadly fatigue. The technician, the mechanic, the engine specialist, the armoury girl, the flyers who didn't take part in the sortie, swarmed all over the cockpit like bees.

"Are you wounded, Comrade Lieutenant?" The armourer Dousya Nazarkina shouted. "You've got blood on your face!"

"No", I said, "My lips are cracked and bleeding."

The mechanic shows me a huge hole in the left wing: "Lucky that the shell didn't burst – otherwise you would have been blown to pieces. Look, the elevator trimmer is broken as well."

And during the flight I hadn't noticed my Il was damaged!

The regiment is lined up. The battle flag is brought out. We, who carried out the Front Command's special mission, stand separately as though it were our name day. The 4th Aerial Army Commander General Vershinin expresses his gratitude to us for our excellent work and pins the Orders of the Red Banner on our chests. And in the evening there is another reward: the accursed Blue Line has been broken through by our troops! We are told that several minutes after we released the 'smoke gas' a white wall of smoke grew up in front of the enemy lines. It fully served its purpose. Moving towards the enemy the smoke screen covered the knots of resistance and made their infantry blind. Not knowing what was happening in front, the Hitlerites abandoned the frontline in a panic. Our troops broke through the lines and advanced a kilometer and a half to two kilometres straight away.

26

My comrades-in-arms

The life of the regiment went on its normal course. Fierce fighting on the Taman Peninsula continued. We had to fly combat missions several times a day, and most of the time we flew towards targets over the waters of the Black and Azov Seas.

I'd feared water since childhood and had always been a bad swimmer. And it seemed to me sometimes when flying over the sea that the engine was playing up. In case of emergency we had been issued with lifebelts but the airmen didn't believe they would save us if we ditched on water. But I, like a drowning man clutching at a straw, would put the belt on without fail, to the jokes and laughter of my comrades, meticulously adjusting it to my figure. Of course by modern standards our lifebelts were far from perfect. Judge for yourself: when a shot-down plane falls into the sea, a pilot has to manage to open the cockpit, to bail out, then open the parachute and the valve on the life belt and wait until it filled up with gas produced by the contact of some chemical substance in it with water. And if the belt didn't fill with gas, what then? That was why the airmen didn't believe in the lifebelts. But when put on, it had a positive psychological effect on me, and therefore I paid no attention to the guys' good-natured joking.

The regimental favourite Borya Strakhov didn't come back after a sortie onto the Choushka Spit. A day later some seamen brought his body to our place and said it had been washed ashore near Anapa. We buried him with a Division lined-up, with all military honours in the *Stanitsa* of Dzhigitskaya. Airmen were rarely buried during the war because they usually died where the action was. I stood next to the coffin of Boris, wept bitterly and could not believe he was dead. It seemed he would get up any minute, look around with his grey-green eyes, twist his non-existent moustache and ask: "What are they taking girls to war for?" and would hand me a field flower. He used to do that often.

During his last combat sortie Boris led a sixer of Il-2s on a ground attack and bombing mission against a ferry carrying a troop train near the Choushka Spit. The *Sturmoviks* flew below the lower edge of clouds at a height of 700 metres. On approach to the target the pilots were surprised: the enemy didn't open fire on the planes for some reason. Strakhov and his wingmen were aware that the enemy flak was zeroed in on the clouds' lower edge beforehand and began to conduct wide anti-flak manoeuvres in course and altitude plane. The flak guns remained silent. The pilots wanted to see them sooner than later, to see the first shell bursts so as to know where to turn the planes but the sky was still clear right up to the clouds. But then Boris Strakhov noticed the ferry near the Choushka Spit – a steam-engine dragging the carriages was creeping off it. Judging by their silhouettes on the open trucks, there were tanks, artillery and vehicles under the tarpaulins, and probably ammunition in the covered carriages. As soon as the leader switched his plane to diving several flak batteries tore the skies with a powerful salvo. The pilots didn't falter and maintained their rapid approach to the target, firing their cannons and machine-guns and launching rockets. The pilots dropped 100-kilogram bombs with delayed fuses from low altitude. In 22 seconds the fuses did their work and a dazzling blaze covered the whole Choushka Spit.

But when the group was on its way home and already flying over the Black Sea the pilots saw that the leader's plane was badly damaged and losing height. Apparently Strakhov was wounded, for his radio was silent. And suddenly four Fokkers[1] leaped out of the clouds. They pounced upon the leader's plane like jackals. Strakhov sharply threw his plane up – possibly he wanted to let the Hitlerites pass forward and attack them himself but his plane was no longer controllable. Hitting the waves with a list, he went to the bottom ...

So Boris Strakhov was no more – a fair-haired bloke from Gorky – the 1st Squadron Commander. Everyone in our regiment took his death hard but his friend Vanya Soukhoroukov suffered harder than anyone. Ivan lost weight, looked drawn and spent all his spare time at his friend's grave. Just recently as an incentive Ivan had got permission to have a vacation at home. Before leaving he told me confidentially that he was leaving to marry his childhood girlfriend and asked me to 'lend' him my trench-coat, for his own was very old, soldier-issue. My trench-coat had been made up from English cloth in a *Voentorg*[2] workshop. "Since you're going to get married ..." I agreed, "take it!"

Ivan had been absent from the regiment for ten days and when he came back for some reason he did his best to stay out of my sight. "What's the matter?" I wondered and decided to 'interrogate' Boris Strakhov. Borya was somewhat hesitant and then said: "You know, it's a very delicate matter. Please don't tell anyone ..."

It appeared Ivan had made it home but his girlfriend had just left for the front. Their wedding didn't happen. When his vacation was over his town-folk presented him with a three-litre bottle of *samogon*[3], a gift for his comrades, the frontline airmen: "Don't be precious, everything we own is yours ..." Ivan saved the huge bottle all the way back, having wrapped it in my 'special' trench-coat. He had to hitch-hike from Krasnodar to the aerodrome, and when he was doing the last leg of his trip the driver shook his passengers so much that all of them flew out of the back of the truck and hit the ground hard. Everyone was alright, and only Ivan suffered: his cherished three-litre bottle was smashed. Of course, the strong home-made drink soaked the trench-coat. Ivan washed it after he came back to get rid of the smell of spirits and hung it out to dry somewhere outside the *stanitsa*, among the vegetable gardens. "As soon as it gets dry, he'll iron it and bring it back to you", Boris finished earnestly, and it suddenly made me laugh: I had imagined Ivan flying out of the back of the truck with arms around the bottle wrapped in my trench-coat. When I finished laughing I suggested: "Not a drama. I'll have to ask for a new trench-coat from the battalion commander, and I'll present Ivan with that one – let it remind him of his town-folk's gift."

That's how it went back and forth in our life on the front: rare minutes of youthful joy and relaxation, and combat sorties, attacks, the grief of losses ...

During one sortie Kouz'ma Groudnyak's shot-up *Sturmovik* landed, barely dragging itself across the frontline. The Il-2 with its damaged engine stood on its undercarriage in a hollow not far away from a ravine, beyond which the enemy's defensive line was situated. The pilot climbed out of the cockpit under a hail of bullets and mortar shell

---

1 Editor's note – the classic nickname for German Focke Wulf Fw 190 fighters in Russian military slang. Indeed, it has nothing to do with the planes of the 'Fokker' design.

2 Translator's note – a network of special shops organised to supply military servicemen.

3 Translator's note – home-made liquor or 'moonshine'.

splinters and lay down. Then he crawled to our lines and reported what had happened, and soon technicians headed towards his plane. But they had to get to the plane on foot. The whole terrain was dug up with trenches and land-mined, and so it was impossible to tow the plane away from the frontline. Only one thing could be done to save the Il: fly it away from the spot after replacing the engine. But how could that be done? You need a run-up and there were endless trenches and minefields all over the place. And it was a dangerous business to replace an engine in sight of the enemy. Finally they decided to work at night, and to disguise the plane with tree branches in the daytime.

So the technicians covered themselves with tarpaulins and began to remove the engine under torchlight. During the next night they installed an operational engine. The pilot had crawled up to the disguised plane too. Kouz'ma Dmitrievich spread out his raglan that had seen better days, lay on it, lit a cigarette and began to think how to take off. Glancing at his cigarette smoke he grasped that the wind was blowing from the enemy side. That was good for the run-up is shorter when taking off against the wind. "Well, is everything ready?" he asked the technicians.

They looked at the pilot narrowly and the Senior Technician Petr Panarin replied: "All nuts on the underframe have been splinted, hoses and pipes connected – I've checked it myself. Water and oil have been topped up, fuel as well …"

"Keep it short, Petr", the surprised pilot cut him short. "You tell me: will it fly?"

"At the aerodrome I wouldn't let it go."

"And why's that?"

"We haven't tested the engine properly, and everything's been done by eye … What if the prop slips? Or something else?

"You check the governor cable thoroughly one more time and just imagine you'll be taking off yourself."

"Aye, Comrade Commander. But how shall we warm up the engine before the start? It's as quiet now before the dawn as at home near Omsk[4]."

"We'll ask the gunners. We'll warm it up under cover of the noise!"

That was how they did it. An artillery battery commander agreed: "Alright, we'll 'rumble' a bit from the reserve positions as if we are zeroing in."

Early in the morning our artillery began its work. Groudnyak turned the engine on and began to warm it up, then revved up – there was no slip. And then he released the brake and rolled! His plane was rolling directly towards the Fascists' dugouts and trenches. At one moment the pilot engaged the booster and just before a German dugout he jerked the control lever. Shortly after the salvaged *Sturmovik* dashed low over our lines and waved its wings in thanks for the hospitability.

One day I was summoned to the regiment CP and ordered to lead a quartet of *Sturmoviks* to that same accursed Choushka Spit – to attack the enemy infantry and materiel reserves that had just crossed the Kerch Straits. I tried to refuse to be the leader and timidly asked the regiment commander to allow me to fly as a wingman.

"And who do you reckon should lead the group?" asked Michael Nikolaevich staring at me point-blank. "There are only inexperienced youngsters left! Usov, Stepochkin, Zinoviev, Tasets, Pashkov, Balyabin, Mketumov are all killed … Bougrov has got burns. Trekin is badly wounded. Who do you think is going to lead the pilots on the mission?"

---

4   Translator's note – a city in Siberia.

The regiment commander turned his face away, wiping his eyes with a glove, and then, quickly repeating the mission aloud, I dashed out of the dugout.

"It'll be nothing but a suicide mission in this weather and on such a target ..." the pilot Zoubov muttered when he found out about the sortie.

And instead of explaining the mission or calming the pilot somehow I suddenly ordered brusquely: "Everyone to your planes! Run!" I had flown off the handle ...

After the take-off all my wingmen joined me, taking up their positions in the formation. The group and I 'called in' to pick up the escort fighters: they were always based closer to the frontline while we, the *Sturmoviks*, were further away. Soon a quartet of LaGG-3 fighters got airborne and joined us.

I knew it would be impossible to reach the Choushka Spit following a direct course through the flak screen. That was why I decided to do it in a broad curve from the direction of the Azov Sea. The low clouds worked for us, but whilst we flew above the marshes and the sea the minutes seemed like an eternity to me: any engine malfunction or damage to a plane meant inevitable death in the water! At last the sandy shallows of Choushka came into view. Death was lurking around here. It might leap out of the clouds as a diving Fokker or come from the ground as a flak shell or a stray bullet ...

Already en route to the target we came under the heaviest flak fire. I glanced back my wingmen were still in formation. "You need to be sneaky with ack-ack", I recalled the words of my squadron commander Andrianov. "Otherwise you'll get shot up or shot down. It's best not to engage them at all but if you're gonna pounce on them attack the one in your way, one protecting the target ..." I got ready to attack: I rocked the plane, changed altitude and speed. The wingmen did the same. We leaped over the first belt of anti-aircraft defence, then over the second ... Here was the target! The Choushka Spit stretches for 18 kilometres and is similar to the embankment of an unfinished bridge crossing the Kerch Straits. And there was so much Fascist scum down on this narrow flat strip washed by two seas, that the spit itself was not invisible – there was only materiel, guns, tanks, men ...

We dived, dropped bombs, fired our cannons and machine-guns. We pulled the *Sturmoviks* out of the attack when we were just above the heads of the Hitlerites, then gained altitude and swiftly dashed into another pass. I saw vehicles burning, something exploding. The infantrymen were on the run, the tanks crawling in all directions, crushing their own soldiers. Take that, you bastards! For everything we've suffered!

The ammo was running low and I turned my plane towards home. I glanced back to check if everyone was still with me – and a nasty chill ran down my back, then I felt hot and my mouth got dry: Zoubov's plane wasn't there ... Where was he? How could that be? A pilot was shot down and I didn't notice? It meant now there were only three of us left. The quartet of our escort fighters was in a dogfight a bit to the side of us.

So, I was flying back and kept watching the ground: maybe, I would see Misha Zoubov's plane? How could it be? And I had shouted at him before the battle ... But as soon as we'd crossed the frontline I saw a *Sturmovik* lying on a hillock not far away from the marshes. The number on its tail was '23' – it was Zoubov's! He and his aerial gunner got out of the cockpit onto the wings and waved to us, then fired a shot from a flare gun. I made a steep turn, banked my wings ("Look, I can see you – wait for help!") and flew away.

We landed safely and, having reported completion of the mission to the commander, I headed to the marshes in a Po-2 to pick up Zoubov and his gunner. Zoubov told us his

Sturmovik had been damaged by ack-ack guns and when he was retiring, shot up, he was finished off by a fighter. Later, when Misha and I had done quite a few combat sorties he admitted to me once: "You know, Anna Alexandrovna, back then I was afraid not of the Choushka Spit or the bad weather but of your presence. I thought: "Well, Michael, no good will come of a 'woman on board'. But when you made the turn above us and then came back to pick us up in a Po-2 all my doubts disappeared. I beg your pardon ...

After that a crew of technicians and engine specialists flew over to the forced landing spot from our regiment and PARM[5]. They were to assess the damage and decide the fate of the *Sturmovik*. Would it be feasible to repair it on the spot or it would be better to disassemble it, load onto trucks and send to workshops in separate units? Such decisions were always taken by the captain of technical services Petr Vasilievich Komkov – formerly engine specialist to V.P.Chkalov[6] himself. He was a jack-of-all-trades but best of all he knew the AM-38 engine. Like a good doctor of diagnostics he would listen to it: tap it all over then sit in the cockpit, turn on the engine and continue listening to it first at low, then at medium revs, and sometimes on booster. At last Komkov would turn the ignition off look into all sections of the engine and only then would he was make a conclusion. We were all confident that our frontline 'academic' would always make the right diagnosis – with him mistakes didn't happen.

It's true Komkov from Gorky had one weakness. He was so very jealous of his wife that more than once she ran to the head of the Division's Political Section with complaint against her husband. Praskovya Semyonovna (just Panya to everyone) from Moscow, very young and pretty, appeared in the PARM unexpectedly but stayed. She went to work in her husband's workshops sewing percale on a machine. And thus Panya sewed up until the end of the war – that was her contribution to the Victory.

---

5   Abbreviation of Mobile Aviation Maintenance Workshop.
6   Translator's note – a famous Soviet test pilot who died in a flying accident shortly before WWII.

27

Frogmarched to training

The division commanders decided to send me on a navigation course in Stavropol. There was no need for navigators in *Sturmoviks* or in fighter planes: every pilot was his own navigator. But each regiment had a squadron navigator position: he was also the deputy squadron commander. Apart from that, there was a position of regimental navigator – the regiment's deputy commander for navigation services.

I didn't care much about these career steps: I only wanted to fly, and categorically refused to go on that course. Then the division commander General Get'man ordered Major Karev to 'frogmarch' me there in a Po-2. I could do nothing and had to yield. And now I was studying. There were six more 'captives' with me: four fighter pilots and two *Sturmovik* pilots. Our course leader was Senior Lieutenant Kalougin – a handsome chap with unruly brown hair, a kind smile and freckles on his nose. He had already become a well-known fighter pilot in our Aerial Army – by that time this lad had more than twenty shot-down enemy planes on his account.

There were as many teachers as students at the course, and the head of the course was a well-educated and kind-hearted man – Lieutenant-Colonel Alexander Petrovich Kilin. In two months the course was completed. We headed back to our 4th Aerial Army on the Stavropol-Krasnodar train. At one station we bought fresh newspapers, and shouted 'hurray!' – our fellow student Senior Lieutenant V. Kalougin had been awarded the title of Hero of the Soviet Union! We'd already known about our comrade's feat from the Army- and Front-level newspapers, and from leaflets dedicated to the fearless aerial fighter. During one battle against a group of enemy bombers intending to bomb our installations the Senior Lieutenant, having expended all his ammo, went for ramming. Choosing the right moment, he moved up against a Junkers and chopped off its wing with his propeller. The Junkers turned over awkwardly and in an instant hit the ground and exploded. The other Fascists turned westward, and the gallant pilot led his damaged plane to his aerodrome and landed safely. Next day Kalougin had to ram again – and again, having destroyed an enemy bomber with a blow to his tail assembly, he managed to make it home. "Two rams in two days!" the newspaper wrote of his feat. "What a striking and convincing proof of the martial valour and high skills of the Soviet pilot, and his indomitable resolve to defeat the enemy at any cost!"

We were very happy about our comrade's high award and decided to celebrate the event. At the station, on the spot, we bought a watermelon and some fruit, and when the train had taken off we began to honour the hero …

The train arrived in Krasnodar where the headquarters of the 4th Aerial Army was located, and from there we flew to our regiments. I returned to my 850th Ground Attack with joy, as if to my kinfolk, but my joy faded straightaway. The 20-year old commander of our squadron, Semyon Vasilievich Andrianov, had been killed in action with his aerial gunner Potseluiko … I remember feeling a lump rise in my throat – I was unable to ask or say anything – there were only memories before my eyes. And among them for some reason I recalled the marvellous drawings in an album my squadron commander once showed me.

"You've got talent, comrade commander", I said him then.

"No, Egorova, you're wrong. We simply had a good drawing teacher in our 11th School in Nizhniy Tagil. He ran a drawing club that I eagerly attended. For as long I can remember I always wanted to draw …"

"Well, join a college of arts after the war, Semyon Vasilievich", I addressed the *comesk* by his first name and patronymic for the first time. "Your drawings are so good! Although I don't understand much about drawing …"

"I love flying, Annoushka", said Andrianov with unexpected affection. "But after the war, when we destroy the Fascists, I will take up drawing seriously …"

But our squadron commander would not live to see Victory. Semyon Andrianov was killed carrying out a combat mission 8 kilometres west of the *Stanitsa* Krymskaya. I was told that on that day a sixer of *Sturmoviks* was ordered to do a bombing raid on a concentration of tanks. The mission was set up by the Regimental Chief-of-Staff Yashin and he appointed Andrianov a group leader. The group was escorted by four LaGG-3 fighters from a fraternal regiment. They were to strike at the tanks from low altitude, for the weather was really complicated – the clouds hung just above the ground and it was raining … Our arms specialists loaded the planes with PTABs[1] – 200 or 250 in each compartment, loaded the cannons and machine-guns, fixed the rockets, and Andrianov took off exactly at the designated time.

By the way, the *Sturmoviks* could not always use all their capabilities when striking from low altitudes. For example, strikes by PTABs upon tanks were usually successful but 100-kilogram bombs had to be dropped with delayed fuses – otherwise your plane might be damaged by shrapnel from your own bombs. And the accuracy of bombing from these heights would be sharply reduced. It was very hard to use cannons, machine-guns and rockets when attacking from such low level. One had to gain height, for the tank cannons had enviable accuracy! But Andrianov's group had no height, and the *comesk* knew the mission had to be accomplished at any cost. He accomplished it at the cost of his own life …

1   Anti-tank bomblets.

28

The aerial gunner and the technicians

In our regiment I flew an old single-seater *Sturmovik* the longest. It seemed to me much lighter and more agile than the two-seater. But really you just needed to get used to it! And now, when I had returned from the navigation course, I was going to fly a two-seater and Boiko the Adjutant of our 3rd Squadron has suggested I choose an aerial gunner. There also was another important factor that has influenced me regarding this issue. In one of the most recent sorties I had quite a close shave with Messers. We'd been flying to Temryuk back then – we had to destroy a bridge over the Kuban river. It seems like it wasn't long ago when Karev with his group had smashed it to pieces. But the damned Fritzes have repaired it yet again! Damn it, how long should we be bothered with it?

Temryuk was situated almost on the coast of the Azov Sea, and the Kuban river flows west of it. At this particular place, a major highway leads from the berth on the Choushka Spit up to the Blue Line. The bridge was surrounded by countless ack-ack batteries, and along the Blue Line there were plenty of anti-aircraft installations. We had already lost three crews over Temryuk: those of Podynenogin, Mkrtumov and Tasets. Our group was led towards the bridge by Captain Yakimov. A tall, sporty guy, with somewhat lordly manners, Yakimov was always keeping himself a bit aside: as if he was looking down on us a bit – although in terms of age he was not much older than us. Having gone over the mission plan with us, he has established an order of the flight and for some reason placed me (flying a single-seater!) to bring up the rear of our formation of six. But orders are not for discussion, and we took off. A quartet of LaGG-3 fighters provided a cover but I have to admit: I didn't feel comfortable bringing up the rear without an air gunner …

After we dropped the bombs on the bridge and leaped out over the Azov Sea our group was intercepted by Messerschmitts. The LaGGs were already tied up in a dogfight with German fighters somewhere aside, so it was up to our air gunners to get busy. They did it with quite some skill, repelling the pressing Messers. Several times they tried to split the *Sturmoviks'* formation, but in vain. We flew tightly, wingtip to wingtip. And it was just me, my plane, that was not protected by a gunner to its rear. No wonder then they had chosen me as a target. I saw a tracer pass on my right, and broke left but too late: a second burst hit my *Ilyusha*. Following that, the 'Messers' had broke, turned and hurled themselves into a second attack from both sides at once, aiming at my plane. Being aware of the power of *Sturmovik*'s forward-firing weapons, the Germans were avoiding my forward-facing zone. Instead, they were hitting my plane (unprotected from the rear) coming at its tail. Once again I saw a stream of fire coming from short range … At this moment I hit the engine boost and simultaneously pushed the control column away. Speeding up I overtook my group and tucked my plane between the leader and his wingman on the right – Volodya Sokolov. And it saved me.

But during debriefing I had to withstand quite a set of reproofs.

"You breached battle formation", Captain Yekimov rapped his words out, enunciating each word and each letter. "Pilot Sokolov might have taken you for the enemy and struck you with his cannons and machine-guns!"

But I had an impudent question to ask a captain: "When seeing the Fascist planes raking me with fire, why didn't you re-form the group into a defensive circle, then drawing a fight to our side of the front?"

Silence fell. Yekimov blushed. And then, breaching the deathly hush, Volodya Sokolov stood up for me. "Comrade Captain! You said I could have taken Egorov's *Sturmovik* for an enemy plane. But could I really? Isn't it seen how the edges of her blue kerchief are sticking out of the earphone helmet? She wears it instead of the liner!"

The pilots burst into laughter, and the heavy atmosphere was dispelled. Battle-hardened airmen, as a rule, recall moments of mortal danger happily. The chill of it felt in their hearts is replaced by the joy of being able to see, to breathe, to live! Maybe that's why they talk jokingly about a mortal danger they've experienced and left behind.

After this incident I was issued with an Il-2 with a cockpit that would fit an aerial gunner. Incidentally, even prior to leaving for the training course I had flown this plane with various aerial gunners available. And not just with the gunners! Once I stealthily took the plane mechanic Tytyunnik for a combat sortie. In fact, air gunners were trained at short-time classes. Anyone who had the will to fly and knew how to shoot could apply. Among those, I have seen engine technicians, mechanics, flight observers from obsolete types of planes, even machine-gunners from ground forces. The future gunners had no flying practice and they knew nothing about the complicated rules of shooting at aerial targets, but all of them had a huge desire to hit back at the Fascists till the victory. In those days, all the regiments of our divisions began to sing an unpretentious song about the *Sturmovik* gunners:

'Il' is turning, 'Il' is flying above a mountain,
A heroic pilot is in control.
There's a young chap on the rear seat
He is an aerial gunner …

There were girls among the 'young guys' as well – Sasha Chouprina, Lena Lenskaya. And some 'young guys' were old enough to be our fathers! In our regiment, for example there was an aerial gunner – a former flight observer Serguey Michailovich Zavernin from the village of Korpogory in the Archangelsk Region. To cut a long story short, when I had returned from the navigation course and the squadron adjutant invited me to choose a gunner I was surprised. "What do you mean 'choose'? If there's one available, send him to me. But to get one from a crew that has already fallen into step – that is no good!"

" Well, we have one not attached to any crew. But he is … he is a bit of a queer chap We want to transfer him out of the regiment to the ground forces. But since you are Deputy *Comesk* now, you have a right to pick a better gunner."

"What's the name of the gunner you want to get rid of?"

"Makosov."

"Give him to me."

"I strongly advise against it, Comrade Lieutenant", the adjutant remarked.

"Send him to my plane anyway, please", I requested.

Soon enough, I was talking at the parking lot with Squadron Engineer Shourkhin and Technician-Lieutenant[1] Stepanov, when a chuckle sounded behind me: "Here I come!"

I glanced back and there stood a boy about eighteen years old at the most, with a round face split by a smile, which dimpled his tight pinkish cheeks. His field cap was pushed onto the back of his head, and the forelock of his fair hair was accurately combed to one side.

"Who are you?" I asked him.

"Sergeant Makasov. Adjutant Boiko had, you know … Had sent me to you …"

"So what? Report your arrival, Sergeant Makosov!"

"It's kinda odd. It's the first time I've seen a female pilot!" And he began to giggle again, shifting from foot to foot, obviously a stranger to standing at attention.

"What for did they send you to our regiment?"

"I am an air gunner"

"Have you ever flown before?"

"I completed a gunnery course and that was it …"

"Do you want to fight as a gunner?"

"I want it very much but they're not assigning me a pilot."

"Do you know well the hardware of the cockpit? Gunnery techniques? Silhouettes of the hostile planes?"

"I do!"

"Alright then. I'll test you tomorrow."

The next day in the morning I saw Makosov in the *Sturmovik* cockpit. During questioning he answered fluently and never stopped smiling. And so it came to pass that we started going on combat missions together.

Personally, I myself would never ever have agreed to be an Il-2 aerial gunner. It was scary! The gunner sat with his back to the pilot in an open cockpit. In front of him there was a half-ring mount with a heavy machine gun. When a Fascist fighter got on your tail and started shooting at you – how could someone withstand it?! After all, an aerial gunner had neither a trench nor a hump of earth behind which he might hide from enemy bullets. Of course he's got his machine-gun but it is the pilot who controls the plane throwing it from one side to another and it doesn't make the gunner's life easy. It may also happen that the machine-gun jams due to malfunction or because it has run out of ammunition[2]… No, no way would I want to be aerial gunner in a *Sturmovik*.

However, Makosov started behaving quite actively right from his very first sorties. Spotting an enemy plane he would immediately shoot a flare at it, warning everyone of danger. When I was gaining in altitude after completing my pass over the target, Makosov would fire his gun to hit a target of opportunity on the ground. I knew that the tail of my plane was covered in a reliable way. Moreover, using an intercom set my air gunner was always reporting whatsoever he saw in the air or over the ground.

"Comrade Lieutenant", I heard time and again now. "A flak gun's firing from the woods on the right!" or "Comrade Lieutenant, six tanks are moving towards 'Lesser Land' from Novorossiysk. They're shooting on the move!" And yet again: "Comrade Lieutenant, *Sturmovik* tail number '6' is hit. It is loosing altitude, going down to the sea …"

---

1   Editor's note – a line used to indicate a corresponding auxiliary branch of military service (technician-lieutenant; engineer-rear-admiral; colonel, medical service, etc.).

2   Editor's note – the normal combat load of ammunition for the rear 12.7-mm machine-gun in an Il-2 was just 250 rounds.

It seemed nothing could escape the attention of my gunner. I was happy for his successes and used every opportunity to support or praise him. For completing 10 combat missions successfully and for damaging a Messer, the regimental HQ awarded Makosov the medal 'For Meritorious Service in Combat'.

My air gunner always kept his heavy machinegun in combat-ready order. He always cleaned and lubricated it in time, performed maintenance check-ups and prevented any jams. Makosov would sit in the *Sturmovik* cockpit for hours and practise by targeting planes flying over the aerodrome. By that time, I had full confidence in him. I was fairly sure: in a difficult situation he will not get lost, will not let me down. Makosov never panicked, never got overexcited. He shot in a calm, business-like manner – and did hit his target. Over the *Stanitsa* Moldavankaya he managed to shoot down a Me-109, jointly with few other gunners. Soon, Makosov was awarded with another medal 'For Valour'. During debriefings he was now being held up as an example for other gunners, but he invariably kept smiling the same way, showing the dimples on his cheeks and blushing. I noticed that our gunsmith and weapon/ammunition specialist girls started looking towards our *Sturmovik* with quite an interest – it was Makosov sitting in its cockpit …

I have to mention that all the girls serving in our regiment were the pick of the bunch – very pretty. Masha Zhitnyak, Yulia Panina, Masha Dragova, Varya Matveeva, Nina Gneusheva, Dousya Nazarkina, Lida Fedorova, Lyuba Kasapenko. Nina Piyuk, Katya Kozhevnikova, Nina Shcwetz, Katya Zelinskaya – they all had come from ShMAS[3]. All of them were locals, from the Kuban area, – it turned out that when we were based in the area the local Military Commissariat had sent them all to us as a bunch. The girls were supervised by armament technicians P.I. Panarin and N.A. Kalmykov, and also by our armament engineer B.D. Sheiko. The days when we were conducting missions in a rapid sequence were incredibly difficult for the girls. How many bombs and rockets they had to lug to a plane! And not just lug but lift and suspend them – and do so without any appliances. It was also their responsibility to load hundreds of cannon and machinegun belts between the sorties, and to fuel every plane scheduled for a combat mission. All that was so impossibly hard that for many years after the war they could not carry a child … Many male technicians would help the girls voluntarily: after completing their own duties.

At the same time, the arrival of the 'best half of the people' in the regiment had surely influenced our male contingent. Prior to the appearance of the girls many pilots of our regiment considered it fashionable to wear a beard. Although it might not have been a fashion but rather a superstition: a bullet will not find you once you have a beard! But once our pretty gunsmiths and weapon/ammunition specialists had arrived – all those beards disappeared overnight, as if they were gone with the wind. The pilots started shaving and changing their clothesmore often, and the technicians followed their example. Their usually oily and dirty overalls became almost snow-white due to washing in buckets of petrol. Some appeared ironed – these were placed under a mattress for a night.

The fact that Technician-Lieutenant Petr Panarin wasn't indifferent to the armament specialist Masha Zhitnyak was noticed in the regiment straightaway. What could you do about it? – he had fallen in love with her at first sight. Petr was attracted to this quiet unhurried Ukrainian girl by her modesty, kindness, diligence, and without procrastination (lest the dashing pilots beat him to it!) he proposed. But … he was rejected. And after a

3   School for Junior Aviation Specialists.

epeated proposal Maria said as if cutting him off: "You, Comrade Technician-Lieutenant, hink I came to the regiment to get married? I won't hide that I like you, but there'll be to wedding until the day of our Victory!"

Many years later, after the war, our former armament specialist Maria Timofeevna Chitnyak (now her last name was Panarina) came to visit me in Moscow. She was living n the city of Chervonograd, close to Lvov. She was as always smiling and cordial as before, lthough the war and age had certainly left their mark on her. We were able to recall a ot during that encounter: how mistrustfully our regimental comrades treated the girls, tow hard their life was at the beginning. Indeed, not everything went smoothly for the emale armament specialists at first. And how hard it was for them... It is true that not verything went right in the beginning: many girls just did not know to use the tools, nd their hands were covered with bruises. But nobody heard any complaints from them! Knowing it was not easy for many, the girls reconciled themselves to all the hard sides of frontline life.

Masha remembered how on the first bath day all the girls, like all the other soldiers, vere issued with high-collared tunics and trousers. They had to make them over and djust themselves individually. Nina Gneusheva – a modest, very pretty and proud girl orn in Kuban – became our seamstress. On finding out about Nina's talent, the male ilots, blushing and hesitant, began to ask her for makeovers, sometimes of their blouses, ometimes of trousers or something else. The Kuban Cossack girl managed to do everything, o hang bombs and rockets, to load cannons, and to carry out all tailoring orders.

The female gunsmith/armament specialists were issued English-made boots, which were icknamed 'Churchills' – for their thick soles. They were issued together with puttees out f which the girls learned to make stockings. The latter had their 'brand-name' – zebras. he homemade stockings were so called for their low-quality dyeing – in stripes. Some vould manage to procure acrichine from the regimental surgeon or ink from Ivanovskiy's HQ administration department, dilute it with water and dip the puttees in it – and rush o wring them out, because the others wanted to dye their own ones. In the summertime he armament specialists did not wear cumbersome 'Churchills'. Instead, they were naking a splash wearing slippers self-made from plane covers. Guard duty was the only luty they served fully uniformed ...

Guard duty deserves special mention. Standing guard was what frightened the girls nost. It was especially hard in the territory of Poland and Germany: there, you had to vatch out, to twirl your neck all the time! And as ill luck would have it, the *Starshina* hkitin would place girls as sentries at the most remote guard-posts. He reckoned they vould be the most vigilant sentinels guarding the aerodrome. Indeed, our beautiful rmourers knew well how to handle submachine-guns and the strict *Starshina* trusted hem with good reason.

Once Yulia Panina came to a meeting of the regiment *Comsomol* bureau, of which he was a member, with a bandaged neck. "What's wrong with you, Yulia? Are you sick?" he bureau secretary Vasya Rimskiy asked.

"No", Yulia replied, "I'm not sick. But I was on a guard duty last night. With fear, I urned my neck so much that I have hurt it ..."

"Are you joking, Panina?"

"Not at all. It seemed to me all night that someone was crawling towards the planes nd I was straining my ears and eyes so much that ... now it hurts." Everyone laughed.

"Everything will close up on the wedding day!" Zhenya Berdnikov concluded joyfully.

"You may well laugh. You're the sterner sex but I often see you standing guard by the headquarters dugout. But we – the fair sex – stand with our machine-guns by night at the outermost plane parks …"

Generally speaking, the regimental and squadron *Comsomol* meetings usually occurred between combat sorties or in non-flying weather, late in the night. The agendas were such as: "All our strength for the destruction of the Fascist beast!", "Strike at the enemy like the *Comsomol* crews of the Heroes of the Soviet Union Rykhlin and Efremenko!", "Mutual help in combat is the *Comsomol* member's law!"

Once, the pilot Bougrov came back from a sortie in plane so damaged, that it would have been better to tow it to a scrap-heap: such holes yawned on its wings and fuselage that a man might have easily fallen through many of them, while the rudders and elevator were barely holding on. After having a look at the machine, the regimental Chief Engineer Koudelin addressed Bougrov: "Tolya, my boy! I am an old aviation engineer. I've seen a lot in my life but I've never seen anything like that. Not only were you flying a wreck now a plane, but what's more you've landed it brilliantly! Honour and praises to you!" And straightaway Koudelin addressed this subordinates. "Shall we try it, guys? Shall we fix it up?"

This appeal by the Chief Engineer played a positive role. The impossible was done – in a week the pilot Bougrov took off in that plane to strike at the enemy. Everyone knew that every repaired plane, its every sortie, meant death for dozens of Fascists!

But in the tension of combat work my regimental comrades nevertheless knew how to find time for relaxation and rest. The aerial gunner Zhenya Berdnikov was an indefatigable and constant organizer of regimental amateur performances. A merry fellow and a live wire, he could tell all sort of cock-and-bull stories and jokes for hours. And when, goggling his eyes and turning his toes out sideways, Zhenya began to dance imitating Chaplin and singing songs from his movies, it was simply impossible to keep from laughing!

Once, Berdnikov suggested putting on stage in the *Stanitsa* Timashevskaya's club a sketch of Leonid Lench's[4] called 'The Dream Comes True'. Most of the roles were taken willingly by the amateur performers, but no one wanted to act as the demoniacal *Führer*. Finally the *Comsomol* organizer Rimskiy had to accept it. The staging went of successfully, and then it was decided to show it to the locals. The concert in the club went well. The mechanic Vanya Koulikov danced the 'Yablochko'[5], then, together with the female armourers Nina Piyuk and Dousya Nazarkina, 'The Russian Folkdance'. Masha Zhitnyak and Vasya Nazarov read aloud humorous stories, and Berdnikov and Panina sang the 'Ogonyok' song to the accompaniment of the flyer Pavel Evteev. Everybody liked how Vadim Morozov recited the poem 'Wait for Me'[6]. Then the sketch 'The Dream Comes True' began, but at the moment of conversation between Napoleon and Hitler loud cursing resounded through the complete silence, and some object flew across onto the stage and accurately hit 'Hitler'. The club audience burst out laughing but the actor didn't feel like laughing: he'd got a good smack from a gumboot. Apart from that, his wig with its renowned forelock on his narrow forehead flew off his head.

After that incident the sketch was not performed anymore: no one wanted to play the despicable person! And when after the concert a very old man came up to Rimskiy and

---

4   Translator's note – a Soviet playwright.
5   Editor's note – 'The apple', a then-famous folk dance.
6   Translator's note – one of the most famous and emotional wartime poems in the USSR.

began to apologize: "My boy! Forgive me, I didn't mean to hurt you. I'd strangle Hitler with my own hands! The Fascists shot my two brothers, burned my house down …" How could we not sympathize with this human grief …

29

A heroic place

On 16 September 1943 our troops liberated Novorossiysk, on 9 October the Choushka Spit was cleared of Fascists and troops were landed North of Kerch on the Enikale Peninsula. Troops also landed near Eltigen. On the maps there is no such a place as Eltigen now, but there is a place named Geroiskoye ('Heroic'). And back then, when on the night of 1 November 1943 huge waves were violently smashing the rocky cliffs, the fearless landing party went ashore there. They were to sail thirty odd kilometres across the tempestuous Kerch Straits in unseaworthy tubs. Thirty-odd kilometres under endless artillery barrage, under the beams of searchlights …

We airmen knew nothing about the Eltigen landing. The weather prevented flying and all our field aerodromes had become slushy. There were several attempts to take off but nobody had any success: the Ils' undercarriage went into the mud up to the wheel hubs. We managed to join the combat only on November 7.

The group was led then by the regimental navigator Major Karev. During the briefing before take off he instructed us: not to brake during the run-up – otherwise the six-ton *Sturmovik* would bog down, bury itself in the mud, and might turn over. The undercarriage might not retract for it would be jammed with mud and, even if retracted, might not extend before landing – the mud would suck it back. In that case one would have to lower the undercarriage with the emergency winch, making 32 turns with the right hand, while controlling the plane with the left. Karev warned that we would all would have to take off with the oil cooler's shield shut, and open it immediately after take-off, or the mud would block the cooler's cells, the engine would cook and break down.

And off we went. A solid morass of mud lay under the wings. Not all of us managed to break out of its clutches. Seven machines out of nine took off for the combat sortie two of them nosed over during the run-up …

Our course lay towards Eltigen. This fishing village was situated between the Chourbashskoye and the Tobechikskoye Lakes – where the spurs of the coastal hills come up against the sea. The port of Kamysh-Bouroun was situated next to Eltigen, a little bit to the north of it. The Fascist naval ships were based in the port. But this time we carried not bombs but containers of ammo, food, medicine. Stormy weather was preventing the timely supply of reinforcements to the bridgehead, and this was weakening the Eltigen landing contingent. Our task was to drop the load precisely on the bridgehead. So as not to miss we would have to take everything into account: wind speed and direction and the speed of our own planes. And meanwhile the Fascists were shooting at us from the ground with all kinds of weapons – so we would have to return fire as well. But that time we dropped the containers of ammo, food and medicine to the landing troops at Eltigen right on target!

Now we would fly from the Taman Peninsula, cleared of the Hitlerites, to the Kerch Peninsula. One day I was ordered to lead a group of six *Sturmoviks* to the area of Baksy north to the Mitridat Hill. But we hadn't been assigned an actual target and had been set the task of flying along the frontline, finding a target of opportunity for ourselves and giving it a whole-group 'workout'.

And now we were flying. I stubbornly repeated through the radio the same word for my wingmen: "Manoeuvre, manoeuvre, manoeuvre!" I wasn't snoozing either – I threw the *Sturmovik* from side to side, slowed down and sped up from time to time. I knew if the ack-ack guns struck, I as the leader would get the largest share. And now they opened up. It flashed through my mind automatically: that means something is concealed down there. I looked closely – down there, in the gardens there were disguised tanks! I went into a dive: there was a tank in my gun-sight and I launched rockets. "Attack, with a manoeuvre!" I yelled to my wingmen via the radio.

Now I see a loaded truck in the gun-sight. I pressed the triggers and the fire of my automatic cannons poured onto the target. The earth quickly came closer: it seemed to be rushing towards me. Again my fingers touched the buttons triggering the launch of rockets, and at the very same moment the lethal missiles dashed towards the ground from under my plane's wings. I pulled the control column and the *Sturmovik* obediently pulled out of the dive. Having dropped a batch of bombs, I switched the machine to climbing, and my aerial gunner *Starshina* Makosov began to strafe the Fascists rushing about below with his large-calibre machine-gun. Now that was an attack!

Having finished working over the target we turned back but at the very same moment the Messers pounced on us. One of their groups engaged our escort fighters, and another struck at the Ils. We formed a defensive circle stretched towards our lines. But there were only six of us against ten German fighters – the odds were clearly unequal. I saw two fighter-planes fall into the sea a bit aside from us: one with red stars, another with a black-and-white cross on its fuselage. Before my eyes an Il-2 hit the water and went to the bottom...

We had to hold out, hold out all costs! And we shot at those who were heedless, who slid forward and exposed their bellies to our cannons. One Fritz emitted smoke and pulled aside. One more was struck so badly that he went straight to the ground like a stone ...

The Messers retired, but the German flak guns opened up at us again. A scorching splinter of flak passed in front of my face, having pierced the Plexiglas cheek of the cockpit. Glancing back I saw blood on the reinforced glass panel separating me from the gunner's cockpit. Was Makosov wounded? And at the same time I felt the plane drifting to the right – the rudder control rods had been smashed. From bad to worse! My wingmen were on their way to the East, home, and my plane was no longer obeying me, it was turning west, towards the enemy. I felt shivers treacherously running down my spine ... I was on my own.

I strained all my strength and skills to straighten out my Il. And on top of that the skinnies', sensing easy prey, smothered me from all sides and kept peppering my badly damaged machine with the bursts of fire! Nevertheless, I managed to turn the *Sturmovik* towards our lines. The engine missed time and again but kept pulling, still pulling, holding on! Clenching my teeth, I held on too and keep steering my unruly machine. Losing altitude I flew at the lowest speed possible. The earth was coming closer and closer but I still needed to cross the Kerch Straits!

Suddenly I saw some objects fly up from the trenches. Hand grenades? No, not that – it was helmets, thrown up by our soldiers who were rapturously greeting my red-starred plane. They were happy for me, for the infantry's beloved *Sturmovik*. I'd made it to our lines after all. I'd made it after all …

When I was above the Straits our fighter planes came in time to drive my pursuers away. At last I saw my aerodrome and landed the machine on the run without closing in by the rules. I didn't care about the rules now: I just wanted to land my plane that was barely staying in the air!

…Silence. How wonderful silence on the ground can be! But what was that? My hands were bloody for some reason, and my blouse was bloody as well … It appears that I hadn't noticed being wounded by the shell splinter during the battle … And what about Makosov? He was alive, wounded but alive! My heart soared …

Airmen ran across the aerodrome field to my plane, an ambulance car with a red cross rolled at full speed, a tractor followed it to tow the crippled plane away from the airstrip as soon as possible. Swallowing tears I held onto its wing and whispered: "Thank you, my friend *Ilyusha*".

They put Makosov on a stretcher. He tried to get up and repeated over and over: "Comrade Lieutenant! Don't send me to hospital – let our doctor treat me. I'll recover soon and fly again. Don't get yourself a new gunner!"

"Alright, alright, Makosov", I calmed the gunner. "I'll ask them to treat you in our [Aerodrome Services] Battalion medical unit. Try to get well quickly. I'll wait for you!"

The next day I went to see my gunner and suddenly heard someone sobbing. I came closer and saw the gunsmith Dousya Nazarkina sitting on a shell crate and crying bitterly her face buried in her knees. "Someone's insulted her!" I thought, but then immediately rejected my assumption. Dousya was loved very much by everyone in the regiment. The frolicsome, cheerful and very hard-working armourer had become highly-regarded by everyone. It was sheer pleasure to look at her when she was hanging bombs and rockets loading cannons and machine-guns. Dousya would flash around a *Sturmovik* in her sun faded but always clean and ironed blouse, with extraordinary speed and deftness. I'm still puzzled how she managed to hang hundred-kilo bombs under the fuselage by herself. But Dousya used to joke: "I used to work at the 'Krasnyy Bogatyr' Works in Moscow before the war and even trained in a weight-lifting club!"

And now the 'weightlifter' was in tears … I shook Dousya by the shoulder but she did not respond. Then I sat next to her on the crate, took Dousya's head in both hands lifted it a bit and lay it on my knees. The field cap Dousya was squeezing in her hand was wet and crumpled. I silently stroked the armourer's head. About ten minutes elapsed, and then she, not wiping away her tears, began to tell me about her love for Serezha Bondarev Being a plane mechanic, he had flown today with the pilot Khmara as an aerial gunner They hadn't come back from the mission …

"I don't want to live without him! Just yesterday we told each other about our love kissed for the first time, and decided to get married when the war is over. And now he's no more. Serezha's killed!"

She fell on the ground moaning, covered her face with her hands and sobbed noiselessly I ran to the headquarters dugout, brought her water and liquid ammonia from the medicine kit. Dousya began to calm down little-by-little, and then suddenly shouted: "Comrade Lieutenant! Anna Alexandrovna! I request, I beg you, take me on as your aerial gunner I know all the aspect angles and estimations, I know the enemy planes' silhouettes, I'm a good shot. Take me on! I want to avenge Serezha!"

"But I have a gunner – Makosov", I said, perplexed by Dousya's unexpected request.

"But he's wounded. Will he be able to shoot after such a wound? His right hand's broken."

I began to talk Nazarkina out of it, told her how scary it was to fly in a *Sturmovik* as a gunner, how many of them get killed[1].

"We pilots are protected by armour", I tried to convince her, "but the gunner sits in front of a Fascist fighter-plane in an open cockpit. And your Serezha may still be alive. After all, you know many cases of our pilots and gunners "coming back from the dead.""

But Dosya seemed not to want to hear me: "Take me on! Support my application before the regiment command, I'll write the application now."

I failed to dissuade Nazarkina. And in about two weeks the head of the Corps Political Department Colonel Toupanov arrived, and the issue was decided: Dousya Nazarkina was appointed as aerial gunner in my crew. Thus the only all-female crew in ground-attack aviation was formed. Later I was to find out about another female crew for the *Sturmoviks* that had been formed in August 1944: it was made up by my abovementioned aeroclub friend Tamara Fedorovna Konstantinova (later Hero of the Soviet Union) and the aerial gunner Shoura Moukoseeva.

Back then I was sorry to part with my seasoned gunner, and he didn't want to go to another pilot. But an order is an order, and I obeyed it. I was to discover Makosov's fate only after the war. During the reunion of the veterans of the 230th Kuban Ground-Attack Aviation Division, Twice Hero of the Soviet Union Air Force Major-General G.F.Sivkov, who had fought in the 210th Aviation Regiment of our division approached me and said: "You had a great gunner in Kuban. He was assigned to our regiment after Nazarkina was appointed to join you."

"Makosov?" – I exclaimed gladly.

"Yes, Makosov. After the war your former aerial gunner quit the forces, got married and raised five sons with his spouse. But then what misfortune befell their grey heads. One of their boys was killed in action during the frontier conflict at the Ussury river in 1969[2]..."

And back then, in 1943, I began to fly with Dousya Nazarkina and was greatly surprised – from the very first combat sortie she handled her gunner's duties not the least bit worse than Makosov. I heard her voice in the intercom time and again. Dousya became my second pair of eyes. Occasionally through the reinforced glass separating our cockpits in which we sat back to back, I saw her operating her machine-gun. Its barrel would now lift up, now dip at an angle, spitting fire. I was lucky with gunners!

---

1   Editor's note – this is indeed true: the ratio of losses in *Sturmovik* pilots and gunners was about 1:5.

2   Translator's note – a conflict between the USSR and the People's Republic of China.

30

Off the front

The fighting near Taman had ceased: now we were attached to the 1st Byelorussian Front. The relocation of the regiment to Karlovka near Poltava went without incident. As usual, the HQ and the technical personnel met us with a prepared airfield, parking lots, and billets for the airmen.

Somewhere in those parts Peter the Great defeated the Swedes.[1] And just recently our troops had smashed a large Hitlerite force here. For our training, the HQ found us a natural bombing range near the ancient Russian redoubts, where the rubble of abandoned enemy materiel remained. They built an observation tower there, marked the trenches with wooden dummy 'soldiers', installed wooden 'cannons'. On this dummy enemy defence line there were also tanks marked with crosses, and vehicles.

Over the period of our action over Taman, our regiment had been reinforced by planes and flying personnel three times. And now a new reinforcement arrived – many new pilots, whom we would have to get into shape: to teach them how to bomb, to shoot to seek out targets – in other words, all we'd been taught once upon a time by the veterans of the ground-attack regiment at the Ogni aerodrome. Experienced, though not battle hardened pilots had arrived in our 3rd Squadron. All of them had come from the Far East: Stepanov, Sherstobitov, Khomyakov, Ladygin, Ivnitskiy, Khoukhlin, Moustafaev Kirillov, Evteev, Ivanov, Tsvetkov, Konyakhin … We – the 'oldies' – did not enjoy working with the youngsters. Leaving the frontline we had hoped to have a short rest in the rear Attacks on the bombing range dummies with cement bombs did not make the seasoned front-liners enthusiastic, and for the younger guys these exercises were only a continuation of their boring school lessons. They were striving to go to the front too. Only once did I come across a pilot who didn't want to fly. I asked him: "Tell me honestly, what's your problem?" And he said: "I'm afraid". That pilot was released from the regiment … But in general the mood was: "Let's go to the front!" We would fly with the young pilots in two-seaters two or three times – they were mostly well-trained, but it was required that they study the plane in detail! Moreover, many of them were used to open cockpits, but the Il's cockpit was closed, and at first one felt sort of boxed in. We also got clumsy ones and we had to 'polish' them up. You would fly with them time and again, they would do their best but there would still be big problems …

There were changes in the regiment: an order was issued for the appointment of "the Regimental Navigator Major Karev Petr Timofeevich as Deputy Commander of the 805th Ground-Attack Aviation Regiment, Lieutenant Egorova Anna Alexandrovna as Navigator of the same regiment". I was still a Lieutenant but this was a lieutenant colonel's position! This promotion horrified me and I rushed to the commander "to sort it out". Not long before, Kozin had visited his family somewhere in the deep rear. Upon his return he showed me a photo of his daughter. Wide-open trusting childish eyes, very

---

1 Editor's note – in this area the historic battle of Poltava, between Peter the Great's army and the Swedish army of Charles XII, took place in 1709.

similar to her father's, two plaits, a kerchief tied under her chin, looked at me from the picture. "The heiress!" Mikhail Nikolaevich said laughing.

We loved our commander very much. A gallant pilot, fair to his subordinates and strict in moderation, he carried in him so much vivacity, joy, sincere gaiety! 'Batya' (Daddy) was what we called him between ourselves in our friendly collective. He sang with us, danced, shared griefs … Showing me the photo of his daughter Mikhail Nikoilaevich confided: "You know, Lieutenant, when my wife found out that there was a female airman in the regiment, she became jealous."

"Let her be like that. It's good sometimes", the regiment *zampolit*[2] Dmitriy Polikarpovich Svydkiy, appointed to replace the fallen Ignashov, laughed then.

It seemed, after Ignashov, who had won great respect in the regiment for his tactfulness, after his kind treatment of people and his fidelity to principle, that the new *zampolit* would find it hard to gain people's confidence and win the same level of fondness and respect from the personnel. But time went by and Dmitriy Polikarpovich, while still a combat flyer, won many people over. He had a marvellous feature – he knew whom to say an encouraging word to, whom to rebuke, whom to praise. And he would do all that at the proper time without delaying till tomorrow, and somehow inconspicuously and tactfully. And flying combat sorties with one or another group and frequently finding himself in difficult situations, Shvidkiy certainly knew the aspirations and the mood of the airmen.

Debriefing of combat sorties had changed its character after Shvidkiy's arrival in our unit. Whereas before we had spoken mostly about the accuracy of our strikes now we began to talk more about the pilots' actions, their fortitude, initiative, battle tactics. Dmitriy Polikarpovich paid a lot of attention to combat camaraderie and cohesion. Our new *zampolit* liked to repeat Suvorov's words "Perish yourself but rescue your comrade!" – how that was to reverberate around in the regiment I will tell of later …

But in the meantime I had to talk to the Regiment's Commander about my new appointment and I walked down into the headquarters dugout. "Comrade Commander, may I address you?" I pronounced, saluting according to the regulations.

"You may", Kozin nodded in agreement and glanced at me somewhat reproachfully.

"What have you appointed me Regimental Navigator for? I won't handle it. I'll be a laughing stock! There's Berdashkevich, the 2nd Squadron Commander, there's Soukhoroukov, Vakhramov. It'll be handier for them to be Navigator of a male regiment!"

"Have you said your piece?" The lieutenant-colonel asked brusquely. "Then about turn and march! Double-quick to carry out your Regiment Navigator duties. And don't bring this matter up to me again."

Now in my new capacity I ran training with the flying personnel: sometimes I would direct an 'attack' by radio from the bombing range observation tower. My duty was to make sure everyone had their maps in order. During preparation for a mission I had to make a meticulous study, tell the airmen how we'd be flying, where the targets would be, what we were going to bomb. That's preparation for a sortie too. I began to like the navigator's duties a bit too, they grew on me. After all, I had graduated from the Kherson Aviation School as a navigator, when working in the Kalinin aeroclub I used to teach aerial navigation for several hours a week, I had done a navigator's course in Stavropol. In a word, knowing about my navigator's 'classes' and taking into account my combat experience

---

2   Translator's note – a deputy commander in political affairs.

the regimental commanders had not appointed me for the position by an accident. Apart from that I was promoted to the rank of Senior Lieutenant.

So, here I was standing on the tower, and there was such a wonderful panorama around me! The planes were taxiing over the green carpet of the airfield, from the Poltava side the American 'Fortresses'[3] were taking off to bomb the common foe. A small river was visible not far off, one of Peter the Great's redoubts towered just nearby, and skylarks completely filled the sky …

The telephone rang. I took the receiver and heard the voice of the flight controller: "Get ready, taking off shortly!"

The radio-station's engine under the tower began to work. I took the microphone, blew into it for convention's sake and spoke: "Hallo! Hallo! Hallo! 'Birch' here! Do you hear there?" "'Mignonette-2' here"! 'Mignonette-2' here"! I hear you loud and clear. Request two hundred …"

'Mignonette-2' was Major Karev's callsign, and two hundred was permission to carry out bombing and ground attack. I'd always wondered why Regimental Signals Commander Matyshenko gave the men call signs like 'Mignonette', 'Violet', 'Lilac', 'Volga'[4]. And once he gave me the call-sign 'Hawk' – enough to make a cat laugh!

A group of *Sturmoviks* was already over the training ground – it made a circuit and steeply dived on a target. The pilots carefully caught the targets in their gun-sights and shot short bursts at the scattered dummies, then dropped bombs and circled to gain altitude. Karev, Mignonette-2, calmly gave orders and carefully watched every pilot's work.

"Khoikhlin! Reduce your diving angle …"

"Ageev! Don't fall behind …"

"Tsvetkov! Slow your plane down or you'll shoot ahead of the group."

"Well-done, Kirillov!"

The voice of Mignonette-2 flew over the training ground and, seeing Karev's painstaking work with the young pilots, I involuntarily thought of that steadfast man with deep respect, remembering my flights with him over Taman. I have never seen a bolder and more gallant flyer over the battlefield than Karev.

After repeating the pass, Karev's group retired towards the aerodrome.

"Birch, Mignonette-17 here, Mignonette-17 here …" A different voice was heard now from the microphone. "Permission for two hundred?"

"Granted!"

And suddenly I heard: "Birchie, are your teeth bothering you?" I did indeed have a toothache. I was standing on the tower with a bandaged cheek, but I furiously cut off the insolent son of the airwaves: "Mignonette-17, mind your own business! Reduce your angle!"

But the pilot didn't obey and dropped his bombs diving at a steep angle.

"Mignonette-17! Stop acting willfully! Otherwise I'll shut the down the range!"

"Roger", the pilot replied gaily and closed in for another attack. You had to admit, he attacked the target deftly, but then he left the range descending, hedge-hopping, leaving a Ukrainian song behind him:

You played a trick on me,
You've gone and let me down,
You've gone and turned me,

3   American B-17 Flying Fortresses flying missions over Eastern Europe sometimes used Poltava.
4   Translator's note – words of the feminine gender in Russian.

From a boy into a clown.

By now I knew the pilot was Lieutenant Ivan Pokashevskiy. That fellow with the broad face and mop of dark hair and mischievous grey eyes had stood out among the newcomers. He was out of uniform: on top of an old-fashioned blouse and civilian trousers he had a wool-lined jacket, worn, seasoned jackboots, an ear-flapped cap set on the back of his head – just about to fall off … Ivan told us he had been shot down in combat and taken prisoner. When the Fritzes were taking the POW airmen to Germany he and two of his comrades broke a hole in the wagon floor and at night time leaped out of the moving train. They then ran into the woods where they managed to find the partisans. Pokashevskiy fought alongside the partisans for seven months and was even awarded the Order of the Red Star. Then the airmen were transferred to Moscow and assigned to aviation units, and thus Ivan found himself in our regiment. When his father learned his son was alive (he and his mother had received the death notice a year before) he sold his bee-hives and bought an aircraft with the proceeds. Ivan's father very much wanted his son to fly that plane: he reckoned it would be safer that way.

Pokashevskiy was fitted out in our regiment and appointed as a pilot to the 2nd Squadron. And then his father – Ivan Potapovich Pokashevskiy – arrived in Karlovka and brought with him his eldest son Vladimir – a *sovkhoz*[5] director.

"Let my laddies serve in your unit", he said to the regimental commander trustingly, in Ukrainian. "Volod'ka[6] has been in 'armour'[7] as irreplaceable – enough is enough! It's time he does his duty! But only on one condition – don't make it cushy for my sons, put the heat on them like it says to in the Army Regulations …"

The weather was wonderful that day. There was not a single cloud in the blue sky, the sun was as warming as in summer. A lot of people were gathered at the aerodrome – locals from Karlovka and the neighbouring villages with banners and portraits of Party and State leaders, and the heroes of the occasion themselves. And there, aside from the other planes, stood a brand-new *Sturmovik* with an inscription on the fuselage 'To the Pokashevkiy sons – from their Father'.

The head of the Division's Political Department Lieutenant-Colonel I.M.Dyachenko and the Pokashevskiy family climbed up on the plane's wing. The sons helped their father to get up on it and stood next to him: Ivan to the right, Vladimir to the left. The meeting was opened by Dyachenko who had two Orders of the Red Banner on his chest. Ivan Mironovich had been badly wounded defending Moscow, and after that the doctors ruled him out of flying operations.

Dyachenko spoke passionately and excitedly about the *kolkhoznik*[8] Pokashevskiy's patriotic deed, about the coming battles and our future Victory. Then he let Ivan Potapovich have the floor. The old man gave a start and was just about to step forward, but his sons held him back so to stop him tumbling from the wing. And he said only two words: "Brothers and sisters!" and there he fell silent. His sons leant towards him and said something, apparently encouraging him … I would long remember that simple

---

5   Translator's note – a state-owned collective farm in the USSR.
6   Translator's note – diminutive form of Vladimir.
7   Translator's note – a slang word for exemption from military service.
8   Translator's note – collective farmer.

peasant's short speech in Ukrainian: "I've got two sons. I'm giving them away to my dear Fatherland[9]. I'd like to join you beating the invaders but I'm a bit past it..."

The old fellow wanted to say something else but, unable to cope with the emotions that had engulfed him, waved his hand, bowed from the waist in all four directions and kissed his sons three times. Uproar and applause from the whole crowd, – and the orchestra took up a flourish. "Chair him, chair him!" a cry came from the crowd and they picked the old man up in their arms.

From that day on Ivan and Vladimir Pokashevskiy were assigned as the crew of their dad's plane: Ivan as pilot and Vladimir as aerial gunner. And now I was watching through my binoculars: the bombing range team was checking the results of the Pokashevskiys' work – excellent! All the hits were on target! Suddenly a *Sturmovik* flew up and approached the range without my permission. "Birch's here! Birch's here!" I said rapidly. "Advise who's flying over the range?"

There was no reply, and by now the plane was already making a turn and diving at our tower. Had he gone mad? He seemed to have confused the 'T' sign on the tower with a cross on the range. "Everyone to the trenches!" I ordered and saw the two-way-station driver, a technician and someone else throw themselves into the trench.

A bomb exploded: the blast wave swept away a tent standing nearby and rocked the tower – bomb splinters also hit it full on. For some reason I grabbed not the rails but the microphone and the telephone, and rushed here and there with them, shouting:

"Signaller! Send a red flare, a flare! Send him away from the range!"

The flares soared. The pilot understood his error and retired. Well, he hadn't done a bad job at all – it was just a pity that it had not been on the right target. But ... training is training!

The next group was led to the range by the *comesk* Captain Berdashkevich – a kindhearted Byelorussian from Polotzk. Misha was heartbroken: his father, a partisan, had been killed in action, and his mother had been shot for her partisan connections.

"Flak from the right!" setting the scenario for his group, and the novices conducted an anti-flak manoeuvre, changing both their altitude and course. "Out of the sun, right – four Fokkers!" The leader's voice was heard again, and the whole group rearranged itself into a defensive circle.

A 'life-buoy', as we called such a circle, is a variety of battle order worked out for defending against Messers. Let's assume that an enemy fighter tries to attack our *Sturmovik* – then a plane following him along the circle is in a position to cut the attacker off with his frontal fire. We may pounce on targets from this circle too – I saw twelve *Sturmoviks* already diving, their rockets darting at the ground, and a ripple explosion resounded mightily over the area. Then cannon and machine-gun fire destroyed the targets and, at the moment of pulling out of the dive, bombs separated from all the aircraft at once. When the dust settled I saw no targets through the binoculars ...

May flew by imperceptibly. The young pilots had learned to shoot and bomb accurately, and begun to keep formation not only when flying straight but also when manoeuvring. They'd learned to attack targets in groups up to a squadron in size. Now the regiment was ready to take off to the front and at last we received approval. The 197th Ground Attack Division, which now included our 805th Ground Attack Aviation Regiment, had

---

9   Editor's note – in Russian, one would say 'motherland'.

just been formed. It was destined to join the 6th Aerial Army commanded by General F.P.Polynin: we knew that we would fight as part of the 1st Byelorussian Front.

The 197th Ground Attack Aviation Division was commanded by Colonel V.A.Timofeev. Many pilots remembered him from aviation schools such as Postavskoye and, during the war, Orenburgskoye, which he had been in charge of. When Timofeev was introducing himself to the flying personnel he seemed to me to bear some resemblance to a Tsarist officer as they had been shown in the movies. His tunic and breeches were strictly fitted to his figure, the box-calf jackboots with high heels and knee caps shone as if lacquered, there were leather gloves on his hands.

"You can tell straightaway: he's from the rear", said my plane's mechanic Gorobets, standing next to me.

"No! Don't you see, the Colonel's got the Order of Lenin and a 'XX years of the RKKA'[10] medal on his chest?" Pilot Zoubov objected. "He fought on the Kursk Salient, was a Deputy Division Commander there. And he received his Order of Lenin back in pre-war times in Transbaikalia. He was in charge of an aviation brigade after graduating from the Air Force Academy and made it the best in drill preparation in Blucher's[11] Far East Army."

"Why are you mentioning Blucher? He was an enemy of the people, after all!"

"He was no enemy of the people at all", "Misha declared stubbornly. "He was a real people's hero: my own uncle – my mum's brother – a *kombrig*[12] used to tell me about him when I was a kid – and I believed him and still do. And Timofeev, by the way, was arrested in 1938 too and spent two years in Chita prison before he was released as a baselessly victimized man, restored in his rights and appointed head of an aviation school. Shvernik[13] himself – a teacher of Vyacheslav Arsenievich – backed him! But apparently there was no one to stand up for Blucher …"

"They say Timofeev fought during the Civil War?" someone asked Zoubov.

"He did. He was a scout on the Eastern Front, then a Deputy Commissar in the 15th Inzenskiy Regiment."

"How do you know all that?"

"How could I not know? I was a flying cadet at the Orenburg School. Vyacheslav Arsenievich used to tell us about the Civil War, gave very interesting lectures."

"What about?"

"Various things – I'd never heard anything of the kind before. And how to hold your knife and fork properly, how to smoke elegantly without leaving marks on your fingers. We were taught how to dance and how to invite a partner to a dance."

"What's this, the war had been on for two years and you were learning to dance?" Tolya Bougrov, a pilot with extensive burn scars on his face, asked angrily.

"Maybe, he also taught you how to choose a good wife?" Zhenya Berdnikov grinned.

"Sto-o-op the chatter!" The regimental Chief-of-Staff Major Kouznetsov loudly cut off our *sotto-voce* conversation, and everyone fell silent. Such was our introduction to Vyacheslav Arsenievich Timofeev …

---

10 Translator's note – abbreviation for the Workers and Peasants Red Army.
11 Translator's note – one of the Soviet Marshals executed during Stalin's purges in 1937.
12 Translator's note – brigade commander.
13 Translator's note – one of the senior members of the Soviet Government.

The 197th Ground Attack Aviation Division successfully relocated to the Byelorussian aerodromes. The weather wasn't spoiling us those days. A layer of thick fog lay dolefully over the airfield, and the *Sturmoviks*, having taxied out to the start point, had to turn their engines off. But then the wind blew and dispersed all the misty haze. The airmen of our division took off on combat missions one group after another. The *Sturmoviks* were bombing the vanguard of the enemy's defences, neutralising the enemy's artillery fire, blocking them on the roads, burning vehicles and tanks, wiping out infantry … Our routine work had started.

We co-operated with the famed General Chuikov's Army (the 8th Guards)[14] – from the Czartorysk field aerodrome. It seemed to us, the airmen, to be a bit quieter over here after the fighting over Taman and the Kerch Peninsula, but it was far away from being so. On one sortie Captain Berdashkevich was leading a group of nine *Sturmoviks* to the target. They'd been given a complicated mission – to destroy a ford on the Bug river, and thus to impede the retreat of the enemy troops. Misha had meticulously 'played out' the whole route with the pilots: he had shown it them on the map, scribbled on the ground with a twig the distinctive landmarks, the flak guns' estimated positions. Then each of the wingmen repeated the 'flight', and only when Berdashkevich had made sure that everyone had understood everything, did he order: "Off to your planes!"

On approach to the target the pilots heard his calm and gentle voice again: "Safety locks off. Spread out, keep freer …" "Manoeuvring, guys! Manoeuvring!" Berdashkevich ordered and in a dive threw his machine at the ford.

The others followed him and the target was carpeted by bombs. But fiery tracer from the ground criss-crossed over the *Sturmoviks*. The pilot Khoukhlin's plane somewhat clumsily, as if unwillingly, aimlessly, with a smashed wing and a destroyed stabilizer climbed up, and then abruptly lowered its nose and went towards the ground with a dead engine. Nevertheless, Khoukhlin managed to straighten out and then land the badly damaged Il-2 on a small, crater-pitted field beyond the ford on the enemy side – and the Hitlerites rushed towards the *Sturmovik* from all sides like carrion crows. The group leader Berdashkevich saw all this, and sent the remaining eight Ils to help his wingmen. The *Sturmoviks* diving one after another were beating off the Hitlerites surrounding our plane, and Andrey Konyakhin – a faithful and inseparable friend of Victor Khoukhlin – closed in for landing where the shot up *Sturmovik* stood.

Konyakhin's plane touched down very close to the Khoukhlin's Il, jolted over humps and bumps and stopped. The Fascists, scenting a double prize, rushed into another attack, but Berdashkevich and his group drove them off again. In the meantime Andrey, defending himself from the closely pressing submachine-gunners, was firing his plane's cannons and machine-guns at them, but his trails of fire were going too high, missing the enemy. Then Konyakhin's aerial gunner leaped out and … lifted the *Sturmovik*'s tail with a superhuman effort! The pilot now began shooting at the Hitlerites on target. In the meantime Khoukhlin set fire to his badly damaged Il, ran to his friend's plane and climbed into the rear cockpit with his gunner. Konyakhin turned his machine around, gave it full gas and a boost, and the *Sturmovik* rushed at the panicked Hitlerite sub-machine-gunners and then climbed into the sky.

---

14   Translator's note – this Army distinguished itself during the Battle of Stalingrad.

Later Andrey told how after the take-off he began to doubt whether he had enough fuel to make it home. He glanced back at the gunner's cockpit and went numb – two legs were sticking out of it next to the machine-gun! Dumbfounded, he didn't understand at first that it was his own gunner, who had jumped into the already occupied cockpit on the run and had not managed to turn around in the tight space – he'd got stuck upside-down.

After the landing the engine stalled. Everyone who was at the aerodrome rushed to the motionless *Sturmovik*. They pulled one aerial gunner from the rear cockpit, then the other, then the pilot. Konyakhin was sitting in his cockpit, pale, his head thrown back on the protective screen, his eyes closed, his wet curly hair stuck to his temples. Major Karev was the first to rush to him and began to kiss him. Then, straight from the plane wing, he addressed his regiment comrades excitedly: "Comrades! The pilot Konyakhin has adhered to the great commander Suvorov's precept: "Perish yourself but rescue your comrade!" He's observed this commandment three times – he's brought his *Sturmovik* back to the aerodrome, saved his friend and stayed alive himself! Let's chair the hero!"

The pilots and gunners pulled Konyakhin out of the cockpit and carried him over to the headquarters dugout on their hands. The next day photojournalists from the Army and Front-level newspapers arrived unexpectedly. They wanted to photograph Andrey, but he hid from them and sent his total refusal via a friend: "They won't get me! This is a combat airfield, not a photo studio and I'm not gonna pose."

So, a piece in the paper was published without Konyakhin's portrait. Later I became a witness of this dialogue between the friends: "You're still alive?" Konyakhin asked Khoukhlin.

"I am, but how come they haven't shot you down yet? They should have smacked you with shrapnel you-know-where to make you go to bed on time and not sit up late with Katyusha from the field ambulance."

The city of Kovel was liberated from the Germans by July 7. Following that, we relocated to one of its aerodromes situated in the area. Once on a new field, I was immediately ordered to make a reconnaissance mission over the enemy's communications, to detect his troop concentrations and to record that on a photo film accordingly. After taking off, I passed over the next airfield to join the fighters about to cover me. A couple were already waiting for me with their engines running. While I was circling the field, they took off and started climbing up. I quickly established a radio link with a flight leader of the fighters and without catching my breath ordered:

"I will run both a visual recon and make some photos. Please do not move far away from me – keep me covered. Is that clear? Receiving!"

Usually on such occasions the leader would of the fighters reply: "Understood!" and either repeat the task or specify if something was unclear. But this time after a short pause, there was a hoarse young tenor, full of sarcasm: "Hey, you, a 'hunchback'! Why are you screeching like a milksop?" And after some silence he added with annoyance: "And you pretend to be a *Sturmovik* pilot? It is disgusting to hear you!"

In the end, the fighter pilot attached a salty word.

The offensive 'milksop' outraged me! In a fit of temper I wanted to respond in a similar manner, but managed to hold myself in check. After all, they didn't even suspect that they were subordinate to a 'milksop'. So after a minute I resumed my high spirits.

I had carried out the task successfully and on my way home contacted the guidance station, reporting the situation in the reconnoitred area. A familiar officer from the guidance station thanked me for the intelligence data with the words: "Thank you, Annoushka!" And it was then, when the fighters went mad. They started an amazing performance around my plane! One would make a 'barrel' turn; another would roll over his wing! After calming down a bit, they rejoined my Ilyushin closely and, vying with each other, began to cheer me from their cockpits waving their arms. Flying past their aerodrome I thanked the fighter pilots in farewell: "Thank you, brothers! Go and land! I'll make it home on my own now …"

But my 'bodyguards' accompanied me to our very aerodrome. Only after seeing me land did they circle our field, waggle the wings of their planes and vanish over the horizon. I was reporting 'mission accomplished' to the commander at the CP when I noticed something. Yes, everybody was listening to my report, but first smiling – and then suddenly bursting into a laugh. "Lieutenant Egorova has started bringing her admirers straight to her base!" Karev genially commented on the event. The pilots laughed, and I laughed too, pleased with the successful reconnaissance. I had come back without a scratch.

31

Fighting after a lull

Polesie[1] was now behind us, and our army moved forward liberating long-suffering Poland. Fields with narrow strips of unharvested rye, stretching from one farmstead to another like streamers, shot past under the wings of my *Sturmovik*. I could see villages with roofs covered with shingles, *Kościóls*[2], wooden crosses at every road intersection.

We were on our way to attack the enemy reserves near the City of Chełm. On the radio I heard the voice of our group leader, Regiment Commander Kozin: "Egorova! On the right there are disguised artillery pieces in the shrubs. Strafe the scum with your cannons!"

I made a steep right turn, switched the plane to diving, pinpointed the target and opened fire. And at the same moment German ack-ack went to work blocking our way. "Vakhramov!" The commander ordered, ignoring the call-signs. "Give it to the battery with your rockets!" This was an ordinary combat operation. On the road near Chełm there was a mechanized column: armored cars, tank-cars, trucks and tanks …

"Manoeuvring, guys, manoeuvring …" The leader reminded us and led into the attack from a turn. "Aim well and fire!"

Strips of smoke stretched from the ground towards our machines – it was the small-calibre guns that had opened fire, and quadruple-barrel flak guns began chattering. I'd have liked to turn a bit and send a couple of bursts at them, but an armoured car loomed in my gun-sight too alluringly. And it would have been too late – we had already rushed past them.

We closed in for the second pass having lost our group's rearguard, Victor Andreev. A guy from Saratov – reticent, unsmiling but kind-hearted and respected by all as the best 'hunter' in the regiment – he used to fly as Volodya Sokolov's partner. Volodya had not come back from the previous 'hunt': a shell hit his plane, and the *Sturmovik*, chopping the trees with its propeller and cutting them down, fell into the forest behind enemy lines. And today we'd lost Andreev …

We gained altitude for bombing. There were more and more black bursts in the sky, but paying no attention we dropped our bombs. It was time to pull out of our dive but the leader continued his rapid rush towards the ground. Suddenly there was a volley of flak, and Kozin's plane seemed to stop in the air. Something blazed up for a second, and his *Sturmovik* crashed in a midst of enemy vehicles. A huge pillar of fire shot up …

It is hard to convey in words now the state that engulfed us in those moments. We were violently throwing ourselves into one pass after another. It seemed there was no force that could stop us! Only after expending all our ammunition did we leave the battlefield – and no more shots came at us from the ground. The crews came back without any coordination, one at a time. We felt bitter guilt inside – we had failed to protect our Batya … We were met gloomily at the aerodrome – the fighter pilots had already

---

1   Translator's note – a woodland in Byelorussia.
2   Translator's note – Polish Roman-Catholic churches.

145

despatched the terrible news by radio. Usually the plane mechanics greeted us delightedly, but today, with tears in their eyes.

The Regimental Commander's mechanic sobbed violently, and not knowing how to make himself busy was throwing about the caponier tools, blocks, plane covers and whatever came into his hot hands. Men moved spontaneously from all stations towards the Regimental CP. The Chief-of-Staff came out of the dugout, stepped up on a shell crate lying nearby and said: "Comrades! The Regiment's Commander would not be pleased with us. Where's your combat spirit? Where's the battle readiness of the regiment? A terrible war is on! We can't forget about it. I ask you to disperse to your places. The airmen of the 3rd Squadron – stay for a combat mission assignment. We will avenge our dead: Mikhail Nikolaevich Kozin, Victor Andreev and our other comrades who have made the supreme sacrifice for their motherland"…

Our assumption that conditions would be quieter than over Taman had not been justified. On the second day after the death of the Regiment Commander, Ivan Pokashevskiy was killed together with his aerial gunner, Hero of the Soviet Union Junior Lieutenant Ivan Efremenko. It was a reconnaissance flight. Pokashevskiy's brother Vladimir had fallen ill and hadn't flown that day. The observers from the guidance station told us later that a lonely *Sturmovik* with the inscription 'To the Pokashevkiy sons – from their Father' across the fuselage leaped over the frontline just above the ground, made a steep climb and disappeared behind the lower edge of the clouds. Enemy flak guns struck, the shooting was heard to move away from the frontline into the depths of the German defence and then die away. Some time elapsed, and the pilot transmitted that he had seen camouflaged self-propelled guns and tanks in such and such a quadrant – and that the enemy was obviously drawing up his reserves. Soon all the enemy arms rattled again, pouncing at the *Sturmovik* coming back from scouting. The pilot gave as good as he got – he dived, and then his cannons and machine-guns worked furiously, the rockets left from under his wings like thunderbolts.

They began to worry at the guidance station: why the pilot had engaged in combat?

"Vistula-5, finish up!" They transmitted to Ivan's radio, and suddenly saw the *Sturmovik* begin a slow (like that of a wounded man) turn towards its lines. The tip of his left wing was bent up, there was a huge hole in the right one, and the rudder had been torn off together with the antenna which was now dangling behind the tail. Pokashevskiy's plane was descending lower and lower – Ivan was trying to drag his machine over to our side. He made it over the frontline, and immediately his plane crashed on the ground, with a thunderclap …

Group after group of *Sturmoviks* took off that day to destroy the enemy tanks Lieutenant Pokashevskiy had managed to report on. The first sixer was led by Victor Gourkin with the aerial gunner Berdnikov. Prior to the sortie he addressed the airmen:

"Let's avenge the death of our comrades-in-arms – the two Ivans. Death to the Fascists! To your planes!"

Ivan Soukhoroukov led a group of the same size, following Gourkin, and I led the third one to attack the tanks. We destroyed the Hitlerites' tank column, and every pass we made in that battle was dedicated to the memory of our comrades, who had made the supreme sacrifice for the liberation of the land of Poland …

32

Poland

The 1st Army of the *Wojsko Polskie*[1] which had been formed on the basis of the Tadeusz Kosciuszko[2] 1st Polish Division, was initially raised in May 1943. The Polish National Liberation Committee was formed in the Polish City of Chełm, which we used to fly to for strafing and bombing. Following the liberation of the cities of Lublin and Dęblin our 6th Ground Attack Aviation Corps was given the honorary title 'Lublinskiy', while the 197th Ground Attack Aviation Division (which included our 805th regiment) – 'Demblinskaya'.

One of Hitler's death camps, Majdanek, where a million and a half women, children, elderly people and POWs had died, was located in Lublin. Delegations from many units visited Majdanek, and so did representatives of our regiment. We saw with our own eyes the gas chambers, in which the Hitlerite butchers had been exterminating people. I remember us entering long barracks and standing petrified: piles of children's footware of different sizes lay in front of us, ladies' handbags from the mothers killed with their children ... I couldn't hold back the sobs, and I wasn't alone ... When we returned to the regiment a meeting was summoned. At first all honoured the memory of the dead with a minute of silence, then my comrades made short speeches calling for the ruthless struggle against the enemy!

After completing the operation our regiment relocated. Now we were based near the Polish town of Parczew. The hostess of the apartment in which Dousya and I were billeted, Pani Juzefa, met us every day with a jug of milk. On the spot, on the doorstep, she would pour a glass for each of us and ask us to drink it. Then the host would appear – a tall and proud Pole in homespun clothes – and would also insist we drink it. It was impossible to refuse, the more so when our hosts treated us to big lumps of cottage cheese.

Once I came back from the aerodrome alone, and my hostess met me with frightened eyes: "*Matka Boska!*[3] Virgin Mary! Where is *Panenka*[4] Dousya?" she exclaimed in alarm.

"Dousya is delayed at the aerodrome. She's the orderly at headquarters today", I lied, trying not to look at the Polish woman.

Pani Juzefa began to blow her nose into her apron and hurriedly wipe her eyes, and crossed herself. As for me, I rushed out of the house – my heart was so unbearably heavy: that day Dousya Nazarkina did not make it back from a flight ...

It so happened that our commissar (as we, in the old style, called our *zampolit* Shvidkiy) had flown on a combat mission in my plane, and taken my aerial gunner. The pilots with whom he had flown, and the group leader Berdashkevich, reported after returning form the mission that the commissar, not having reached the target, had turned away, and none had seen him since ...

---

1   Translator's note – Polish Armed Forces fighting on the Soviet-German Front.
2   Translator's note – a Polish, Belorussian and American national hero, 1746-1817.
3   Translator's note – mother of God.
4   Translator's note – little Miss.

A plane was dispatched to search for them, but Shvidkiy and Nazarkina were not found. The next night they came back to the regiment – worn out but unharmed. It turned out that when they were approaching the target the *Sturmovik*'s engine began to play up. Shvidkiy managed to turn the machine around and glide down to our territory. He landed the machine on a marsh near a lake. They barely got out of there … "Anna Alexandrovna!" Dousya appealed to me. "I only want to fly with you. Don't give me away to anyone anymore!"

"Alright, Dousya, alright", I calmed her. "Just don't be angry at the Major. It could have happened to any pilot!"

But after the unsuccessful flight with the *zampolit* Dousya was clearly upset: "The regiment has people capable of flying combat missions. Let him deal with his ground stuff!"

I did not agree with her: from my point of view when a political officer flew himself, he could better understand a pilot's soul and all the hardships of his work. There had been cases: a *Sturmovik* pilot returned from a mission, and not yet chilled out after combat, having suffered badly himself, losing a comrade, might commit some breach of discipline on the ground, make a simple blunder – and he would be slated! And how vexing it was for a pilot when the political officers couldn't understand him and on top of that would give him instructions on flying techniques, knowing nothing about it! No, Dousya was wrong: our ground attack regiment was really lucky that our *zampolit* was a combat airman.

On 20 August 1944 we had no combat missions in the morning. By tradition we were going to celebrate our aviation holiday, Air Force Day, and Aerodrome Services Battalion Commander Belousov suggested we utilise Count Zheltowsky's estate for this purpose. Just recently a conference of the pilots of our division and fighter pilots had taken place on this estate. They had discussed co-operation – providing cover to the *Sturmoviks*, mutual aid, tactical skills.

Adjusting his tunic with its two Orders of Lenin, our Division Commander Colonel V.A. Timofeev was first to take the floor: "We have analysed the combat operations of the regiments. It looks like we've lost more planes from the enemy's anti-aircraft artillery fire than from their fighters. It happens this way because our crews make themselves ready to encounter with the enemy fighter planes, they know all their silhouettes, and the escort fighters help us properly during sorties. And yet we give in to the flak guns: the *Sturmoviks* are not always ready for their salvos. I reckon", the *comdiv*[5] continued, "it is essential the pilots study before each sortie the enemy's anti-aircraft defences around the targets. To do this Headquarters and the Operations Department must prepare intelligence data for the future target areas."

Major P.T. Karev, acting as Regimental Commander after the death of M.N. Kozin, said that the escort fighters were always alert for the foe, beat off their attacks on *Sturmoviks*, and gave no quarter to the Messers or Focke-Wulfs. But there were times when they failed to guess the enemy's intentions, engaged a diversionary group, and in the meantime another would pounce on the *Sturmoviks* with impunity …

I was given the floor as well, and as an example I told about the combat sortie of a sixer I had led to smash enemy materiel and manpower in the area of Puławy. Whilst we were operating over the target making one pass after another, the escort fighters had been carried away in a dogfight against a group of Messerschmitts somewhere off to the side. We

---

5   Translator's note – division commander.

had already finished up and pulled away from the target when a pack of stalking Focke-Wulfs attacked us. We would have been in trouble if two La-5 fighters had not appeared. They struck at the Fokkers from above and attacked them with such determination that soon they shot down two of them, and two others trailed smoke and retired to their lines.

"As a woman", I pointed out, "I feel uncomfortable asking men not to abandon me. And it's even more annoying when they desert me!"

"You shouldn't pretend to be poorer than you are", Misha Berdashkevich whispered to me, when I'd taken my seat. "Do you remember how our fighters protected you over Taman? There was even an order distributed throughout the Army about 'chit-chat in the air', and the example they brought was: "Anechka![6] Don't go too far ...""

Indeed, there was such a case. Back then I was leading a group towards the Choushka Spit and decided to converge on a target from the rear. The fighters' leader Volodya Istrashkin thought I had got lost, and somewhat courteously, in the old style, started a conversation with me by radio ...

Our conference on the Count's estate lasted for five hours, and then there was a concert of real artists. After much effort they'd been 'acquired' from our Army by the Head of the Division's Political Department.

Fear is typical of all people, but not all are capable of suppressing it. I had never seen dismay amongst my regimental comrades during combat, nor had I seen the traces of ordinary human weakness on the faces of pilots or gunners. They knew how to protect themselves from it with a smile, a joke, a song ... So, the pilots had prepared an amateur concert for our holiday. Each squadron had worked out solo pieces. A song written in the 7th Guards Ground Attack Aviation Regiment back at Taman was particularly beloved in the regiment. The regimental navigator, Hero of the Soviet Union V. Emelyanenko, formerly a conservatorium student, had written music for it. He was a marvellous man, a superb pilot and a great commander.[7] The refrain of the song was as follows:

Hey, *Ilyusha*, friend of mine
Let's attack them one more time!

But the *Sturmoviks'* feast at the Count's manor came to nothing. Already at mid-day the airmen of the division were beating off violent German attacks at the Magnuszew bridgehead on the other side of the Vistula south of Warsaw, where Chuikov's Guards were containing the enemy's onslaught. The support of *Sturmoviks* at the bridgehead was needed like air. Our 805th Regiment was assigned a mission to fly in echelons, in two groups. The order was to load our planes with anti-tank bombs.

There were three of us at the CP: the Regimental Commander P.T.Karev, the *zampolit* L.P.Shvidkiy and I – the Regimental Navigator. "I will lead the first group of 15 *Sturmoviks*", said the Regimental Commander. "Egorova will lead the second one after a 10-minute interval. All crews of the regiment will join. Which group will you fly with, Dmitriy Polikarpovich, mine or Egorova's?"

Shvidkiy stood silent for quite some time, and then forced himself to speak: "I won't be flying!"

6   Editor's note – another common diminutive for Anna.
7   Editor's note – see V. Emelyanenko, *Red Star against Swastika. The Story of a Soviet Pilot over the Eastern Front* published in 2005 by Greenhill Books, London, UK.

We were stunned by his response, but the flight time was pressing, and the regiment commander just said angrily: "What kind of a commissar are you if you abandon your comrades in a hard moment, at a dangerous sortie?"

We quickly left the dugout and saw a green flare already in the air – it signalled the take-off of the leading group. Karev rushed to his plane, and Shvidkiy quietly disappeared somewhere. Uneasily pensive, I sat on a stump, and to drive away 'spiteful' thoughts began to hum a song: Mishka, Mishka, where's that smile of yours?

I awaited my take-off with anxiety. It was to be my 68th or 70th combat sortie, taking into account only sorties in *Sturmoviks*. Oh, those minutes of waiting! They dragged on for hours. I always wanted to take-off straightaway after receiving a combat mission. It's true what they say – waiting and chasing are worst of all.

I walked towards my plane's parking bay from the CP and from afar I noticed my gunner Nazarkina. I had not seen her smiling so happily for a long time: her cheeks were flushed, her eyes were shining. Well, thought I, my gunner is gradually recovering from the shock she's been through!

The plane mechanic Gorobets reported the plane ready, and then made a covert nod to the side and whispered: "Comrade Senior Lieutenant, Sergeant Nazarkina has secretly stowed two anti-tank bombs with detonators in the rear cockpit …"

"She's gone mad, has she?" I burst out. "Clear the cockpit immediately!"

I looked at my watch: there were three minutes left till the take-off. "She won't let me come near her", Gorobets approached me again. "She's threatening me with the pistol …"

I came up to Nazarkina. Dousya rushed to cover something with her hands like a broody hen with its wings, but I gently moved her aside and shoved my hand down to bottom of the cockpit. The bombs! Pulling out a kilo-and-a-half one, I handed it over to the mechanic, but when I was going to take out the other one Dousya said anxiously: "Comrade Senior Lieutenant! Let me have them. In a direct hit these little bombs'll go straight through any tank: King Tigers, Panthers, Ferdinands. Don't take them away! Over the target I'll drop them by hand when there are no Fascist fighter planes around and there's no need to beat them off. After all, it's tank attacks we're flying to beat off. Leave them with me!"

"Mechanic! Clear the cockpit immediately!" – I ordered …

A green flare blazed up and curved in the air. Hurriedly putting on my parachute, I sat in the cockpit, turned the engine on, checked the two-way and taxied out. Through the intercom I heard Nazarkina's voice – she was too cheerful for some reason. Why was that? Had Gorobets managed to pull all the bombs out from under her feet? I took off, and 15 *Sturmoviks* went into the air following my lead. The Vistula with islands in the middle of its course was visible ahead of us. On the right, as if in a fog, was Warsaw … Yesterday, coming back from a sortie, I had seen the city burning, engulfed by flames and clouds of thick smoke. And our pilot Kolya Pazukhin – a chap from a town with a poetic name, Rodniky[8] in the Ivanovskaya Region, died in flames over Warsaw. Kolya was transporting foodstuffs and arms to the revolted people of Warsaw. A Polish pilot Major T. Wiherkewicz didn't come back from the mission either. He had broken through the infernal flak barrage and dropped his load on a parachute but was shot down as he turned, and crashed with his plane on the scorched buildings of his dear Warsaw …

---

8   Translator's note – Springs.

The Polish airmen from the 'Krakow' and 'Warsaw' aviation regiments fought shoulder-to-shoulder with the Soviet pilots. They did their best not to fall behind our aviators and fought courageously and skilfully. Many a time the fighter pilots from the Warsaw' regiment flew as escorts for the *Sturmoviks* ...

Now I was in the air, looking with sorrow towards Warsaw. I felt really sorry for the betrayed people of the city, sorry for their ruined capital, the former beauty of that old city.

"Four Fokkers on the left above us!", came Nazarkina's voice. She was the first to notice the enemy's fighters and shot out a flare towards them so everyone would take notice.

Long-range flak guns blocked our group's path with their fire. We took evasive action, but their shells exploded so close that it seemed that the splinters were rapping on the Il's armour. Then AA tracers flew towards the *Sturmoviks*, like red balls. They looked so beautiful from a distance that it was hard to believe each of them meant death. Petr Makarenko was flying wingtip to wingtip with me. The ground fire was getting closer with every second. If you converge on a target directly you'll face an even denser wall of fire, that's why I made a decision to turn right. My wingmen followed me in the turn, and the powerful barrage was left to the side. But we had distanced ourselves from the target, and the enemy was just about to zero in again having made their adjustment. That's why we now turned left and flew with evasive action against the curtain of flak. Looks like it's time to attack! I start a dive. Now I had no time to keep my eye on my wingmen, but I knew that they were following me. Attack! We pounced on the enemy tanks with our rockets and cannon fire, pelted them with anti-tank bombs. The earth below us was on fire. In the heat of the battle I paid no attention to the enemy ack-ack guns, didn't see the flak, saw no fiery traces from machine-guns.

One more pass, then another ... Suddenly my plane was thrown up as if someone had kicked it from underneath. Then another blow, a third one ... It became hard to control the plane. It didn't obey me, it was climbing up. I was now flying without taking any evasive action: all my efforts, all my attention were concentrated on trying to put the *Sturmovik* into the dive again and to open fire. I managed to do that, and I led the group again for another pass directed at the tanks. But my wingmen could see better the condition my plane was in. Someone yelled to me over the radio: "Get back to our lines!"

"Apparently the plane is shot up", I thought, and suddenly everything fell silent. Communications with Nazarkina vanished too. "Has she been killed?.." flashed through my mind. But the plane shuddered as in a fever: the *Sturmovik* wasn't obeying the controls. I wanted to open the cockpit but I couldn't. I was choking from smoke. My spiralling plane was on fire ... I was on fire along with it ...

33

"She died a hero's death"

The pilots who had returned from the sortie reported that Egorova's crew had been killed in the target area. As was done in such cases, they sent a death notice to my mum, Stepanida Vasilievna Egorova in the village of Volodovo in the Kalinin Region However, this time death had missed me again: miraculously, I'd been thrown out of the burning *Sturmovik*. When I opened my eyes I saw that I was falling with no parachute canopy over my head. Just above the ground (I don't remember how it happened myself) I jerked the ring, and the smouldering parachute opened up, although not completely ..

I regained consciousness with terrible pain engulfing my whole body – it was so strong that I couldn't move. My head burned like fire, my spine hurt unbearably, as did my arms and legs, scorched nearly to the bone. When I half-opened my eyes with difficulty I saw a soldier in a grey-green uniform over me. A terrible realisation shot through me stronger than any pain: "A Fascist! I'm in the Fascist's hands!" This was the one thing I'd feared most of all in the war. The moral pain was a hundred times more dreadful than fire, bullets, physical pain. Only one thought pulsated feverishly inside my head: "I've been captured!" Helpless, incapable of resistance! I couldn't even stretch my arm towards my pistol! And the German set his foot against my chest and pulled my broken arm for some reason. Oblivion ...

The next time I came to my senses was from hitting the ground: the Hitlerites had tried to seat me in a vehicle but I couldn't stay upright. I was falling as soon as they let go. Then they brought a stretcher and put me on that. As if in a dream I heard Polish. "Maybe the partisans have snatched me away?" the hope flashed through my mind. No, I saw the Hitlerites again and heard them conversing. "Schnell, schnell!" they were rushing two Polish medics, urging them to treat my wounds faster: a raid by Soviet aviation was on. Again a tiny ray of hope glimmered in me – our planes were around! I'd be happy if they hit this place where I was lying ...

The Poles gave me no medication, they simply bandaged me, deftly hiding all my decorations and Party membership card under the bandages. I had to gather all my strength so as not to let out a moan in front of the enemy ...

The Polish medics were conversing in whispers and I caught something about the Radom concentration camp. Then among the gaps in my memory there was an endlessly long shed, and when I came to my senses I found myself on the floor ...

"What have they done to you, the freaks? It'd be good to put some ointment on now ..." I heard a young female voice.

"Where would I get it from, this ointment? The Germans haven't stocked medicines for us", a male voice replied and asked straightaway: "And you, girl, who are you anyway, how did you end up here?"

"I'm a medical orderly, Yulya Krashchenko. I ended up here from the Magnuszew bridgehead beyond the Vistula, just like you. A tank ironed out the trench I was bandaging wounded men in, and then the Hitlerite submachine-gunners took us prisoners ..."

"You know what, sister, I do know you. You're from the 2nd Guards Battalion. Your commander, Captain Tskayev, is from my neighbourhood. Move over here closer to us, Orderly Krashchenko, let's talk. We've examined a female pilot here, and found decorations under the bandages ... We'd better take them off and hide them so as not to let the Fritzes have them. You do it, sister, it's easier for you – the Fascists could accuse us of God knows what."

"I understand. But where can I hide them?"

"Let's put them into her burned flying boots – the Fascists won't want them – they prefer new stuff", someone else suggested.

When I heard my native speech, a spasm squeezed my throat and the first word burst out of me with my first groan: "Wa-a-ater!"

From that moment Yulia was with me all the time. The Hitelerites couldn't drive her away from me with curses, nor with blows ... I remember lying on a trestle-bed in some room of the shed, and a tearful Yulia sat next to me. Three men in rubber aprons, and with gauze bands on their faces, tore from my scorched arms and legs the bandages the Poles had put on me, tipped some powder over them and went away. As Yulia told me later, I began writhing in pain, dashing my head against the bed, yelling, losing consciousness ... The Poles held in the Radom camp for participation in the Warsaw Uprising stood up for me. They began smashing windows and breaking everything indiscriminately, demanding a halt to the torture of the Russian pilot. Then these three 'physicians' appeared again and washed my burns of all they'd tipped on them before.

On the second day they loaded us into a freight car and rode us somewhere. Apparently the frontline was getting closer – after all it was September 1944. "Us" meant me, Yulia, a barely alive soldier from a penal company and a battalion *zampolit* – a completely fit Captain. He dreamed of escaping, but there had been no suitable chance, and the Captain was taking fatherly care of the dying soldier. We, the POWs, occupied one half of the car: all laying on the floor. Huge bunks were built in the second half where lay, slept, ate, played cards, sang and told jokes two German soldiers and three Ukrainian *Polizei*[1]. The Germans behaved reservedly, but the *Polizei* lacked any mercy at all towards us, their compatriots.

Fortunately, Yulia the medical orderly was nearby. I tossed in delirium: it seemed to me all the time that I was falling to earth in a burning plane, that flames were licking my head as if they encircled it, that I should do something to break out of their strong grip ... But when I regained consciousness I saw Yulia sitting next to me. "Be patient a bit longer, sweetie, one day they'll get us somewhere. We'll find medicine, we will for sure", she wept and wailed.

For five days the SS guards rode us through Germany. At stops the freight car door would open with a rumble. "Look!" an SS guard would yell and many eyes, spiteful or sympathetic or indifferent, would look where on the floor lay the dying POW soldier and I.

I was very thirsty. But how could I quench my thirst when instead of my face there was a dreadful mask with its lips stuck together? It was hot. Festering appeared on my burns, I was suffocating. I wanted this agony to end fast ... Five days of hell ...

At last the train arrived at its destination. A column of POWs, surrounded by numerous escorts, passed through the gate of the Hitlerite 'SZ' camp. Fellow-sufferers carried me on

---

1   Auxiliary policemen.

a stretcher as they carry the dead to the cemetery. The gate closed behind us, they put the stretcher on the ground – and at that moment many Germans rushed up to have a look at the dying female Russian POW. I lay helpless, burned, with broken bones. I was dying ..

Later I was told that the whole camp was overwhelmed by the news as if by an exploded bomb: "A Russian female pilot!" The Germans surrounding me were arguing loudly about something. I understood one word: "lockup". Then they carried me on the stretcher through a narrow corridor made of barbed wire: I could see watch towers with submachine-gunners on them. From behind the barbed wire on both sides I heard a sort of buzzing, and something flew onto me. It appeared that the French, Italians, British POWs of the Küstrin[2] camp were throwing me pieces of bread and sugar as a sign of support and solidarity. Yulia, walking beside the stretcher, collected everything and put it into the lap of her Army skirt.

Yulia Krashchenko and I were placed into an isolated stone cell. There were smooth concrete walls, two-tier bunks by one of the walls. There was a low cement ceiling with a wooden crossbar and a bulb on it, two small windows with double bars. The lockup was formerly located on these premises.

Yulia tipped off onto my legs (there was no other place) all the pieces of bread she had picked up, and at that moment a huge Gestapo man, who could speak reasonable Russian, came in, two German soldiers with him. "You will be fine here!" he addressed me and added straightaway: "What kind of rubbish is this?"

The German pointed his knout at the bread lying on my bunk: "Take it away!" The soldiers scooped everything up, not leaving a single bit. Yulia began to ask them to leave us the bread and sugar, but the Gestapo man was implacable. Then they left, but a submachine-gun-armed Hitlerite with a wooden look stood by the door of the lockup. Yulia had hidden under me (to be precise, under my bed, in a scorched flying boot) my Party membership card, two Orders of the Red Banner, a medal 'For Valour' and one 'For the Defence of the Caucasus'.

Thus began my nightmarish existence, full of mental anguish and physical pain, in the 'SZ' Fascist camp.

The lockup, according to the Hitlerites' point of view, was the most appropriate place for a person who was between life and death. Everything they were doing to me was in the spirit of Nazism. They didn't torture me, didn't torment me – no, they simply threw me into a damp concrete casemate, and threw me on the mercy of fate without elementary medical aid. They didn't kill me straightaway but with Jesuit cruelty gave me the chance to die on my own, slowly and agonisingly. But I was saved from death by something they hadn't thought about – human solidarity. The very same day I was put inside the lockup a real battle for the life of the Russian female pilot began – a battle joined in by dozens and hundreds of people representing the most varied nationalities. By that time a strong, deeply conspiratorial clandestine resistance organisation was operating in the camp. Its members were conducting a broad propaganda campaign among the inmates, delivering them the truth about the situation on the fronts, organising acts of sabotage, unmasking traitors, supporting the sick and wounded. From the first minute of my presence in the camp I, all unsuspecting, found myself observed by the organisation, one of whose leaders was Doctor Sinyakov, known as 'The Russian Doctor'. He had been head of a hospital in

Kiev, and when our troops were leaving the city, all who could walk left. Only soldiers badly wounded during the siege of Kiev – there were a large number of them – were left. He got to someone on the phone, carts arrived to pick the wounded men up and transport them to the rear. All the other doctors had scattered, and the nurses and medics also fled in fear. Kiev had already been occupied, the sound of shooting was already heard nearby, but together with one nurse and some slightly wounded men assisting them, he carried down and loaded the badly wounded into the carts. The Germans had already begun to fire at the convoy – they managed to set out, but the Germans caught up with them ... They shot dead everyone, leaving only him and a wounded female nurse. Both were placed in a cellar, and the nurse died in his arms: that was how he told his story. Then he found himself in the camp ...

Doctor Sinyakov's first concern was naturally my medical condition. For the experienced doctor even a brief glance at me at the moment I was being carried through the camp on a stretcher was enough to be sure that I was in the most serious condition. If no immediate aid were provided, then ...

The clandestine committee instructed Doctor Sinyakov and a Belgrade University Professor Pavlo Trpinac to try to get the camp administration's permission to treat the wounded POW. Then Sinyakov reported to the camp office and appeared before the Commandant. Looking at the Doctor from outside, it was impossible to ascribe to him the power, energy and firmness he really possessed. Not a tall man, emaciated, slow in his movements, with a shock of half-grey unruly hair ... He spoke German unhurriedly, but in his every word there was steel and self-confidence.

"A badly wounded female Russian pilot has arrived in the camp ..."

"And what of it?" The Fascist said. "New parties of prisoners arrive here daily. The Reich needs labour ..."

"She's not like all of them, she's maimed and burned all over ... She's had no medical treatment for ten days."

"It's not a hospital here ..."

"On behalf of all the camp prisoners I demand that Doctor Trpinac and I be given access to the wounded woman."

"You demand, do you?" The Gestapo man went purple. "For that one word I could simply ..."

Yes, here in the camp everything was simple ... Death called up new victims from the POW ranks on a daily basis. Insubordination – a bullet; refusal to work – a bullet. Any guardsman was a judge. Everything was as simple here as in the Stone Age. Sinyakov knew all that, and yet he looked directly into the Hitlerite's mad eyes ... The Doctor was protected from the Nazi's fury by his hands: the cunning, strong, capable hands of a surgeon ...

When Georgiy Fedorovich had arrived in the Küstrin camp in another party, he was walked to what they called the *revier*[3] or just the infirmary, protected by guards in the middle of the camp behind the barbed wire. The Doctor was greatly surprised seeing in this hell, in this stationary Fascist execution truck, a surgical table, a scalpel, bandages, iodine and other stuff. But then it became clear: the infirmary was here not because of humanism. It was just that 1944 was coming to an end, our army had entered Europe,

---

3   Abbreviated from the German word 'Krankenrevier' (meaning 'sick bay' or 'dispensary') this was a barrack for sick concentration camp inmates. Most of the medical personnel were inmates themselves.

and the Fascists could no longer kill all the POWs ... The front was gobbling up Hitler's divisions. Germany badly needed labour, but the POWs living in hellish conditions were dying in their hundreds and thousands. This situation had become disadvantageous to the Reich, and that was why the hospital had been established. Actually, there was another reason. POWs were carriers of disease, and the Fascists were terrified of infection in their densely populated country. For this reason people would be sent over to the *revier*, behind the third row of barbed wire, on the smallest suspicion of disease.

When Doctor Sinyakov was appointed as a surgeon, he was ordered to operate on the stomach of a maimed, burned, dying tankman who was barely breathing. All the camp Germans, headed by Doctor Koschel, came to see the 'Russian Doctor's' first operation. Koschel brought along his fellow German surgeons and along with them the French, British and Yugoslav specialists from among the prisoners. Let them, he said, see for themselves what sort of medics these worthless Russians are! The patient was brought in. The hands of Georgiy Fedorovich's assistants were shaking from worry – behind their backs someone among the Fascists was loudly holding forth about how the best Russian doctor of medicine was no better than a German medical orderly. And Doctor Sinyakov, his legs barely holding him up, pale, barefoot and ragged, was performing a stomach resection. His movements were accurate, confident and those present understood that this surgeon didn't need an exam. After a one-and-a-half-hour long operation, superbly performed by Georgiy Fedorovich, the Germans left. The French, British and Yugoslavs remained. Standing up, they cheered the Russian doctor's first victory in captivity. "*Tovarich*[4]..." said Pavle Trpinac, the only Russian word he knew, and shook Sinyakov's hand.

Trpinac, like a campaigner, began to talk about the Russian doctor in the camp, and people from all blocks began to come to Sinyak one after another for treatment: they said he knew how to raise the dead! Georgiy Fedorovich cured perforated ulcers, pleurisy, osteomyelitis, performed surgery for cancer and thyroid diseases. Each day there were up to five operations and more than fifty dressings. The doctor was terribly tired, but the knowledge that there were more than a thousand and a half sick and wounded men in the hospital did not allow him to take any rest.

And so Sinyakov had no fear of the Commandant's threats, and repeated his demand ... Finally the Gestapo men allowed Doctors Sinyakov and Trpinac to treat me ...

Twilight. The door opened with a creak, and a German *Feldwebel*[5] came in like a ghost.

"Wow! It smells of a dead corpse here already", he said, taking a drag on his cigarette, then leaned over the bunk and exclaimed, astonished: "A thousand devils! What does it take to kill these Russian witches! She's breathing ... skinned alive but still breathing!"

I really did smell like a dead corpse. The heavy burns on my face, arms and legs were covered with pus. Later that would save me from rough scars formed where the burns were.

"Come in!" The *Feldwebel* told a man standing by the door. It was the 'Russian Doctor' – that was what they called 2nd Class Army Surgeon Georgiy Fedorovic Sinyakov.

---

4   Translator's note – comrade.
5   Sergeant.

34

The infirmary

Carrying out instructions from a clandestine organisation of Russian POWs, Doctor Sinyakov was preparing escapes. In the hospital there were always five or six weakened POWs, who were to be fed up before an escape, helped to dry some bread for the journey, provided with a watch or a compass.

The first escape was organised in the camp in the spring of 1942. Then 5 men escaped, and three of them were airmen. Sinyakov said that he would remember for the rest of his life one of those escapees – a chap aged about 23. He'd been brought to the camp in very bad condition, with frostbitten toes on both feet and a high fever. His plane has been set afire deep behind the lines and he had to use a parachute. The pilot had walked through the forest for more than two days and had got his feet frostbitten: his fur-lined flying boots had been torn away during the jump from his plane. Having worn himself out he decided to have a rest, dozed off, and then two German shepherd dogs pounced on him … The Gestapo men transported him to the camp hospital. The guy had a large scalp wound on his head. Sinyakov told the Gestapo men the POW had skull and brain damage, and that he was unconscious. The doctor knew that the German doctors would easily notice his deceit the next day, but was doing it with his eyes open. In the night Georgiy Fedorovich and the medics replaced the pilot with a soldier who had died of wounds. They amputated half of the pilot's feet, for gangrene had already set in. And then, having recuperated, the pilot first learned to walk and then made an escape. It had become another of the doctor's victories.

Later I found out that once an alarmed guardsman with an interpreter from the POWs appeared unexpectedly before Georgiy Fedorovich and shouted: "To the commandant, immediately!"

You didn't argue in the camp: if you were ordered to the commandant – you went. Why was there such a rush? But indeed business had been really urgent: some object had fallen into the trachea of the son of one of the Gestapo guards – a button or something. No one, actually, knew what the boy had swallowed. The boy was choking, immediate surgical intervention was required, but all the doctors were dismissing it as hopeless. Then the Germans remembered the 'Russian Doctor', remembered that this wonder-physician had been curing hopeless patients in the camp environment without essential instruments or assistants. Of course, he was a Russian – a representative of a 'lower race', but the Nazis had no choice. And did Doctor Sinyakov have a choice? An escort walked him – barefoot and ragged – to the spot. The Gestapo man said to him: "If you don't save my son – you'll be shot immediately", and summoned all the camp doctors as witnesses. Had Sinyakov been ordered to operate on the father, a Gestapo man, a sadist and a notorious scoundrel, he would have said "No" but this was a child. Granted he was a German but all the same a child who was not to blame for his father being a Fascist. And he agreed to operate, immediately at that, for the child was nearly passing out. Georgiy Fedorovich asked for a piece of wire, did some trick with it, inserted the wire down the trachea and pulled out the button.

The man, staggering from constant malnutrition, suffering physically and morally every day but capable of preserving his clear mind and his craft, had saved the boy. And when death had retreated from the latter, another miracle occurred. The boy's mother – a 'pure-blooded Aryan', haughty and swaggering, fell on her knees in front of the Russian doctor and kissed his hand, which had just put the instrument aside. Since then Doctor Sinyakov had obtained a kind of independence and right to state his requests. It had also played a role in Germans allowing him and Professor Trpinac to treat me.

Not knowing yet who these people were, having barely seen them at first, I understood that there were friends in front of me. Georgiy Fedorovich and Pavle Trpinac not only healed me, procuring medication for me, they tore off bread from their meagre camp ration. I will never forget that human generosity! I remember Trpinac bringing biscuits himself or sending his compatriot Zhiva Lazin – a peasant from the Banat – with a small bowl of kidney beans. In spite of everything, all the POWs except for the Russians were receiving food parcels and medication from the International Red Cross. The Soviet Union had withdrawn from that organisation. Stalin said then: "There are no POWs of ours – there are traitors …"

When Trpinac managed to get a *Sovinformbureau* communiqué, he would put on his gown, shove a cigarette into the guard's hands so the latter would let him through to me, and would step quickly into the cell. "Oh, good news have I", Pavle would say, mixing words in his native tongue and Russian ones, "The Red Army is gloriously advancing westward …"

Once he brought me a topographical map. The line of advance of the Soviet troops towards the Oder river was shown on it with a red pencil. Pavle fell to his knees, his back to the door, and showing me the red arrow directed with its point towards Berlin, said: "Soon they will come for us!"

At that moment the door opened and the *Feldwebel* ran into the cell cursing, but Trpinac managed to hide the map, and, pretending he had finished the dressing, walked out in silence. Next time the professor brought a piece of the *Pravda* newspaper[1] in which there was a report about some Colonel Egorov's heroic feat.

"Good news is a medicine too", he said assuming my namesake was my husband or a relative. My dear Pavle of course did not know there as many Egorovs in Russia as Ivanovs or Stepanovs!

Sometimes Trpinac told me about his wonderful homeland, Yugoslavia – told me about his family and sighed heavily. His sister, Melka, was hanged by the Fascists in 1941. His second sister, Elena, joined the partisans with her daughter, in the future a national poet of Yugoslavia, Mira Aleckovic. The fascists had arrested Pavle himself on the podium where he was giving a lecture on Biochemistry at Belgrade University. Pavle's wife Milena was still in Belgrade. Trpinac had been in the Küstrin camp since 1942 and before that he had been tormented in various jails. Trpinac hated Fascism with all his soul and fought against it as best as he could. He strongly believed in the final victory of the Red Army, made no secret of it and with no concerns for his own safety actively spread anti-Fascist propaganda among the POWs.

---

1   Editor's note – for many decades, the most popular Soviet newspaper.

The medications I needed were found in the barracks of the French, British and American POWs who had been allowed to get parcels from the Red Cross and from home. Once, a high-ranking SS man who could speak Russian came to see me.

"Rotting away, girl?" he asked me with an insolent grin. I silently turned to the wall. The SS man tapped me on the shoulder with the handle of his rubber knout: "Oh, I'm not angry, kid! We respect the strong", and, after a silence, added: "A word from you, and tomorrow you'll be in the best Berlin hospital. And on the day after tomorrow all the newspapers in the Reich will be talking about you. Well?"

"Eh, you beasts! She's, one might say, at death's door, and you've got only one thing on your mind," came Yulia's sonorous voice.

"Shut up, you Russian swine!" The SS man exploded.

"You're a swine yourself. A German one!"

"You can rot!" the Hitlerite shouted and ran out of the cell.

Later Georgiy Fedorovich came to see us. I told him about the SS man's visit. "You need to be cunning with the enemy, but you were behaving like silly little kids. I can't hide it – you are in trouble", he said, and then I admitted to Sinyakov: "There's a hiding place in my flying boot. Please, hide my Party membership card and decorations. If you make it back home, hand them over to the proper authorities …"

Sinyakov left, and we began to listen guardedly to every knock and rustle. We were very uneasy. We were silent for quite some time, each busy with our own thoughts. Then, interrupting the silence, I asked Yulia to tell me how she had ended up on the front.

"Very simple", she began. "As soon as I had graduated from the 7-year school in my village of Novo-Chervonnoye in the Lougansk Region, the war broke out. Our village of Novo-Chervonnoye (near Donetsk) was occupied by the Hitlerites. Oh, it was a terrible time! My mum and I were kicked out of our house, and for a long while we lived in a shed. And when our troops had come back, first of all I grabbed my badge and certificate 'Ready for Medical Defence' I'd got while I was still at school, ran to see the unit commander and asked him to take me along with them to the front.

"I can do bandages, take me!" I said.

He said "My girl, what are you talking about? They'll kill you!"

"No way will they kill me!"

"So how old are you?"

"Seventeen …"

Seventeen-year old Yulia Krashchenko was an army medic. Short and agile, she would rush about battlefields, hurry to any groan, any call of: "Sister! Help!"[2] It might seem that it was beyond her strength to drag out even one casualty – often a big and heavy man. But she had dragged out more than five and more than ten …

During the forcing of the Southern Bug river the Fascists tried to break the thin river ice and drown her company that was striving to reach the occupied river bank. The bank was steep, the water was cold – and all around her were fire, groans and entreaties: "Sister, help …" Yulia was bandaging wounded men, but dragging them not to the rear but forward: it was impossible to crawl back – the enemy shells had already smashed the ice. She met the dawn of 23 February 1944 on the high bank of the Bug. It was then that Guards Sergeant Y.F. Krashchenko was awarded the medal 'For Valour. And later,

2   Editor's note – 'Sister of Medicine' is a term for nurse in the Russian language.

several months after that, a battle broke out on the Vistula river, which had been turned by the Germans into an impregnable defence line. One night a group of Soviet troops crossed the river and consolidated their grip on the opposite bank. Yulia Krashchenko was amongst them. The German artillery battered them incessantly, dozens of Fascist planes bombed the small bridgehead, trying to throw the troops into the Vistula. The company commander was killed but they held on, trying to keep the bridgehead. Like steel wedges, columns of Tigers, Ferdinands and Panthers advanced onto our lines pressed against the Vistula. During all those difficult hours our Air Force was helping the land troops. Yulia didn't know that up there, in the skies, in a *Sturmovik* cockpit there was I – a woman with whom a shared misfortune would soon bring her together ...

The Fascist tanks flattened the trench in which the medic Krashchenko was dressing the wounded. That's how she had found herself in captivity. And then, after our conversation with the Gestapo man, towards evening two strong Germans appeared and said, pointing their fingers at Yulia: "Kommen. Schnell, schnell!"

I asked the Hitlerites where and why they were taking the girl? One of them, pressing a finger against his temple, squeezed out: "Pif! Paf!" and off they went.

They locked me inside. Silence. How terrible silence can be ... Grief stripped all my strength. I wanted to shut my eyes and not open them again. A condition of extreme apathy twisted my last forces and will into a tight knot. And who knew how it all would have come to had I not sensed the tenfold strong support of friends. The POWs began to demonstrate their sympathy to me by different means, and even through the walls of the casemate I felt their fraternal handshakes. The Englishmen passed me a trench coat and the Poles tailored a jacket 'in the latest style' from it; the Yugoslavs found me a warm scarf, and our Russian guys hand-made me slippers out of trenchcoat cloth, with red stars on the toes. Had the camp administration found out about any of these gifts, severe punishment would have befallen the donors. But what is death by shooting against the great force of human solidarity! And the will to live arose in me again. To live so as to see the end of hateful Fascism with my own eyes!

They then banned Sinyakov and Trpinac from treating me, and a traitor with the black eyes of a brigand began to dress my wounds. But my comrades in misfortune didn't abandon me even then. Miraculously once they passed me a bread ration with a note inside: "Hold on, sister!" That unforgettable bread ration ... I won't enlarge upon what that meagre piece of bread meant back then. He who has been hungry knows, and the one who has never starved – as they say – God forbid! Two hundred grams of ersatz bread and a litre of soup from unpeeled and badly washed turnips – such was the daily ration for the Russian POWs of the 'SZ' camp. And a starved man, reduced to dystrophy, had sent me his bread ration ...

On one excruciating day of my solitary confinement my attention was attracted by a tall skinny guardsman – a youth of about seventeen. That was not his first day of guard duty, and each time he studied the 'flying witch' with unhidden curiosity. I saw that the guard wanted to talk to me but was hesitant. But once, looking back at the door, he produced a wrapper from his pocket, pulled out a piece of pie and actually stepped towards the bunk. Swiftly putting the pie on my chest, he smiled.

"Bitte essen, Russische Frau!" the youth said cordially and went back to his place straightaway. "Bitte ..."

"Take it back! I don't need anything of yours!" I replied more by gestures than by words.

"Nein! Nein! Ich bin Fascisten nicht!" The guard exclaimed and hurriedly began to explain that his mother had come to visit him from the countryside and brought him presents ...

It was already January 1945. On the last day of that month Major Ilyin's 5th Shock Army tanks liberated the accursed camp 'SZ', but two days before the arrival of our troops the SS guards drove out of the barracks all those who could still stand on their feet. Only the dying men and some doctors and medics headed by Doctor Sinyakov were left in the camp. Working together, they secretly dug a deep hole under the operating room and hid underneath till the liberation.

Through the bars on the window I saw a Gestapo man and two submachine-gunners with him were running into the French barracks and shooting: apparently they were finishing off those who couldn't walk ... But then the cannon shots, previously reaching the camp like a far-off roar of thunder, began to resound just nearby. The shells were bursting right and left of the punishment cell, which had been locked. There had been no one on guard for quite some time already. And suddenly everything fell silent. A lull set in. Suddenly the door swung open and I saw our tank-men in it ... How happy I was! "They'll fix me up for sure", I thought. "I'll get better myself – such is my character!"

Major Ilyin – the tank brigade commander – advised me go to hospital with the wounded tank crews who were about to be taken away in carts. He knew that I would be going through hard times – apparently he was aware of our SMERSh[3]. That's was why he recommended I lose myself among the wounded tank-men. He said: "You were flying at tanks when they shot you down!" But I found out the 16th Aerial Army in which I used to serve was operating towards here. That was why I declined:

"I will be looking for my regiment. It must be somewhere here, on this sector of the front."

With the tank crews' field mail service, I immediately sent letters to my mum in the village of Volodovo, Kouvshinovskiy Region, and to the regiment. Because of the happiness, that day I got to my feet and walked. I remember I put on those gift slippers with red stars on the toes, made by an unknown friend for me, braced my hands against the bunk and moved forward. But my legs were trembling like strings, my flabby muscles wouldn't obey me, my burns had just grown over and began to crack and bleed straightaway ... "Stop! Sit down for a bit, have a rest", I said to myself and then carefully shuffled around the floor again. One more step! I swayed but didn't fall, stayed upright and walked on, although holding onto the wall ...

And the ex-POWs of the camp, those who could hold weapons, climbed up on the tanks and went into the battle for Küstrin. Sinyakov organized a field hospital in the camp at the tank crews' request: their rear lines had fallen behind during their rapid advance. Georgiy Fedorovich did more than seventy operations on wounded tank-men over several days. And back then, in the camp, immediately after the liberation he brought my Party membership card and decorations and handed them over to me ...

3   Translator's note – abbreviation of a special security service of the Soviet Army, also nicknamed 'Death to the Spies'.

35

The SMERSh

I am careful with my memory – generally I try not be carried away by recollections. Memory is memory and life is life. Nevertheless, I have to tell my grandchildren and great-grandchildren the truth. That truth that when the fighting near Küstrin had died down and the rear lines had caught up, all of us survivors, now ex-prisoners of the Küstrin camp, were ordered to walk to the city of Landsberg – for a check-up. I could barely walk, but there was a horse-driven waggon on the road, and Doctor Sinyakov talked a coachman into giving me a lift to the nearest town, to where the soldier was heading. Georgiy Fedorovich told me to wait for them by the first building at the entrance to the town. The soldier helped me: he lifted me off his wreck, took me to the proper place, helped me to sit down. But I didn't have to wait long. As soon as I had sat down on a bench, an officer with a sabre and two soldiers with submachine-guns on both his sides came up to me. "Who are you?" I explained: "Doctors are coming to pick me up shortly. They will assist me in getting to the town for a check-up". "You know, we should feed you! You must be starving!" I thought it was a bit strange. He was behaving in an unpleasant affected way. And he also had quite a 'professional-looking' face. And they lifted me up under the arms, took my straw handbag and off I strode through the prostrate German town. The dashing officer was in front of us, and the two soldiers were holding me under the arms … I plodded along and the tears were running … I was wearing the jacket 'cut to the latest Warsaw fashion', that gift from the British POWs. On the jacket were my two Orders of the Red Banner, the Order of the Red Star, the medals 'For Valour' and 'For the Defence of the Caucasus': the Party membership card was in my breast pocket. My hair, singed by the fire, had just begun to grow out and that was why I'd covered my head with the warm scarf – it was a gift from the Yugoslav peasant from the Banat province – Zhiva Lazin.

So I walked through the town – in such a uniform, slippers made of trenchcoat smooth woolen with red stars on the toes, escorted by a 'guard of honour'. "Soon you will have a dinner and everything else!"

I was brought to a commandant's office – to a Soviet officer who was a town major. Without hesitation, with no particular formality or interrogation of a 'suspicious person' he ordered me shoved into a vehicle, and then under a reinforced escort carried to the SMERSh Counter-espionage Section of the 32nd Rifle Corps of the 5th Shock Army. There I was 'billeted' on a trestle-bed in the watch-house and brought some kind of thick broth. Hitlerite POWs were downstairs in the basement, and I, thank God, was not with them but above them. As airmen say, I 'had an altitude gauge'…

The very first night two soldiers with submachine-guns took me for an interrogation. I had to walk up a very steep stairway to the first floor of the building adjacent to the watch-house. My legs were not very responsive, the thin skin that had just appeared on the burns was cracking. The crooks of my arms and knee-joints were stinging and bleeding. But if I tried to stop – a soldier would push me in my back with his submachine-gun …

I was led into the room which was lit brightly. The walls were covered with paintings; a large carpet was placed on the floor. There was a major sitting behind the desk. He had benevolent looks – but he started by taking away my awards and the Party membership card. For a long time he did now allow me to sit: all that time he spent studying the items with such attention – using a magnifying glass. I thought I was just about to collapse but held on by drawing on some remaining strength, and kept asking for permission to sit down. At last the Major gave permission. I thought that no force would tear me off the chair now! But no, the 'benevolent' major suddenly barked:

"Get up!"

I sprang to my feet. And so they started, the questions rained down upon me: "Where did you take the decorations and the Party membership card from? Why did you give yourself up? What was your mission? Who gave you the mission? Where were you born? Who is your contact?"

The major kept asking me these and other questions in that order or mixed up, right up until morning. Whatever I said, he shouted the same thing: "You're lying, you German shepherd!"

This was to go on for ten nights in a row! They escorted me to the toilet. Food was brought to me once a day at the same place – the watch-house, on the trestle-bed … I was snubbed with the dirtiest words … My name was forgotten: I now was 'the Fascist Shepherd'.

I cannot forget how after the war was over I told about my 'stay' with the SMERSh to Petr Karev – the former commander of our regiment. It was the first time I ever talked to somebody about it – and I was crying almost hysterically And then Petr yelled:

"And you did what?! Why didn't you remind him about flying reconnaissance missions in 1941 – on an unarmed U-2?! When in the same year your U-2 plane was set on fire, shot down by the German fighters – but being scorched with fire, you delivered the orders to our troops! And wasn't it ever worse? All you have passed through? We took Kovel, Lutsk, Warsaw … Why didn't you, a *Sturmovik* pilot, throw something at the mug of that scoundrel rear trooper!?.."

Karev angrily axed the air with his hand and suggested: "Let's drink, Anya Egorova. Let's have our 'frontline 100g ration'! "

On the tenth day of my stay with the SMERSh I ran out of patience. I rose off my trestle-bed and without saying a word moved towards the door. . I made it to that wide stairs and rushed to the first flour – straight for that major.

"Freeze, you whore! I'll shoot!" That was a 'fine hint' a guard gave, rushing towards me. But I kept going up the stairs almost at a run. Where did I gain the strength for that? I think in the 18th century the Englishman John Bradman remarked: "Beware the anger of a patient man". How right was he …

I flung the door open and from the doorway shouted (or was it that it only seemed to me that I was shouting?): "When will you quit taunting me?.. Kill me, but I won't let you taunt me!"

I came back to my senses lying on the floor on the carpet. There was a glass of water next to me, but no one was in the room. I quietly sat up, drank the water, somehow dragged myself to the divan standing by the far wall, and sat down. Then the door opened and Major Fedorov entered. By that time I already knew his surname.

"Have you calmed down?" he asked politely.

I didn't reply.

"Nine days ago the former POWs of the Küstrin 'SZ' camp – the doctors – were looking for you. They wrote all they knew about you. How you were captured, how you behaved and how they'd been treating you. They requested you be allowed to go with them to the Landsberg camp for a check-up, but we couldn't do that then. It looked too suspicious – to preserve your decorations in such a hell. And moreover – to keep the Party membership card! To cut it short, you are now free to go. You are considered as being checked. If you want, stay with us and we will find you a job ..."

"No, no", I said hurriedly. "I wish to go back to my regiment. It is somewhere around there, fighting in the same sector ..."

"You are free to go wherever you want", snapped out the major.

"How will I go without a certificate? I would immediately be taken again, and placed somewhere once more!"

"We do not provide any certificates! If you want to go to your regiment, I advise you to come to a checkpoint at the road. You could then ask them to give you a lift to a proper place."

"You have been taunting me major – and now you are laughing? Can't you see: I can hardly walk! And who would get me into a car without a document? My regiment is in this sector – so give me a horse or a carriage. Or give me some certificate and a lift to the checkpoint – I beg you for Christ sake!"

The major had softened and did me a favor. He made a certificate with my whereabouts one saying I had passed the check-up. Following that he ordered to get me on a carriage bringing me to the checkpoint. There, I was advised where the headquarters of the 16th Aerial Army was located. They then put me onto a passing vehicle.

But from the Army personnel section I was immediately transferred to the Army-level SMERSh. "We will send an inquiry to the 34th Rifles Corps of the 5th Shock Army where they checked you out", they told me. But the room I was placed into had all the utilities and I was fed in the officer's mess. The SMERSh chief's wife brought me magazines and books. Some more women visited me, Army HQ officers, the pilots ... They congratulated me on my return 'from the world beyond', I received many gifts. A whole pile of various things accumulated in my possession, and I remember someone joking: "So, Comrade Egorova, you've been to hell, now paradise awaits you ..."

And one day Captain Tsekhonya came to see me. Unfortunately, I don't remember his first or parental name but I will never forget his kindness! He had served in our 805th Ground Attack Regiment as an Adjutant in the 3rd Squadron. That was what they then called the position that is now called 'Squadron Executive Officer'. As Deputy 3rd Squadron Commander I used to curse him over all sorts of 'trifles' although they say that there're no trifles in the Air Force. But he was such a sluggish chap that I used to 'push him' a bit. Tsekhonya would not get angry at me (or would just pretend not to), but either way he would not repeat his mistakes. And now, having found out I was alive and that I'd been found, he came to visit me. The captain brought me a gift of some beautiful dresses and said: "I put together a parcel for my wife, but I found out you were alive and I've brought it to you ..."

"What do I need dresses for?" I said apprehensively. "You'd better send it home to your wife, they are in great need after all, but those are useless here. Probably the quartermasters will supply me with a uniform blouse and a skirt?"

"You need treatment, Annochka", Tsekhonya said affectionately and ... burst into tears, staring looking for a handkerchief in his pockets ...

Having received my letter, they reported from the Regiment to my Division: 'Senior Lieutenant Egorova is alive and is on our sector of the front'. The division commander Colonel V.A. Timofeev then ordered our regiment *Zampolit* D.P. Shvidkiy to mount an expedition' to search for me. And now we were to meet...

I was sitting on a bench in the staff department of the 16th Aerial Army, waiting to be called. My crutch that assisted me in walking was next to me, there was also my straw handbag with the Soviet Air Force emblem and my initials, 'A.E.' This bag had been woven for me by the airmen – POWs of the Küstrin camp (currently it is stored in the Central Museum of the Armed Forces of the Russian Federation). Shvidkiy was first to notice me. Leaping out of the car, he rushed towards me with his arms flung open and nearly knocked me over! And I for some reason failed to recognise him straightaway: short, in a fur-lined flying suit and flying boots (it was still chilly) and an ear-flapped hat on his head, he was just like a bear cub! The surname Shvidkiy[1] corresponded pretty well to the lively character of Dmitriy Polikarpovich. He quickly kissed me, sobbed through his nose, and ran to arrange documents for me so as to take me to the regiment immediately.

"No, no, don't rush ..." I told him.

"No, I'm going all the same, I'll get you out of here!"

"The SMERSh here have still got me."

"What SMERSh?"

He started making a noise, cursed, then ran away to draw up the documents. A group of submachine-gunners accompanying the *zampolit* approached too, then our aerial gunners, dressed in fur flying suits. They mobbed me, greeted me noisily, interrupted each other telling me the regiment news and only one man stood aside and, not hiding his grief, wept, while repeating: "And my Dousya was killed ..." I looked closely at the crying man and recognised the aerial gunner Serezha whose death Dousya had bewailed so much. She had been stowing anti-tank bombs in the cockpit before her last sortie so as to avenge Serezha's death ...

During those same days my mum received a letter from me – it had been sent when I was still in the camp, by the tankers who had liberated us. Having received the letter, she read it several times, crossed herself and decided she was losing her mind. After all, there had been a death notice, pension had been given her instead of my pay, a reliable fortune teller had visited her and, finally, there had been a funeral in the church and an entry in the church commemoration book for the peace of soul of the 'Warrior Anna'! "I'm going mad," mum finally decided, crossed herself once again and headed to her neighbour's. There she began to ask, handing the letter over to the boy: "Tolyushka, read this! I seem to be imagining things ..."

It seems when they brought my death notice to mum, she was prostrated by grief, but refused to believe in my death. Some of the locals told her confidentially that there was a very reliable fortune teller who charged a lot, but told true fortunes and only true ... Mum was warned that the fortune teller's services would be dear, but mum collected some bric-a-brac and some money, and wrote a note to her elder daughter in Kouvshinovo,

1   Translator's note – 'quick' in Ukrainian.

where the latter worked and lived with her family: "Manyushka! I need you badly for a day, take a day off from work and come around and stay the night".

With difficulty Maria got permission to be absent from work and came to Volodovo by night. "My little girl, go to Spas-Yasinovichy. Our last hope is the fortune teller. Whatever she says we will go with."

And Maria headed off at first light in the morning – 30 kilometres one way and as many back – all on foot. She had to do it in one day, for on the next day she had to be at work for the morning shift. The daughter carried out mum's instructions, but the fortune teller divined that I wasn't among the living. It looks like she didn't pay her enough! Generally speaking, it's rare for a fortune teller to divine bad news and not instill hope in a person. And my sister, instead of sparing mum with a white lie passed her the fortune teller's 'truth'. We had had a tradition in our family – always tell only the truth to mum no matter how hard it is …

After such news mum fell seriously ill again. And on top of that the Kalinin Region Military Commissariat had assigned her a pension instead of the pay mum had been getting from me. After that her faith that I was still alive was ruined completely …

Later, about five years after the war, I was called to the Noginskiy District Military Commissariat, where I was registered. Here they gave me, against a receipt, a writ to read, from the Kalinin Region Commissariat, in which they demanded a debt be recovered from me to the sum of three thousand roubles, allegedly for wrongful payment of pension to my mum over a period of five months. In case of non-payment they threatened to take the matter to court …

"I won't pay", I said then to a major – the head of the Commissariat's 1st Department. "Nobody asked them to assign my mother a pension instead of my pay."

But then this idea entered my head: "However, let the Kalinin Region Commissariat exact my unpaid bonuses for combat sorties successfully carried out from the Air Force. Take as much as you need out of it, and send the rest to my home address!"

"Write a memo!" – The major ordered. I did. But more than half a century has gone since then, and not a peep out of them!

After more than a month of illness, mum made it to the church with difficulty and arranged with the priest to read the Orthodox burial service over me for the peace of the soul of the fallen 'Warrior Anna'. By the way, the commemoration record – a booklet with a cross on its cover, in which there are records of prayers for my health, and separately, for my repose – is still kept in my desk. In the box for 'repose' is written 'Warrior Anna', and then (angrily!) the record is crossed out in a different sort of ink, by mum's hand …

After the 'funeral' there was a wake. Only old women gathered for it: there were no young people at all in the village. Aunty Anisya – mum's sister – told me about this wake later. She was a wonderful character! Whilst my mum was strict, truthful in everything, Aunty Anisya was a mischievous and merry jester. Sisters they were, but polar opposites. My Aunt had worked at the Kouvshinovo paper factory from the age of twelve – she'd bound notebooks. She married a seaman from the Baltic Fleet, her countryman, but he was killed during the Kronstadt rebellion[2]. All that Aunty Anisya had left from him was an enlarged photo of the dashing seaman and their two kids – Kolya and Panya, who she

---

2   Translator's note – the rebellion of the Red Baltic Fleet naval personnel against the Bolshevik dictatorship 'for Soviet Power without Communists' in 1921, thwarted by Red Army troops.

had had to raise on her own. With the years the pain of his loss had begun to pass away, and Anisya had acquired her cheerful character again.

After all my misfortunes I had at last arrived at mum's in the village of Volodovo … We were sitting with our arms around each other, with my Aunty at the table covered by a festive homespun white tasselled tablecloth. A *samovar* polished with brick dust to a glitter close to gold – as it had seemed to me in my childhood – was boiling on the table. This *samovar* was the 'medium' one. It was called that because we had three *samovars* at home, presented by the priest Gavriil – mum's uncle, brother of my Grandmother Anna. The first *samovar* was the biggest – a bucket of water would fit into it; the medium one contained half a bucket, and the smallest five glasses. Mum used to boil it up quickly early in the morning, and first of all drank tea from it. The big one would be heated up with charcoal beforehand, and only when the whole family was together. It was especially good at home on Saturdays. The *banya*[3] would be heated, and at the beginning, when the heat was highest, the menfolk would bathe, and after that the womenfolk. After the *banya* we would drink tea till we sweated. On the table there would be dishes of soaked red bilberries, cranberries and whortleberries …

We had a lot of fiction literature at home. Where had those many books come to a remote village from? That same priest Gavriil used to bring them to us kids, as presents, and a lot of books had accumulated at our place. He used to tell us a lot of history, geography, knew plenty of verse. I remember Father Gavriil advising us what to read. And now, in 1945, when with my Aunty I sat at the festive table laid in honour of my 'resurrection from the dead', and when mum had come out of the kitchen bringing plates of snacks, Aunty announced loudly (so mum would hear it):

"And now, my little niece, I'll tell you how your mum held your wake. I won't tell a lie", my Aunty began. "There was plenty of food on the table, there were wine glasses, and she went and took the decanter from the locker, poured each of us a full wine glass, and put the decanter back in the locker, and then turned the key around to lock it up!"

"What you're saying is not true, Anisushka!" mum beseeched.

But Aunty Anisya, giving me a wink, went on: "What do you mean, not true? It's the truth, the plain truth!"

Mum was distressed, having failed to understand another of Anisya's jokes, but Aunty kept clowning, and so cheerful, so warm was it in my soul after all I had been through, that now I can't convey all this, I can't find the right words …

Here is another episode from that distant time. When mum had received a message from me, and the neighbours had confirmed that she hadn't lost her mind and that her younger daughter Anyutka was alive, mum put on her holiday clothes in celebration and headed to the District Military Commissariat.

Later the military commissar would recall that visit: "A *babushka*[4] came in agitated – and went straight to me. 'Sonny', she says, 'get me rid of this accursed pension!' I begin to question the *babushka*, 'what's your surname, who are you, who is the pension for', but she kept on about the same thing: "Get rid of the pension, and that's it!' At last I sorted out what was what, gave her a seat, gave her some tea – and she left, pacified …"

---

3   Translator's note – Russian steam-bath.
4   Editor's note – Russian nickname for grandmother.

36

The Colonel's suit

When the *zampolit* of our regiment, Major Shvidkiy, found me in the 16th Aerial Army Headquarters, he handed me a letter. It began with somewhat unusual words:

Dear Annoushka! I am very sick, writing from bed, but it's a pleasure to write to you. When we'd lost you, I couldn't come to my senses from grief for quite some time. Do you understand that feeling? I don't understand it clearly myself, but I know for sure that you mean a lot to me. Maybe it's not the right time to write about it, because you've got other stuff to think about. I've been doing everything I can for you and even a bit more than that. Be as cool-headed as you can, but be persistent. I hope Major Shvidkiy will bring you back to the regiment! I beg you to come and see me first thing, for otherwise I'll be offended. Everyone in the regiment is waiting for you. If they don't allow you to come – be patient and remember that you're always on my mind and I will be nagging the commanders. But I do want to believe that you will come ...

I embrace your slender shoulders as a friend and wish you well.
With deep respect,
V. Timofeev
21.02.45.

This letter was written by the Commander of our 197th Ground Attack Aviation Division Colonel Vyacheslav Arsenyevich Timofeev. His words amazed and delighted me, and its content made me pensive. Why was he writing to me like that? I didn't know much about him ... Moreover, I'd always related to the commanders with a certain alienation and mistrust. They even joked in the regiment that Egorova simply ignored the commanders, and because of that still hung around with the lieutenants while acting as a lieutenant-colonel. I had even had a 'conflict' with the Division Commander. Back then the regiment was relocating to the Dys aerodrome near Lublin. I'd been scheduled to move there with the last group. Whilst I was standing and talking to the pilots, the Division Commander appeared out of the blue. He came up to us, and I reported by the book and said that an Il-2 would soon be ready after repairs and we would be taking off.

"Take me up with you", the colonel asked as if joking.

"What do you mean 'take me up'? You're welcome to fly with us. But you, as the senior in rank, will be the leader", I replied.

"Oh, no, I don't want to be leader. I'd better form up at the rear of your group", the colonel said again, – overacting a bit, as I thought.

"I don't like the superiors looking over my shoulder!" I rapped out without stopping to think. The colonel took offence, turned around and left, saying nothing. After that he did his best not to notice me, and I was glad of it: one way or another I was further out of the commanders' sight.

But nevertheless I was cheered by that letter. I was pleased to know that there was someone in the wide world who thought and cared about me, was trying to improve my lot. It turned out that Timofeev had requested Shvidkiy take me to the Division Headquarters, which was based in Zamtera. We did so, and the Division Commander received me joyfully and cordially. He kept my hands in his for some time, looking closely at the burns, and then suddenly kissed them. I quickly jerked my hands back and blushed, and he began to invite me and Shvidkiy to have lunch with him. The *Komdiv*[1] called an orderly and instructed him to bring three lunches from the aerial personnel mess, and produced a bottle of wine from somewhere. After lunch the Komdiv said: "Now, Annoushka, you need to stay in our army hospital, get treatment and then, when the doctors give their verdict and depending on how you're feeling, we'll decide the question of your further service …"

They kept me in the army hospital a short time and sent me to Moscow at the disposal of the Air Force Personnel Department (my position – Regimental Navigator – was scheduled to the Air Force Personnel Department). The head of the Personnel Department General Shadskiy told me I would be sent to the disposal of the Serpoukhov Military Commissariat for my further service.

"There will be a Lieutenant going with you", the personnel man explained. "Head off tomorrow by train, the Lieutenant will pick you up from home with your personal papers in a package."

Indeed, in the morning a lieutenant with Air Force shoulder boards popped in and off we went. On arrival at the spot we visited the Military Commissariat where an orderly opened the package. Another one with a wax seal was found inside it. "You have to go to the school. It's next door to our building. You'll see it – it's behind barbed wire. Reception is on the opposite side from us", the man on duty directed us further.

At the checkpoint, when the Lieutenant showed the package, they let us through to someone in charge. To be honest, I still couldn't figure out where they were taking me. And suddenly the lieutenant told me: "Sit a while in reception, and I'll go into the office by myself first."

He went in, and I heard someone behind the door coarsely cursing the lieutenant over and shouting: "Why are you escorting a criminal with outa firearm?" The Lieutenant calmly explained: "Comrade General, she's wounded, in uniform, with medals. And look what a reference she's got … She was put forward for the rank of Hero of the Soviet Union posthumously …"

But there was obscene language again – and the lieutenant flew out of the office like a bullet.

"Let's get out of here quick! They're bastards in your Air Force. They're sending a checked-up person for a trial …"

For the rest of the trip on the train we were silent. I felt completely run-down, and the lieutenant barely managed to walk me to the Arbat. I never met my escort again.

Having recovered under the all-seeing eye of Ekaterina Vasilievna – my brother's wife – I went to the Directorate-General of the Air Force, to the personnel department, to see General Shadskiy. I was heading there with the firm intention of spitting in his face

---

1   Translator's note – Division Commander.

and then what would be would be … But he would not see me, as if having guessed my intention. In the medical department they gave me a referral to the Medical Examination Board. They said that after the examination, they would send me to a sanatorium.

After that everything went simply. The doctors quickly concluded: 'Unfit for military service – disabled war veteran, 2nd category'… Of course that was a great shock to me. But my youth and natural optimism won: I decided to take some treatment and go back to my dear *Metrostroy*.

At the end of April 1945 Colonel Timofeev returned from Germany on leave, found me on the Arbat staying with my brother Vasiliy's family and offered me 'his hand and heart', as they used to say in the old days. His offer both surprised and frightened me. I was surprised for he was a man more than twenty years older than me, who had asked me to become his wife. I was frightened because he was doing it hardly knowing me at all. I'd been crippled by the war, and the wound in my soul, that had appeared after Victor Kroutov's death, had not stopped bleeding …

"Are you joking?" I asked Timofeev then.

"No, I'm in no laughing mood. I'm making the most serious step in my life."

"And how many such steps have you fitted into your adult life?" I asked saucily. "The pilots who had studied in schools under your command used to say you'd had a few such steps!"

The Colonel blushed but told me that he had a wife and daughter, but when he'd been demoted from the position of Aviation Brigade Commander in Transbaikalia and out in a jail in Chita in 1938 as an 'enemy of the people', his wife had married another man …

"I married once again after I'd been exonerated with restoration of rank and the Order of Lenin I was awarded in 1936 for excellent drilling of the brigade personnel. We divorced in 1942. There was no issue. Now I'm single …"

My brother's wife Ekaterina Vasilievna, at whose place I was living, told me as if snapping: "Don't be stupid! Who else is going to be interested in you, a cripple? He loves you, pities you, protects you, helps you. You can see he's a good man. Marry him, Annoushka, and forget, or rather try to forget, all your memories … You need to live!"

And then the war came to an end. I still remember sitting in my home on the Arbat and crying … After all, I was still under investigation, they were checking on me! We had no wedding as such in the way they are celebrated nowadays. We signed up at the Kiev District Registry Office in Moscow, and then had dinner in the restaurant of the 'Moscow' Hotel where Timofeev lived. Then we were given places in a sanatorium on the seashore in the Caucasus, and we spent nearly a month there. Upon our return to Moscow we decided to go and see my mum in the village of Volodovo. Mum was so happy then, so joyful, and during those days I didn't know I was seeing her for the last time in my life …

My husband's holiday was nearly over, he had to go back to Germany, and I decided to spend some time at mum's place. He left, but returned three days later in a light vehicle and took me away with him. I had no pass, and we flew over to Warsaw in several hops. From there General Polynin provided us with a U-2 two-seater. The pilot was in the front cockpit, we squeezed ourselves into the back one – and off we flew like that. Near the Oder river the engine stalled, we ran out of fuel, and the young pilot lost his head and sent the plane over a woodland reserve. Fortunately, we still had some altitude. With lightning speed, my husband leaned towards the pilot, snatched the control column from his hands and managed to turn the plane away from the forest. We landed on a field jolting (the plane was now jumping up and now falling down having lost speed), but the colonel had lost his Air Force peaked cap in the air. We looked for it in the field and in the bushes for quite some time. All that happened not far from Frankfurt-an-der-Oder. The pilot stayed by the plane and we headed towards the city on foot. The local commandant gave us a vehicle and by night we had safely arrived in Cottbus, at my husband's duty station.

37

Where are you now? My regimental comrades

In Germany, in the city of Cottbus, despite all the doctors' prohibitions, I gave birth to a son whom we called Petr. After the delivery I was sick for a long time, couldn't walk – apparently my unsuccessful landing with the parachute that had failed to fully open had taken its toll. In Cottbus Professor Molitor warned me – I had spinal injuries in the sacrum area. I was happy about one thing: the boy was healthy.

In a year my husband was called to Moscow and we headed for the Soviet Union by train. In Moscow, in the Air Force Personnel Department Timofeev was offered a General's position, as Commander of the Aviation Corps in … Kamchatka. He said that he couldn't move there because of his wife's illness. "We can't offer you anything else!" the head of the Personnel Department cut him off. A medical examination followed, my husband had wounds from the time of the Civil War – and we both became pensioners. I was a disabled ex-serviceman, and he had become a pensioner per 'order #100'.

We had no place to live, and with difficulty we settled in the outskirts of Moscow, in Obukhovo near Monino: we wanted to hear the roar of planes' engines if nothing else … In Obukhovo I gave birth to another son – Igor – and again 'unauthorized'. I say 'unauthorized' for the doctors had banned me form bearing children most strictly. But I hadn't turned to them any more, right up until the delivery. Before giving birth to Igor I had taken fright and requested admittance to the maternity hospital of the town of Elektrostal: its doctors saved both me and my child. I also have to thank Kalistov, the Director of the 12th Plant, who obtained some medication for me from the 4th Central Medical Board with which the 12th Plant was in partnership …

I had no communications with my regimental comrades: our 805th Order of Suvorov Berlin Ground Attack Regiment[1] had been disbanded.

And then one day, not believing my eyes, I saw two Captains in Air Force uniform in front of me. They were Andrey Konyakhin and Leva Kabisher. My God, there was so much talk, so much news! It appeared that when our regiment had been disbanded many airmen had stayed in service. Konyakhin, Kabisher, Makarenko, Tarnovskiy, Mazetov found themselves in the Moscow Military District. Their unit took part in aerial parades and major manoeuvers.

"And how is Makarenko?" I kept questioning my comrades.

"He's alright. He married Katya – an instrument mechanic. Do you remember her – she served in our 3rd Squadron – a serious girl? By the way, during your last sortie, when we were flying onto the bridgehead across the Vistula, Makarenko seemed to see something white, similar to a parachute just above the ground near the target. Our guys got it hard then! Karev was shot up and barely landed on an island in the middle of

---

1   Editor's note – where Order of Suvorov stands for the unit award (as was the practice) and Berlin is an honorary title.

the Vistula river, south of Warsaw. That evening he turned up with his gunner right in Meljanuw for our festivities – the Air Force Day celebrations. But that celebration was a very sad one. I remember the *Comsomol* deputy of the Division Political Department showing your leather gloves that you'd thrown to him before the sortie. He had invited you then for the first dance in the manor-house that evening. You thanked him, threw him the gloves and said: "It's gonna be hot today ..."

That day from Andrey Konyakhin and Leva Kabisher I found out about the death of several comrades-in-arms whose fate I had not known. Pavel Evteev – our regimental singer and *bayan* player had met his death – the regiment was bereft without his songs, without his warm-hearted music. And his regimental comrades would keep Pasha's *bayan* for quite some time after that, carefully carrying it from one aerodrome to another ...

"Well, and how are things between you and the Party?" my friends asked me after all the stories. "We've heard you managed to save your Party membership card."

"Yes, I did. But it was taken away from me in our Division Political Department when I returned from the camp. I'd been in captivity for five months, and, of course, no membership fees had been paid for those months. Some instructor took away my card from me and gave me a reference instead. I gather the card was sent to the Central Political Department without being cancelled."

"And what about Dyachenko, the head of the political department – was he present during this 'procedure'?"

"No, he wasn't. He wasn't in the department then. He had no time to deal with that matter – he was taking his 'honeymoon' with a typist from the department", Konyakhin entered the conversation. "He'd become totally shameless! He'd left a wife and three kids in the Ukraine, and here he was courting ..."

"Well, what happened then with your Party business? Tell us."

"Listen to me and I will ...

Upon arrival in Moscow I applied with that reference to the Central Political Department of the Soviet Army. They didn't find my Party membership card there and recommended looking for it in the Political Departments of different branches of the forces, including the Air Force. I wrote lots of letters and finally found my Party membership card in the Moscow Garrison Depots and Construction Political Department, somewhere near the Manège[2]. I came and showed the reference given to me in the Political Department of the 197th Ground Attack Aviation Division. They received me politely and amicably. I was in military uniform with Senior Lieutenant's shoulder boards, my decorations and my walking stick ...

'Yes, your party membership card is kept here. I'll hand it over to you now!' A man from the Political Department moved to a safe as he said it. 'By the way, in which hospital were you treated?'

'I was in captivity ...'

The officer's face became stern, he slowly opened the safe and locked it straightaway: 'I'm not giving you the Party membership card! Apply to the Party Commission.'

'Which one? Why?'

'We don't have POWs, we have traitors! Leave the premises ...'

---

2   Translator's note – the former riding school of the Tsars in the centre of Moscow.

I went out. I felt so bitter, so insulted … I walked by the Kremlin wall, sat on a bench in the Alexandrovskiy Garden. There was a roaring in my ears … Then I seemed to calm down, but the tears kept falling. I couldn't stop them at all, I was shivering as if in a fever, my teeth were chattering … I remember a militia man[3] came up to me and asked: 'What's happened? Are you alright? I'll call an ambulance now!'

'No, no', I replied. 'Help me get home …' Thus, in a militia vehicle, I made it to my home at Arbat Street, 35. Ekaterina Vasilievna saw me, began to wail, put me to bed, gave me some powders to drink and I fell asleep …"

"And what happened next?" Andrey Konyakhin asked impatiently, clenching his fists. "What happened next?"

"Next? Two days after my visit to the Moscow Garrison Depots and Construction Political Department I was urgently summoned by telephone to the Moscow Military District Air Force, which was under the command of Vasiliy Stalin[4]. Why 'urgently'? Because Vasiliy Iosifovich had written with his own hand on my letter to the Military Disctrict: 'I think Egorova is right'."

"And what happened after that?"

Here my husband begged: "Guys! Let's change the record. It'd be better for you to tell what's happened in your lives after the war, for Anna is getting upset telling you all this, and you're grinding your fists into the table yourselves! Everyone's nerves are at breaking point since the war …"

"You're right, Vyacheslav Arsenievich", Kabisher said. "It's not easy to relive that abuse with her."

But I decided to finish my story about the Party membership card … "So, there was no decision after the Party Commission in the Moscow Military District. The Party Commission of the land forces was inquiring into it, and were at a loss."

"And then what?"

"Then there was a Party Board session in the Central Committee of the Communist Party, chaired by Shkiryatov – the head of Party Control. We were living in Obukhovo by then. The Board consisted of thirty men, if not more. In front of me the Chairman advised this Board that I had parachuted from my plane to the Germans … with a mission [from them]! I stood up and shouted: "Lies!" Everyone looked at me as if at a sworn enemy … In a word, they decided in the Central Committee: 'You will receive a verdict in the Noginskiy District Party Committee at your place of residence'."

"And what was the verdict?" My comrades asked in one voice.

"It was clear 'Refusal of reinstatement as a Party member'. But I was pleased even with this verdict. They might have put me behind bars! They could have done anything … And I had already had two kids then."

"And after that you sat as quiet as a mouse?"

"No, not at all. A year later I wrote another letter to the Party Central Committee, although all my friends and acquaintances were talking me out of it. 'What do you need all this for?' my husband was saying too. 'Take care of your health, to raise our sons!'

And then they summoned me to the Party Central Committee again. There was another Party investigator this time – KGB Colonel Leonov. He received me very civilly: seated me on a couch, sat down next to me, showed me photographs of his two daughters,

---

3   Translator's note – policeman.
4   Translator's note – Stalin's younger son – an Air Force General.

asked me about my husband and children. And then he began to question me on how I had found myself in German captivity.

'Is it all really true?' The Colonel wondered then. 'Just yesterday an airman was sitting here and telling me he was as clean as a new pin, and at that time in my desk there were documents that discredited him.'

'I am confident, Comrade Colonel, that in your desk there are no documents discrediting my name!' I said sharply.

'Alright, you may go now. Now wait to be summoned to the Party Board of the Central Committee of the Communist Party.'

This time the Party Board was very formidable – about twenty-five men. My thanks to Colonel Leonov: he reported everything honestly. And such was the verdict: 'Taking into account her services to the motherland, she may join afresh in accordance with standard procedure'. Finding out about such a resolution of my case, people began to send and bring me recommendations: Dyachenko, the former head of the Political Department of the 197th Division; the Chief-of-Staff of our 805th Ground Attack Regiment Colonel Yashkin; the senior surgeon of the local hospital in Obukhovo – a Communist since 1917 who had done 10 years in the camps as an 'enemy of the people' and been exonerated during Khrushchev's 'thaw'; Leonov and many others ... But I was obstinate again and didn't want to join the Party afresh. And on top of that the Poles sent me the 'Silver Cross of Merit' which I had been awarded in May 1945. The Awards Department of the Ministry of Defence found me and handed over their debt – the Order of The Great Patriotic War, 1st Class ...

The kids grew up healthy, but I was sick very often back then, so my 'menfolk' learned to do everything themselves at home. Igor would go shopping, Petya would do the housework and cook lunches. Vyacheslav Arsenievich had already written two books: 'The *Sturmoviks*' and 'Comrades Airmen'.

"After the XX Party Congress[5], I wrote to the Party Central Committee again", I went on. "I requested justice be done. They replied very quickly with a phone call: 'Your letter has been received. When will you be able to come and see us?' I replied that my son had a cold and I was unable to come for now.'

'Write down our phone number. When you have a chance to come – give us a ring, we'll order you a pass.'

On the second day I couldn't restrain myself and rang them up myself. "Come to Moscow", they answered, "to the Staraya Square, 4", and they gave me the entrance number, telling me the floor and the office ...

I went. They received me very civilly again, but I kept my ears pricked. First they asked me about home, family, how my medical treatment was going, enquired about many other matters. Then they asked a short question: "Do you feel hard done by?"

"It would be quite an underestimation to put it that way ..."

"Well, Comrade Egorova Anna Alexandrovna, we will be reinstating you as a Party Member ... You will have to come to the Party Board once again."

"No, I won't do that! There have already been two trials, a just one and an unjust one!" – and I told them about Shkiryatov's 'Star Chamber'.

---

5   Translator's note – held in 1956, Stalin's 'excesses' were condemned there for the first time.

"It'll be a formality", they said gently. "There will only four or five people. A verdict in your presence is required – and that will be it."

"Alright then, I'll be there."

When I arrived and saw in reception the former head of the Political Department of the 197th Ground Attack Division Ivan Mironovich Dyachenko, by whose orders his deputy had taken away from me my Party membership card, I felt ill at ease. But I saw that for some reason Dyachenko's hands and legs were trembling. I began to calm him down as best I could, and at that moment they called us to the Boardroom.

As they had told me, only five people were present from the Board, and two of us. The Chairman of the Board Shvernik asked Dyachenko to explain how Egorova had managed to preserve her Party membership card in the Hitlerite hell and then he had taken it away from me.

Ivan Mironovich stood up and began to say confusedly that a mission had been set up, that Egorova had led into action 15 *Sturmoviks* escorted by 10 fighters … The Chairman interrupted him and demanded: "Keep it short, answer my question!"

Dyachenko began to talk about my sorties again, but at that point Shvernik stopped him loudly:

"Enough! You may go."

Ivan Mironovich went out, and Shvernik, addressing the Board members, said that he had spoken to Marshal S.I. Roudenko in whose Army Egorova fought in the last stage of the war, and the latter had given me a good reference: "Egorova fought honourably!" And he went on:

"Comrade Egorova, we reinstate you in the Party. Your length of service is preserved. You will be paying your dues from the day the Noginskiy *raikom*[6] of the Party hands over your new Party membership card. Unfortunately we are unable to have it done by the October celebrations – only five days are left …"

After the meeting with my comrades-in-arms Captains Andrey Konyakhin and Leva Kabisher I began to receive letters from my regimental comrades. Our former commissar Dmitriy Polikarpovich Shvidkiy sent me a letter as well. He said he was living in Kharkov, worked at a tractor plant and was looking for the document in which he and former head of the Corps Political Department Colonel Tourpanov had recommended I be awarded the Golden Star of a Hero of the Soviet Union. Then the commissar 'reported' that they had already written to many authorities and even to the Presidium of the Supreme Soviet of the USSR. At the end of the letter Shvidkiy asked me if I had seen the movie 'Clear Sky', directed by G. Choukhray, and advised me to be sure to see it, for this movie was about my fate and that of people like me.

In those months I got many letters form my regiment comrades, and they all advised me to see 'Clear Sky'. "What kind of movie is it?" I thought and at last went to see it. I remember watching it and weeping, and my sons, sitting next to me, were urging me in whispers so as not to disturb the other viewers: "Mummy, stop crying. It's only a movie, those are actors …"

In those days the *Literaturnaya Gazeta* journal published a piece 'Egorushka' written by Leonid Kashin. The editor of the magazine *Starshina, Soldat* told me on the phone that a Polish writer Janusz Przmonowski had arrived in Moscow and brought me a letter

---

6   Editor's note – District Committee.

from Warsaw. The writer was eager to see me, and on the next day Lieutenant-Colonel Souvorov from the *Starshina, Soldat* magazine and Janusz Przymonowski sat at the table in our apartment. Przymonowski spoke excellent Russian. He asked me in detail about the war and was surprised that I fought in a *Sturmovik*: "It's far from being a ladies' plane! And to lead men into action? Unbelievable ..."

And the letter Przymonowski had brought for me was from a Polish writer Igor Neverli. There was a photocopy from a West German magazine *Deutche Fallschirmjäger* ('German Paratrooper'). Neverli addressed me:

Dear Friend!
I am hastening to forward you a document which must of interest to you. Colonel Janusz Przymonowski, when working on the literature for a monograph about the battle of Studzianki, read in a West German magazine *Deutche Fallschirmjäger*", No.5, 1961, memoirs of former officers and soldiers of Hitler's army. One of the respondents of this magazine tells of his experiences in the area of Warka-Magnuszew in 1944 and about the feat of a Russian female pilot. The place and time point to it being you, Anna Alexandrovna. I am forwarding you the story of the enemy witness and a photocopy.
My best regards!
Igor Neverli
Warsaw, 5.04.1963

A former officer of Hitler's army had written in the *Deutche Fallschirmjäger* magazine:

Our Parachute division was relocated from sunny Italy to the pandemonium of the Eastern Front. We had a terrible experience under the hammer of Russian aviation that day. More than once I needed something at the dressing station, and there I witnessed the following:

They had brought a Russian pilot from the frontline in a medical cart. The guy looked badly maimed in his burned, torn flying suit. His face was covered with oil and blood. The soldiers who had transported him told me the pilot had bailed out of a burning plane and landed near their position. When they took off his helmet and flying suit, everyone was astounded: the pilot turned out to be a girl! All present were amazed even more by the behaviour of the Russian pilot who made no sound when pieces of skin were removed from her during treatment ... How was it possible that such inhuman self-restraint had been fostered in a woman?

Thus, many years after the war, I found out a bit more about that tragic day of my life – and that was a view from the enemy's side ...

On 7 May 1965 a phone call resounded in our apartment. I took the receiver and quietly, so as not to awake my sleeping sons, said the usual: "Listening ..."

"Hurray! Hurray! Hurray!" the excited voice of the poet Gilyardy flew through the lines.

I asked, laughing, "Why are you celebrating so early in the morning, Nikodim Fedorovich?"

I heard in reply: "Annoushka, turn on the radio! They're broadcasting the Decree conferring on you the title of Hero ..."

Then another call resounded ... In a word, I was being congratulated by comrades-in-arms, public organizations, schools, editorial staff of newspapers and magazines, in which pieces about me and my brothers in arms had been published at different times. I will always remember the lines of the Decree of the Presidium of the Supreme Soviet of the USSR conferring on me the title of the Hero of the Soviet Union: "For exemplary fulfilment of combat missions on the fronts of the struggle against the German-Fascist invaders during the years of the Great Patriotic War and for displays of valour and heroism during that ..." I read the words of that document, and before my eyes I saw my regimental comrades who had gone forever into the inferno, roaring formations of *Sturmoviks*, the troubled years of my youth ...

"What are they taking girls at the front for?" I heard the voice of Borya Strakhov, and it seemed that he stood in front of me on the aerodrome with field daisies in his hands and smiled boyishly, shyly and so brightly and joyfully. And after him the *Sturmovik* pilots rose in my memory: Pashkov, Andrianov, Usov, Stepochkin, Zinoviev, Tasets, Podynenogin, Pokrovskiy, Rzhevskiy, Mkrtoumov, Groudnyak, Balyabin ...

The terrible years of the war have long gone. Our children have already become men and grandchildren have grown up. How fast the time goes by ... Recalling the past battles and my frontline friends I think about their courage and nobility, their high sense of duty, contempt for death and the lofty feelings of frontline camaraderie, and more – their love for the motherland. There's none better than her in the whole world!

I dedicate this book to those who didn't return, and those who survived, and who passed away after the war – my dear comrades from the 805th Berlin Ground Attack Aviation Regiment. And forgive me, my comrades, that I didn't see everything, haven't remembered everything, haven't written about everyone ...

Photographs

Technical school, early 1930s – Anna is standing second from the right, rear row.

Anna as a cadet at a flying school.

Anna as a mechanic repairing pneumatic hammers and drills
during the construction of the Moscow Metro, 1937.

Anna in the cockpit of a Po-2.

Glider school cadets – Anna is seated front left.

Anna receiving final instructions before a Po-2 flight.

Alexei Cherkasov, navigator in the 130th detached Aviation Signals Squadron.

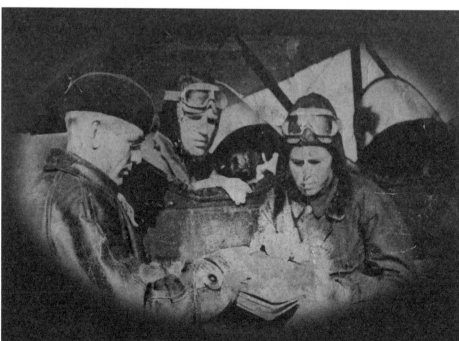

Anna receiving orders alongside her Po-2.

Early single-seat Il-2s in flight.

German anti-tank guns viewed
from the cockpit of an Il-2.

Pilot Vasili Baliabin, 805th Ground Attack Aviation
Regiment (805 ShAP), killed in action 1942.

Squadron commander Vasily Rulkov, 805 ShAP, killed in action 1942.

Pilot Viktor Khukharev, 805 ShAP, killed in action 1942.

Il-2s taking off, 1943.

A destroyed Il-2, with the body of one of its crew lying on the wing.

Boris Strakhov, commander of the 1st Squadron in the 805th Ground
Attack Aviation Regiment, killed in action in 1943.

Anna, summer 1943.

A member of Anna's 197th Ground Attack Division receives an award.

Anna's Il-2 mechanic
Mikhail Korzhenko.

Pilots and heroes from the 805th Ground Attack Aviation Regiment – Victor
Khoukhlin, Victor Gourkin and Andrey Konyakhin (left to right). Konyakhin daringly
landed his Il-2 and rescued Khoukhlin and his rear gunner in the heat of battle.

Pilots from 805 ShAP - I. Sherstobitov, V.Khomyakov, N. Ternovskiy.

An enemy train burning after an Il-2 attack.

Il-2s lined up on an airfield.

A dramatic but blurred shot showing an enemy train under attack.

An Il-2 undergoing maintenance.

Some of Anna's comrades from 805 ShAP photographed before embarking on a mission.

Commanders of 805 ShAP, from left to right: Regimental navigator Petr Karev, Regimental commander Michael Nikolaevich Kozin, political deputy Dmitriy Polikarpovich Shvidkiy.

Pilot Ivan Stepochkin, 805th Ground Attack Aviation Regiment, killed in action 1944.

805 ShAP Regimental commander Michael Nikolaevich Kozin, killed in action 1944.

Pilots from 805 ShAP after a combat sortie.

Mechanics and armourers from Anna's Regiment, 805 ShAP.

A damaged Il-2 from the 820th Ground Attack Aviation Regiment (820 ShAP).

Wrecked German vehicles and equipment – the work of Soviet aviation.

The wreckage of destroyed German aircraft.

Two unknown members of 805 ShAP, c 1944.

Anna next to her Il-2, c 1944.

Doktor G. Sinyakov known as 'The Russian Doctor' (centre) and two POW
pilots saved by him N. Maiorov (left) and D. Kashirin (right).

Anna proudly wearing her awards and decorations, 1960s.

Anna standing beside an Il-2.

Anna grasps the propeller blade of an Il-2 – machine and woman needed to work in unison to ensure both made it home safely after each mission.

Related titles published by Helion & Company

*After Stalingrad. The Red Army's
Winter Offensive 1942-1943*
David M. Glantz
536pp, photos, maps
Hardback
ISBN 978-1-906033-26-2

*The Last Rally. The German Defence
of East Prussia, Pomerania and Danzig
1944-45, a Photographic History*
Ian Baxter
112pp, photos, maps
Hardback
ISBN 978-1-906033-74-3

Forthcoming titles

*A Military Government in Exile. The Polish Government
in Exile 1939-1945, a Study of Discontent*
Evan McGilvray   ISBN 978-1-906033-58-3

*Barbarossa Derailed: The Battle for Smolensk 10 July-10 September 1941
Volume 1: The German Advance, The Encirclement Battle, and the First
and Second Soviet Counteroffensives, 10 July-24 August 1941*
David M. Glantz   ISBN 978-1906033-72-9

Adventures in my Youth. A German Soldier on the Eastern Front 1941-45
Armin Scheiderbauer   ISBN 978-1-906033-77-4

Entrapment. Soviet Operations to Capture Budapest, December 1944
Kamen Nevenkin   ISBN 978-1906033-73-6

HELION & COMPANY
26 Willow Road, Solihull, West Midlands B91 1UE, England
Telephone 0121 705 3393   Fax 0121 711 4075
Website: http://www.helion.co.uk